THE CONTROL ROOM

HOW TELEVISION CALLS THE SHOTS IN PRESIDENTIAL ELECTIONS

MARTIN PLISSNER

A Touchstone Book
Published by Simon & Schuster
New York London Toronto Sydney Singapore

TOUCHSTONE
Rockefeller Center
1230 Avenue of the Americas
New York, NY 10020

First Touchstone Edition 2000

TOUCHSTONE and colophon are registered trademarks
of Simon & Schuster, Inc.

Manufactured in the United States of America

10 9 8 7 6 5 4 3 2 1

The Library of Congress has cataloged the Free Press edition as follows:

Plissner, Martin.
    The control room : how television calls the shots in presidential
elections / by Martin Plissner.
        p.   cm.
    Includes bibliographical references and index.
    1. Television in politics—United States.   2. Presidents—United States—Election.
    3. Electioneering—United States.   I. Title.
    HE8700.76.U6P55   1999
    324.7'3'0973—dc21
                                                                98-51053
                                                                CIP

ISBN 0-684-82731-X
    0-684-86772-9 (Pbk)

*To Susan Morrison, who calls the shots in my life,
and to Mike, Paige and Sarah*

CONTENTS

THE
CONTROL
ROOM

INTRODUCTION

THE DAY BEFORE THE REPUBLICAN NATIONAL CONVENTION OF 1992 opened in Houston, Texas, officials of the Bush-Quayle re-election campaign met with a small group of CBS News producers and executives. Earlier in the year the campaign's press secretary, Torie Clarke, had declared that Patrick Buchanan, the President's bare-knuckled primary opponent, would have to "get down on his hands and knees and grovel over broken glass with his mouth open and his tongue hanging out" before he would be allowed to speak at the convention.[1] But now, deeply worried about the party's restless right wing, Buchanan's base in the primaries, these officials had been dickering with the Buchanan camp over an endorsement. Far from groveling over broken glass on his hands and knees, Buchanan insisted on making his endorsement from the convention podium *during prime time on network television.*

Before the President's men would consider that, they had warily insisted on seeing a Buchanan script. They had got it the night before. They had all read it—and loved it. "It's everything we could have asked for," said Jim Lake, the communications director. "The primaries are over," the speech began, "the heart is strong again, and the Buchanan brigades are enlisted all the way to a great comeback Republican victory in November." George Bush and Ronald Reagan, declared Buchanan, had jointly authored "the policies that won the Cold War. . . . Under President George Bush, more human beings es-

1

caped from the prison house of tyranny than in any other four-year period in history."

The man who once fought Bush so bitterly had composed a far more eloquent tribute to his accomplishments than anything the President's own speechwriters could fashion. But where to put it? The networks had scheduled an hour each for their convention broadcasts from Monday through Thursday, with an extra thirty minutes on the final night reserved for the President and Vice President. Wednesday was an obligatory "Ladies' Night"—with Barbara Bush and Marilyn Quayle. Tuesday night was reserved for Jack Kemp and Phil Gramm, both ardent Bush supporters in the primaries. Both were sharply opposed to sharing their long-scheduled hour in the sun with the man who had spent most of the year trashing the convention's nominee— and whose speech would surely overshadow their own appearances.

After a brief huddle, CBS agreed to help out. Buchanan embracing Bush seemed more like news than anything else that year at either party's convention. The original highlight of the Monday schedule had been Ronald Reagan. Buchanan, the current poster child of the party right, back to back with the patriarch of conservative Republicanism, sounded like a swell hour—maybe even more— of television. If Buchanan were slotted at 9:30 P.M. on Monday, ahead of Reagan, CBS agreed to take air a half hour earlier than planned.

For the Bush handlers, CBS's accommodation was the answer to their prayers—especially when ABC agreed to do the same. It could not, however, have turned out in the end more deadly for Bush. As delivered in the convention hall, Buchanan's speech—after its opening applause lines for the nominee—went on to summon not only Buchanan's own following but the entire Republican Party to a "religious war" against gays, inner-city toughs and the likes of Hillary Clinton.

NBC made things even worse—by insisting on its original starting time of 10:00 P.M.[2] In order to keep a commitment that Buchanan would be seen on all three networks, the Bush managers then pushed Buchanan's appearance all the way back to the time originally assigned to Reagan. As a result, the Great Communicator's good-natured, inspirational speech did not get under way till after 11:00— when the damage done by Buchanan was already history.

NBC's executive producer, Bill Wheatley, recalls with relish, "On two separate instances we saw them hold the convention waiting for us to come on the air." The second came Thursday night, when Vice President Quayle was scheduled before the network's 9:30 P.M. start. "They literally stopped the convention at 9:20. The orchestra played for ten minutes. We were still in our opening when they introduced [Quayle]. There was this tremendous roar, and Tom [Brokaw] just picked it up."[3]

It took a number of elections for the country's politicians to learn to wait for television, but learn they did. In 1952, when the TV networks proposed the first coast-to-coast convention broadcasts, the Republican party chairman initially suggested they pay for the privilege. In 1964 Nelson Rockefeller, in the second of his three tries for the Republican presidential nomination, shooed network cameras out of a New Hampshire "meet and greet" because he feared they would be a distraction as he made his pitch to perhaps thirty voters.

By 1976, however, Morris Udall, the most durable of Jimmy Carter's rivals for the Democratic nomination, could leave a breakfast in New York, haul a busload of reporters and technicians, mostly from television, to the airport, fly them five and a half propeller-driven hours to Milwaukee, and bus them to a nice middle-income home in the suburbs where Udall would display a middle-income housing plan. By the time space was found for all the reporters and television gear hardly any of the on-site middle-income voters could see or hear, let alone greet, the candidate. No matter; his soundbites aired on local (and network) television that day. Udall's whole entourage then went directly back to the airport and then to New York, where there was another primary in progress and more television news to generate. The lesson had been learned.

In 1963, a poll by Elmo Roper found for the first time that television had overtaken newspapers as the principal source of public information about "what's going on in the world today."[4] It was the same year in which the CBS and NBC evening broadcasts expanded from fifteen minutes to a half hour, in which television coverage of the Kennedy assassination became the chief experience of most Americans for nearly a week. There would be more such profound national experiences in which television enveloped the people—the

1969 moonwalk, the 1976 Independence Day Centennial—and each of these, along with more routine instances, enhanced the notion of the television broadcast as the essence of the event itself.

For the highly competitive network news divisions, covering landmark special events was the ultimate test of worth. Moonwalks and presidential assassinations, however, do not happen often enough to provide an adequate proving ground. Every four years, on the other hand, presidential campaigns did. Primary, convention and election-night coverage were seen as especially useful in establishing the hands-on reporting credentials of their anchormen. The broadcasts were "live," apparently spontaneous, and living proof that these standard-bearers of the networks' news efforts were no mere script readers but aggressive diggers after facts and captains of their respective teams.

Just as presidential-campaign coverage was found to serve the strategic purposes of television news, the same enhanced exposure came to dominate the strategic thinking of the campaigns themselves. Campaign managers, whose most important connections had once been with contributors and state and local party leaders, now prized the home phone numbers of television correspondents and certain producers and executives. More and more of the campaign managers' day was devoted to reading the minds (and sometimes the communications traffic) of the line-up producers in New York, to promoting "good stories" about their candidates and deflecting "bad" ones—or, to state the goal more exactly: to contain bad stories in the print media, where they often started, and to get the good ones promoted to where they can make a difference—on television.

It was in 1963, the year when television overtook the daily papers as a force affecting voters, that I signed on as an associate producer with the CBS News Election Unit; I became immersed for the next thirty-three years in the network's coverage of national politics. As the network's political director during most of this period, I cultivated party chairmen and regional officials, negotiated debates and interviews, tracked convention delegates, briefed correspondents and producers, kept a close watch on our pre-election polling and election-night calls and—very important—kept in touch with what NBC and ABC were doing. From that experience I have tried to trace in this book the evolution of American presidential campaigns from a party-driven process rooted in a leadership elite to one in which the choices are presented to the voters primarily by television.

———

As this book appears, more than a year and a half before the first president of the twenty-first century is sworn in, the race for that office is already far along. Like the party leaders who used to make all the choices but the final one in November, television news will have the most far-reaching voice on who is plausible and who is not as contenders in this race. It will decide which of the fifty-seven primary and caucus contests are meaningful and which are not and what constitutes victory or defeat in each.

With their polling partners in the print media, the networks will together subject the sitting President to a more or less weekly vote of public confidence—something the framers neglected to provide for. Random samples of likely voters will grade the wannabes of both parties on such traditional yardsticks as leadership, knowledge of the job and ability to handle a major world crisis. There will also be a horde of freshly crafted queries about moral fitness. But most of all they will poll about the "horse race."

Once the primaries and caucuses begin, the much deplored reporting of "who's up, who's down, who's ahead" will get undiminished play. This is not because the perennial resolutions of news anchors and network presidents to rein in horse-race reporting are insincerely taken, but because the networks are in the business of reporting news.

As they do this, they provide a large measure of the information on which Americans make their choices in primaries and on Election Day—and, it is often argued, on whether they vote at all. The quality of that information has long been a matter of controversy, especially in academic circles. So too, in other circles, is the impact on national decision-making which has accrued to what one critic famously described as a "small and unelected elite."[5]

In the pages ahead I will show that those on the political right (of whom there are many) and those on the left (of whom there are some) who worry about this worry too much. The men and women who call the shots at the network news divisions do have an agenda, but it is not a political agenda. Their goals are for the most part (1) the largest possible viewership at the lowest possible cost and (2) the gratification that comes from scoring any kind of competitive edge over their *television* rivals—including, among other things, the quality of their reporting.

CBS and ABC, in granting the best time slot at that Republican convention to George Bush's nemesis in the primaries, were not shrewd enough to foresee that this was a bad idea for Bush—especially since the men supposed to be pursuing Bush's interest were thrilled by it. (Far more thrilling for CBS News, during a very dark period in the ratings wars, was the prospect of launching its convention coverage off a lead-in from the series *Murphy Brown*, then the country's reigning sitcom.) Nor did NBC, in refusing to budge Thursday night for Dan Quayle, have anything against the Vice President. It was just protecting its top-rated broadcast, *Cheers*.

What did occur at that convention flowed from the strategic bargaining between the campaigns and television news, each with their own conflicting purposes, which defines what is seen and heard by Americans as they think about electing a President. For a third of a century, as the rules of this game evolved, I had a privileged position from which to observe how it is played. The account that follows starts with the uniquely American endurance test by which the Democratic and Republican parties, under television's gaze, pick their nominees for President.

1

IN THE BEGINNING WAS
NEW HAMPSHIRE—AND THE NETWORKS

THIRTY-SIX YEARS AGO, SAD TO SAY, CBS, NBC AND ABC created the modern New Hampshire primary. The primary itself had been around since 1952, when spirited campaigns in both parties drew the first primary coverage ever aired nationally on television.[1] But not until 1964 did television go overboard. That year, the network news divisions for their own purposes converted this once marginal political event, involving barely 1 percent of the country's voters, into a unique showcase and proving ground for aspiring presidents.

In February 1964 over a thousand correspondents, producers, technicians and support people of all kinds descended on New Hampshire, its voters and its merchants to confer the special franchise they have ever since enjoyed. This was an era of hardball competition among the network news divisions, in which jobs were on the line. Throughout the 1960s and 1970s, New Hampshire was the first test in every cycle of the networks' speed in declaring winners of elections. In that era, it never occurred to us that there was anything shameful about aggressive coverage of the horse race.

In 1964 the New Hampshire Republican primary was won by a write-in campaign for Henry Cabot Lodge, the party's vice-presidential nominee in 1960, who was then serving as Lyndon Johnson's Ambassador to South Vietnam. The big winner in that year's primary, however—Lodge ignored the hint and remained in Vietnam—was

CBS News. Eighteen minutes after the polls closed, Walter Cronkite declared that the Lodge write-ins had defeated both Barry Goldwater and Nelson Rockefeller—the only national figures who actually campaigned there. It took NBC another twenty-five minutes to make the same call, and nobody remembers when ABC got around to it. It was a turning point for CBS, at the time very much in NBC's shadow as a political reporting institution. A third winner was the primary system itself.

Saturation network coverage in the 1960s brought business as well as national attention not only to New Hampshire but to Wisconsin, Oregon and other states at strategic points along the primary calendar. Across the country, state legislatures adopted primaries specifically to get that business and attention. By 1972 primaries were held in almost half the states, including nearly all the big ones. But to politicians in that era who wanted to be President, winning primaries was only half the battle.

———

For most of American history, ordinary voters had little to say about the choices for President they would face on Election Day. Every four years, state and local officials of the major parties spent a few days at a national convention and decided among themselves what those choices would be.

Those who controlled the votes at national conventions did pay some attention to the primaries. Candidates who did well in them could argue they were more likely to win the election. As John Kennedy told a New Hampshire audience in 1960, "If they don't love you in March, April and May, they won't love you in November."[2] But the influence of primaries, to the extent they were held, was limited. Most were "beauty contests." Delegates were not obliged, at the national conventions, to vote for the winners. Harry Truman, who called primaries "eyewash," proved his point by steering the 1952 Democratic nomination to Adlai Stevenson, the freshman governor of Illinois, who had run in none of them.[3]

At the 1952 and 1968 Democratic conventions, party officials who controlled the votes ignored clear messages from the primaries and chose candidates who had ducked all of them. At other Democratic conventions of the 1950s and 1960s, only when primary voters ratified the inclinations of these party leaders did they get their way. The Republican record was similar.

At about the same time, however, that the networks began aggressive coverage of the primaries, the grip of the traditional party leaders had already begun to slip. In 1964, while Barry Goldwater himself was stumbling in New Hampshire, right-wing backers in the South and West out-organized the local party leadership. After their man won the California primary they took control of the convention away from the national faction whose strongholds in the financial centers of the East had decided every nomination since World War II.

Four years later the Democratic left, largely out of opposition to the Vietnam war, rebelled against the presidential nominating power of that party's city hall, county courthouse and state capital machines. That revolt failed, and very likely would have failed even if Robert Kennedy had lived to lead the fight at the convention. In a concession, however, to the infuriated losers and their supporters in the streets of Chicago (seen charging barricades on network television), the 1968 convention committed the party to cleaning up its nominating act for the future.

The task was assigned to a Commission on Delegate Selection and Party Structure. Chaired by George McGovern, a 1968 Kennedy backer with ambitions of his own, the commission carried its assignment much further than anyone expected. The new Democratic rules did not require every state to hold a primary, but they outlawed a lot of practices that had made it hard for candidates without the backing of local party powers to compete with their hand-picked organization slates. The commission did the same thing for caucuses, which were still used in most smaller states and a few of the larger ones as well.

Since many of the changes ordered by the Democrats were enacted into state laws, they often applied to Republicans as well. As the general idea, moreover, of empowering a party's ordinary voters became contagious, the way in which Republican as well as Democratic nominees are chosen was also radically transformed in the early 1970s.

THE IMPORTANCE OF BEING FIRST

Expanding the nominating power beyond the party hierarchies did not equally enfranchise the rank and file. For the Democratic reformers allowed state parties to decide the timing of these contests pretty much at will, and national Republicans were even less inclined to meddle with the calendar. This reinforced the privilege conferred on a relatively few active party members in New Hampshire and later in Iowa. As the sites of the first caucuses and the first primary, Iowa and New Hampshire would both become the scenes of year-long campaigns by candidates of at least one and usually both parties.[4] As these campaigns got off to increasingly early starts, so did the network coverage. In some cycles as much as 40 percent of the network stories on the contests for party nominations would originate in Iowa and New Hampshire.[5]

Voters in states like Pennsylvania, Ohio, Texas and California—up to thirty times as numerous as those in New Hampshire—would not get their turn until most of the original candidates had been all but eliminated in struggles for the blessing of a few hundred thousand partisans in two of the nation's lesser states. A few weeks later, with most of the primaries yet to come, one of the remaining candidates was usually well in front, and the futility of any further struggle would be reinforced by the networks' abandonment of the story.

The arbitrary empowerment of a few early-acting primary and caucus electorates was widely blamed on a television medium whose mindless doting on them was seen as the source of their great impact. For all the television coverage of Iowa and New Hampshire, however, the combined effect of these two events was seldom to pick the nominee outright. In the Democratic party since 1972, three of Iowa's Democratic winners (Ed Muskie, Richard Gephardt, Tom Harkin) and two of its Republican winners (George Bush, Bob Dole) failed to win the nomination the year they won Iowa. Three of New Hampshire's Democratic winners (Muskie again, Gary Hart, Paul Tsongas) and two Republicans (Lodge and Pat Buchanan) also failed to make it.

Unike later events on the nominating calendar, however, you did not have to win Iowa or New Hampshire to profit from them. In one of the earliest of several controversial cases, President Lyndon Johnson's 50-percent to 42-percent victory in New Hampshire over a relatively obscure senator from Minnesota was found so stunningly inadequate that Johnson left the field before the next primary. "A major setback for the President," Walter Cronkite pronounced it soon after the polls closed, and for Eugene McCarthy "a dream come true." Eight years later, however, a 49-percent to 48-percent victory for President Gerald Ford in that same primary was universally construed as a boost for Ford. It nearly ended, then and there, that year's campaign by Ronald Reagan.

Edmund Muskie won New Hampshire's Democratic primary in 1972 by nine percentage points. Such a win would not normally be thought of as narrow, but it was universally found not good enough. Two months before the primary, David Broder of the *Washington Post* had laid down a marker for Muskie that was eagerly embraced not only by Muskie's rivals but, as tended to happen with Broder, by his fellows in the press. "As the acknowledged front-runner and a resident of the neighboring state," declared Broder on the front page of the paper most national political reporters read first thing in the morning, "Muskie will have to win the support of at least half the New Hampshire Democrats in order to claim a victory." Some time later, Broder, Martin Nolan of the *Boston Globe* (whose most recent poll had Muskie at 65 percent of the primary vote) and some others elicited a plea for mercy from Maria Carrier, Muskie's campaign manager in New Hampshire. "I'll shoot myself," she blurted out, "if Muskie doesn't get 50 percent." Mercilessly, Nolan put that in the *Globe*—from which it flew into every network's clipping file. A week later Johnny Apple put the 50-percent marker on the front page of the *New York Times*, and it was set in stone.[6]

On primary night, an hour after the polls closed, the trap set by Broder and his followers was sprung on all three networks. This is the way it went on one of them: "Good evening from CBS News Election Headquarters in New Hampshire. This is Mike Wallace. The story from here is that Edmund Muskie, the front-runner, the

Senator from Maine, did not do what he set out to do. Anything under 50 percent, he suggested—his staff echoed—would have to be considered a setback."

Muskie, himself, had of course never suggested any such thing. As it happened, he got 47 percent, and George McGovern, a South Dakota senator virtually unknown in New Hampshire when the year began, had scored 38 percent. It was an impressive performance for McGovern. There was no disputing that. Still, the theme of an utterly devastated Muskie marched relentlessly through the broadcast. McGovern, being interviewed, was thrown this softball: "You may be winning the moral victory you've been talking about. How do you feel about that?" McGovern then put the most extravagantly unlikely words yet into Muskie's mouth: "Muskie said some time ago that if he got less than 50 percent of the vote in New Hampshire, it would virtually take him out of the presidential race." When Muskie was shown thanking his campaign workers for "our third victory in a row," Wallace observed drily, "Senator Edmund Muskie, obviously disappointed, exhorting the troops to stand fast."

From the beginning, network election units were sensitive to the influence on later events of their matching primary results, at the moment of reporting them, with prior expectations. This sometimes inspired extraordinary efforts to bring precision to the task. In 1972 Dotty Lynch, who is now Senior Political Editor of CBS News, was a researcher for the NBC Election Unit. Lynch recalls one meeting at NBC just before the Florida primary of 1972. "There was a whole series of scenarios. What if this? What if that? That's how we got to call them 'whiffing sessions.' We'd start with the most plausible scenarios and progress towards the most fantastic. What if [Alabama Governor George] Wallace wins and Muskie's fourth? What if [New York Mayor John] Lindsay's first?" The scenarios looked not only backward on the day's returns but forward to the next primary. " 'If Humphrey has 18 percent in Florida,' " Lynch recalls it being put to the group, " 'what will he need to prove himself against Muskie in Pennsylvania?' "

Each of the scenarios, no matter how hypothetical or wildly improbable, would be fully worked up and written out, entered into a computer and made ready for instant transfer to a Teleprompter screen. It could then be read smoothly by NBC's John Chancellor or

David Brinkley when the actual results dictated which carefully crafted judgment to render.

In later years, the promotion of favorable (i.e., minimal) benchmark expectations by the media became a major task of presidential campaign strategists. Most of this promotional effort was directed at television. At the networks, stories poking fun at the "expectations game" became a routine feature of early campaign coverage. On primary-night specials there would often be some discussion of the propriety of doing what the network anchors and analysts, along with their counterparts in every other medium, never failed to do.

STRAWS IN THE WIND

In 1975, impatient for the caucuses and primaries to begin, network news teams poured into state conventions and party dinners that had no role at all in selecting delegates and reported, as though they meant a good deal, the results of "straw votes" among the participants. Soon these events, at which attendance generally carried a sizable price tag, became a major cost for campaigns—whose only aim was to register wholly fabricated expressions of support on the network broadcasts.

Sometimes, in order to draw the full field of candidates to a party event, the sponsors had to promise not to take a vote. It made no difference. A poll was apt to be conducted anyway for network news. This was a practice in which I myself became quite active. One such vote in the late 1970s, at a Republican conference in Indianapolis, was won handily, to everyone's surprise, by John Connally, a onetime Democratic governor of Texas who had survived the bullet which killed John Kennedy, served as Richard Nixon's Secretary of the Treasury and was now pursuing higher office as a Republican.

Unlike Ronald Reagan, the recognized front-runner, Connally had come to Indianapolis and had worked the crowd. Unlike the other candidates who did show up, Connally gave a pretty good speech. His "upset" victory over Reagan led all the reports out of Indianapolis, and three weeks after my straw poll, Connally was on the cover of *Time*. For much of 1979, until his failure to meet expectations at a straw vote in Florida, Connally was widely recognized as the peer of Ronald Reagan in the first tier of Republican candidates for 1980.

Some candidates (Jimmy Carter in the 1976 cycle, George Bush in 1980) were seen to "emerge" from the crowd long before the first caucuses by upsetting, or doing exceptionally "well" against better known figures in getting supporters to these events. Some of the most highly regarded campaigns, on the other hand (Henry Jackson in 1976, Howard Baker in 1980), were badly bruised by falling short in these dubious tests—whose influence derived almost entirely from television coverage.

With such examples of lightning striking the obscure, and striking down the renowned, the roster of obscure aspirants inevitably grew with each election cycle. Given the finite length of network broadcasts and the need to cover other news during a presidential campaign now measured in years, equal attention to so many contenders was out of the question.

Deciding which candidates to cover, or stratifying the field into the more covered and the less, involved choices with large consequences for the respective campaigns and raised obvious questions of fairness. Aside, however, from the dollar costs involved in casting too wide a net over all the claimants for attention, there was a limit in the competitive world of evening news broadcasts to how much information about the quadrennial turnout of little-known contenders could be thrown at viewers without driving them to other channels.

Normally, in parties without an incumbent president, there were one or more candidates with national reputations and the ability to raise a lot of money. More often than not, one of them led handily in polls of his party's voters, and was crowned the front-runner. Together he and the candidate or candidates who appeared most threatening to him would constitute a first "tier"—warranting close attention in the pre-election year and an assigned crew and correspondent on his campaign plane thereafter.

Sorting out the rest of the field created a second tier of lesser lights with a potential for outshining one of their presumed betters in an early contest. At the bottom, ordinarily, was a third tier given no chance at all. This sorting out was inevitably quite subjective. Into it went appraisals not only of the candidates themselves but of their professional consultants. The were the men and the occasional woman who raised money, probed public opinion and "focus groups" in search of a winning "message," lobbied the news media and steered the campaign through six months of primaries and caucuses randomly strewn across fifty states, the District of Columbia and six overseas territories.[7]

Lapses in assigning candidates to at least the second tier could come back to haunt those who committed them. George McGovern early in the 1972 cycle and Gary Hart in early 1984 barely made the cut. Such apparently sturdy first-tier designees as John Connally in 1980 and John Glenn in 1984 had become hopeless cases by the time the first primary was tallied.

If the networks were having problems with the hordes of candidates enticed by the newly unbossed primary and caucus system, so too were the Democrats who devised it. The nominees who emerged from this ordeal kept losing elections. In the five contests immediately following the reforms, only Jimmy Carter won election, just once and just barely—against a Republican incumbent hobbled by a tough primary challenge and by his pardon of the predecessor who appointed him.

As conventions, moreover, lost their historic role in picking the nominees and became instead massive rallies for the fall campaign, the onetime power brokers of the Democratic party were not merely shorn of the delegates they once delivered; by the 1980s they were having a hard time becoming delegates themselves. Since these people could be useful in the fall campaign, they began to be missed.

As a result there were relatively few objections in the early 1980s when the Democrats created a new class of "unpledged" delegates, who were soon labeled (by *Congressional Quarterly*'s Alan Erenhalt) "superdelegates." These delegates did not have to be elected but went to the convention and voted as they pleased by virtue of being governors, members of Congress or mayors of large cities. A few years later, the nearly four hundred members of the Democratic National Committee quietly voted the same privilege to themselves. By 1988 there were over eight hundred superdelegates—out of roughly four thousand in all.

That was one major "reform," actually a counter-reform, undertaken by the last of the Democrats' notorious rules commissions. Another, designed to rein in Iowa and New Hampshire, created a "window" opening on the second Tuesday in March, before which no state could hold its primaries and caucuses. When the Republican legislatures in both Iowa and New Hampshire (with the private blessing of the local Democrats) refused to budge from their cherished perch in February, the national party threw up its hands—while leaving the "window" in effect for everybody else.

When the 1984 Democratic ticket lost every state but Minnesota, Democratic leaders in the South were stunned by how far down the ballot their tickets had been battered by the landslide up top. The newly created "window" gave them an idea. For the next cycle, they erected on the opening day of the "window" a wall of twelve southern primaries and caucuses—deciding over a third of all the delegates to the next convention. The idea was that moderate and conservative Southern Democrats would flock to the polls on the freshly created Super Tuesday and stop the next liberal front-runner right at the start.

As often happens with such schemes, nothing went as planned. Facing four white opponents in 1988, Jesse Jackson got a huge black vote to the polls on Super Tuesday and carried five of the primaries designed to launch a "mainstream" moderate, ideally from Dixie. By throwing millions of dollars at the major television markets of Texas and Florida, Michael Dukakis, precisely the kind of old-fashioned liberal Super Tuesday was designed to swamp with its bubba vote, managed to win the region's two megastates. It gave little consolation to the creators of the day that Al Gore, the campaign's designated Dixie moderate, won as many primaries as Jackson.

An even more decisive consequence of Super Tuesday took place in the Republican Party, which had played a largely passive role in creating the event. In the skilled southern hands of Lee Atwater, George Bush's own personal and political links to the region had been carefully cultivated over his eight years in Ronald Reagan's White House. Super Tuesday thus became what Atwater called his "insurance policy," a "firewall" he also called it, against anything that might go wrong elsewhere. If all went well, a Bush sweep of Super Tuesday would become inevitable and enable him to put the nomination away for good. With a little help from television news, Atwater would later insist, it worked out just that way.[8]

The help that Atwater had in mind, if in fact it was that, originated at a Christmas party in Washington, where I told Pete Teeley, the Bush press secretary, about a series of profiles CBS was planning on the presidential candidates. One of them would naturally be on Bush, and I wanted Dan Rather to do that one himself. Would the Vice President agree to an interview? He had not done any since the Iran-*contra* scandal broke a year before.

What happened after that has become one of the landmark events of television news. Teeley said initially that he himself thought that Bush, who after all was running for President, should start doing interviews. He said Bush had a warm feeling about Rather, a fellow Texan, and he'd get back to me. When he did, and the news was good, I put him in touch with Richard Cohen, that cycle's evening news producer in charge of campaign coverage.

There could never have been any doubt that, in the Vice President's first face-to-face interview since Iran-*contra*, he would be pressed on what he knew about Oliver North's arms dealing from the White House. Given that, I myself was a bit surprised when Bush agreed to do it.

The assumption, for all the proposed profiles, was that the subject would be interviewed on tape and the parts which made news or were otherwise interesting would be incorporated in the piece. But Roger Ailes, Bush's media advisor, wanted no part of that. The interview, he insisted, would have to be live. CBS agreed, but at that point the whole premise of the profile collapsed. At a National Press Club appearance and (goaded by former Reagan Secretary of State Alexander Haig) in an Iowa debate, Bush had aggressively rejected queries on what he'd known about the arms deals, insisting he'd already answered them fully in other forums (not true) or that they involved confidences with the President.

If Rather, in a live interview on his evening broadcast, were to have any chance of drawing Bush out where so many others had failed, he could not hope to do it in the context of a broad-based profile. In a series of telephone exchanges between Tom Bettag, the executive producer of Rather's broadcast, and Teeley, Bettag insists he made it clear that the central subject would be Iran-*contra* and that the interview would be preceded by a "long and very pointed story" of Bush's record on that subject.

Just *how* pointed would soon get around. Rather likes to prepare for important interviews the way politicians prepare for debates—by rehearsing with a surrogate. On the weekend before the interview with Bush, he did that with Howard Rosenberg, a CBS producer, highly versed on Iran-*contra,* who had worked on the taped piece to be aired in front of the live interview. One of those who watched, though he didn't say much, was Tom Donilon, a gifted Democratic strategist who at this stage of the campaign did not have a candidate. Rather found Donilon's insights useful, and CBS had retained him as a consultant.[9]

As reports of these preparations reached the Bush camp, Ailes has said a source at CBS told him, "They're running around the CBS newsroom saying they're going to take out George Bush tonight. They're going to indict him by putting him on the screen with some sorry characters who have some problems. Then they're going to hand him a blindfold and Rather is going to execute him. So you guys better be ready."[10] I should say that any predictions that Bush would be driven from the race by Rather's interview never got to me.

When the CBS Evening News of January 25, 1988 began, Rather was at his anchor position in New York. Bush and Ailes were at the Vice President's Capitol Hill office with a CBS crew and Mary Martin, the network's deputy bureau chief in Washington. Ailes, she recalled, "was like a boxing coach. It seemed like he just wanted to keep Bush stirred up. He was waving his arms and telling Bush, 'He's gonna sandbag you.' "[11]

Who exactly got sandbagged that evening is open to argument. Bush, cruelly lampooned by the late-night comics as a wimpish yes-man, was obliged to watch (along with fourteen million outside viewers) four minutes of taped evidence that he could not possibly have been as far "out of the loop" on arms sales to Iran and supplies to the *contras* as he kept saying. When Bush got his turn, he complained that this was not his idea of a "profile" and that Rather had "implied . . . that I didn't tell the truth." "Where did we imply that?" replied the anchorman, a study in injured innocence.

Three minutes of what meetings Bush was present at and who said what led up to:

> *Rather:* How do you explain that you can't remember [Secretary of State George Shultz objecting to the arms sales] and the other people at the meeting say he was apoplectic?
> *Bush:* Maybe I wasn't there at that point.
> *Rather:* I don't want to be argumentative, Mister Vice President.
> *Bush:* You do, Dan.

At this point, off screen, Roger Ailes held up to Bush a legal pad on which he had written, "Not fair to judge career on . . . yours." And, right on cue, the Vice President delivered the soundbite of the 1988 primary campaign: "I don't think it's fair to judge my whole career by a rehash on Iran. How would you like it if I judged your career by those seven minutes when you walked off the set in New York?"

Bush/Ailes had picked the right sandbag—though the celebrated Rather walk-off, when a late-running tennis match preempted the opening of his broadcast, actually took place in Miami. The interview went on for another shrill five minutes, but a thoroughly rattled Rather never regained his composure. History will surely reject, as CBS had, Bush's self-portrait (in this instance) as a potted plant in the councils of the Reagan Administration, but in the short term Bush and his camp were beside themselves with joy.

Their euphoria was tempered, to be sure, when Bush, the presumptive front-runner, two weeks later ran third in the Iowa caucuses. But campaign manager Lee Atwater, who had originally opposed the interview, never wavered from his view of it as a gift from God. It "totally demolished the 'wimp' factor," declared Atwater, and helped Bush "more than any single other event in the campaign" to become President.[12]

THE CAMPAIGN NOBODY LOVED

Over the years, little sleep had been lost at the networks over the harsh reviews of campaign coverage from candidates and a growing host of critics in the academic world. However, 1988 was different. When the campaign ended, the winners joined the losers in trashing the television coverage, and many who did the covering had misgivings of their own.

The early front-runner among the Democrats, Gary Hart, was a victim primarily of his own recklessness and self-indulgence, but the press by almost any standard went crazy in reporting it. On the story of Hart's furtive meetings with a woman campaign follower, none of the networks could even claim credit for enterprise. It was a newspaper, the *Miami Herald*, that broke the original story. Another newspaper, the *Washington Post*, did most of the follow-up reporting. But what assuredly determined that Hart was finished was the sheer quantity of coverage, however derivative, on the evening news broadcasts.

In the five weeknights following the *Herald*'s disclosure, thirty separate stories on the subject appeared on the three network broadcasts—an average of six per night. ABC alone ran thirteen such stories—nearly three per night. On that network's *Nightline*, a broadcast highly regarded by advocates of television standards, four nights out of five were devoted to the story.[13]

In the 1988 cycle's other candidate assassination, the initial blow was struck not by the tabloid press or by ratings-driven network news producers but by the good gray *New York Times*. Joseph Biden's attribution to himself of a poignant moment from a British Labourite's stump speech had gone largely unnoted until the Dukakis campaign supplied videotapes to *Times* reporter Maureen Dowd. Another copy was leaked to NBC as well, though the network hesitated, and the *Times* broke the story first. NBC recovered the very same night, airing a devastating matchup of Biden and the Brit mouthing, word for word, identical tales of their rise from humble roots.[14]

CBS and ABC, with research aid from scholars in other camps, found further unacknowledged borrowings by Biden—from Robert Kennedy and Hubert Humphrey. This led to more pairings of identical soundbites on the evening news broadcasts. CBS then reported that Biden had flunked a course in law school because a large hunk of his term paper was lifted from a law review. Without clandestine sex, Biden rated only eleven network news pieces (five by CBS), about a third of Gary Hart's coverage, but it did the job. Within a week, Biden's once promising campaign was over.[15]

Serious research was applied in 1988 to the sex life of five candidates aside from Hart—the flimsy findings of which broke into print in one place or another, though little turned up on television. Similar feats of investigative reporting on marijuana use by candidates in earlier years produced universal shrugs when half the Democrats, to nobody's surprise, confessed.

As the 1992 presidential campaign began, at each evening news broadcast more airtime was pledged to issues and less to the private failings of candidates. At the CBS fishbowl, around ABC's rim and the NBC bullpen, however, there were more pressing concerns about their campaign coverage. Declining ad budgets during the post-Reagan recession had struck television hard. Large losses from overbids by CBS's Sports division had tightened belts throughout that company. The collapse of NBC's prime-time schedule had the same effect there. ABC was under similar pressures.

On top of that, 1991 brought each network news division $40 million, more or less, in unbudgeted costs for covering the Gulf War. So nothing could have cheered network news managements more than the prolonged delay in starting the campaign. One Democrat after another who might ordinarily have thought about running for President looked at the incumbent's war-enhanced approval numbers and passed. At a staff meeting, CBS News president Eric Ober joked merrily about an unopposed Bush being re-elected by acclamation. Each month that passed with no campaign activity to cover was money in the bank for the networks.

There were other reasons to welcome the unusual stillness on the campaign trail. Starting in the mid-1960s, for nearly a quarter of a century *CBS Evening News* had led the evening news ratings without interruption. Since 1989, however, CBS had not been able to challenge for even a week ABC's boast: "More Americans get their news from ABC News than from any other source."

Some weeks, in fact, CBS came perilously close to the perennial doormat of 1980s television news, once its chief rival for the ratings crown, NBC. Unlike the 1960s, when the networks asserted their muscle over one another with their campaign coverage, in the 1990s politics was seen as poison to viewership. At one point in 1992, noting this fact of life and the virtual boycott of campaign coverage by the front-running ABC, Rather suggested that CBS abandon day-today reporting from the field and just let him *tell* any "breaking news" that our Election Unit staff turned up.

Until nearly Labor Day, the only declared candidate was Paul Tsongas. A former Democratic senator from Massachusetts, Tsongas had been out of politics for ten years, claimed he had overcome cancer, and had written a book on how to turn the economy around. Most years, Tsongas would have been a third-tier candidate. For much of 1991, he was the only tier.

In sorting out the candidates once they appeared, a consensus over the first tier quickly settled on three men, all of whom were unknown to nearly nine out of ten Americans: Senators Tom Harkin of Iowa and Bob Kerrey of Nebraska and Bill Clinton.

Harkin's trademark was a speech in which he rhythmically recited all four names of the President of the United States and then invited his audience to chant, "Bullshit!" Kerrey had a supposed star quality based on his medal of honor from the Vietnam war and his on and off affair with Hollywood's Debra Winger.

Clinton had achieved a certain fame in 1988 with an eye-glazing nominating speech for Dukakis that, many feared, would never end.[16] Still, he was a tireless campaigner who dazzled both campaign audiences and Washington reporters with his detailed grasp of the complexities of government. His stump speech was full of tough talk on crime and welfare—designed to draw white middle-class men ("Reagan Democrats") back from their recent Republican leanings.

In the second tier with Tsongas was the only man who'd ever run for President before. Jerry Brown, a onetime governor of California, had in fact run twice—very poorly the last time. Brown had no staff to speak of; during televised debates he would ask people to send him money; he made up his schedule from hour to hour as he went along—defeating any rational approach to covering him.

If the seeming invincibility of Bush, while it lasted, helped keep news division budgets in the black, Harkin, the Iowa Senator, helped even more. Four years before, with six Republicans and six Democrats stalking Iowa's caucus-goers, that state soaked up nearly a fourth of all the network money (not to mention airtime) spent on the race for the party nominations. With Harkin, Iowa's most popular Democratic politician of his generation, in the race, this year's caucuses were conceded to him from the outset. The Iowa line in the network budgets could therefore be dropped entirely.

With nothing going on in Iowa, and little in New Hampshire, during an eight-week period in October and November the broadcasts paid more attention to the struggle inside the head of Mario Cuomo, the governor of New York, over entering the race than to any of the candidates who actually did. From Labor Day through New Year's, *CBS Evening News* aired only fourteen stories (less than one a week) on the race itself. NBC and ABC did even less.[17]

As a result, by year's end, none of the Democratic candidates was any better known nationally than when he started. As the election year began, Harkin incredibly spent the first two weeks on a holiday in the Bahamas. Kerrey spent most of that time in Washington—rejiggering his campaign staff. Clinton, meanwhile, was campaigning with hardly a pause in New Hampshire. By mid-January, in the New Hampshire polls, Clinton had overtaken Paul Tsongas, the one-time Massachusetts Senator who had camped out in the first primary state for more than a year. Had Clinton won New Hampshire, as then seemed likely, he appeared certain to obliterate his Yankee rivals two weeks later on the South's Super Tuesday.

Just as the mantle of inevitability appeared to be settling on Clinton, however, the *National Star*, a publication that took no part in the hand-wringing over 1988, unleashed Gennifer Flowers and her tale of a twelve-year affair with Clinton on the rest of the press. We all knew that sooner or later we would have to deal with Clinton's women. That he'd had affairs was notorious in Little Rock and on the political grapevine in Washington. Sooner or later there was going to be a story. In the normally cutthroat culture of evening news broadcasts, however, nobody was dying to be first.

At *CBS Evening News*, Executive Producer Erik Sorenson said he did not care if he was dead last when the story broke. When the *Star* release reached his desk on Thursday, January 22, he crumpled it and threw it away. At NBC, on the other hand, there was little choice. A Clinton profile was scheduled that evening. It was hard to devote three minutes (an epic by evening news standards) to the heart and mind of Bill Clinton and not mention the one Clinton story that millions of Americans already knew by way of the tabloid press, and that had dominated local TV coverage of Clinton's own appearances that day in New Hampshire.

As it happened, Clinton himself wanted to tell, that is to deny, the story his way. "Nobody wanted you guys to handle it," said his media strategist and designated bully, James Carville. Thus began a bidding war, which CBS quickly won. CBS offered an interview on an "abbreviated edition" of television's all time top-rated broadcast, 60 Minutes—on a night when its own normally huge ratings would be enhanced further by a lead-in from the Super Bowl, the most widely watched broadcast of the entire year. Not till CBS News announced that 60 Minutes appearance did it, for the first time, report any part of Flowers' story. Sorenson by then had recovered, or replaced, the discarded handout from the Star.

The 60 Minutes interview was seen by more people than, on any given night, ordinarily watch all three evening news broadcasts combined. Steve Kroft, who did the interview, never got an unequivocal statement as to whether Clinton ever had what most people would regard as sexual relations with Flowers. What 60 Minutes did air, out of a prolonged series of exchanges, was a categorical denial of her claim of a "twelve-year affair." That denial was parsed over for years until Clinton, under oath for the Paula Jones lawsuit, acknowledged at least one act of intercourse. Not in the least flustered, Mike McCurry, the White House press secretary, claimed the President had not changed his story a bit—any fool, he implied, knows the difference between a one-night stand and a twelve-year affair.[18]

The day after 60 Minutes, Flowers held a news conference and played her tapes. CNN earned the lasting enmity of Clinton (akin to that of Bush for CBS) by airing that news conference live—though it did not air the tapes themselves as they were played. Soundbites, however, in which Clinton was heard urging Flowers not to answer questions about something and appearing to acquiesce when she likened the Governor of New York to a "Mafioso," were aired by all the evening news broadcasts. At the same time that Clinton staffers were publicly declaring the tapes a fake and reproaching the networks for airing any part of them, Clinton privately apologized to Mario Cuomo for letting the "Mafioso" remark go unchallenged.

After leading with the tapes (there was no obvious alternative), each network followed with stories on the ethics of reporting the private affairs of candidates and on the reactions, mostly bored, of voters in New Hampshire. Nearly all the experts interviewed on the journalistic ethics of the case came down on Clinton's side. Most of the New Hampshire politicians and voters interviewed predicted the story would have little effect. That was the entire network evening news coverage—less than a third of what the Gary Hart scandal inspired four years before.[19]

While the Clintons were berating the networks for having done even that much, Clinton's rivals on the trail in New Hampshire seemed almost as upset. Tim Raftis, running the Harkin campaign, was enraged by Clinton's thirteen minutes in the most watched television time slot of the year—even if it was to talk about his observance of the Seventh Commandment. Bob Kerrey's manager, Tad Devine, saw the Gennifer coverage not as a blow to Clinton but as a distraction that was shoving his own candidate aside at time when Kerrey badly needed to "get into the news mix."

The Kerrey and Harkin managers appeared to have it right. In the week that Gennifer Flowers became a household name, so too—for the first time—did Clinton. In national polls of Democratic primary voters, Clinton now for the first time became a clear front-runner.

This outcome should not have been surprising. Well before Flowers got to make her case on the networks, Clinton and his backers had saturated the airwaves with their denials. Flowers' tapes did not directly confirm her claim, and she herself—with her six-figure fee—was not a compelling witness. Americans had been telling pollsters for years that they could accept a President who cheated on his wife. They apparently meant it—though the definitive test would come in Clinton's second term.

By now the networks were all in New Hampshire, ready to deal with the issues (e.g., health care, the capital gains tax, welfare reform) on which they had pledged to concentrate their 1992 coverage. Once again, however, the central issue of Clinton's career—his personal character—got in the way. It was no supermarket tabloid, moreover, but the *Wall Street Journal* which put the story of Clinton's youthful struggles with the draft in play. Unlike the issue of marital fidelity, this could not be brushed off as having no bearing on Clinton's suitability for office.[20]

Meanwhile, at CBS, Dan Rather was convinced that Roger Ailes, who had no formal role in this year's Bush campaign, had in some way inspired the Gennifer Flowers story. When the draft story appeared in the *Journal*, Rather wanted to break a story on how the Bush campaign had planted that.

Lots of people, as it happened, had been flogging the story of Clinton's efforts to avoid wartime service. Opponents in Arkansas had raised it in the past. Opposition researchers at the Republican National Committee had a substantial file. Still, the most aggressive promoter of the story to me and others in the press was no Republican but a consultant to a rival Democrat—whose need to slow Clinton down was far more urgent than the Bush campaign's.

As Clinton tried to spin a story about his avoiding military service while protecting his "political viability" into one about sneaky Bush tactics, he got help from ABC's Ted Koppel as well as Rather. Having obtained a twenty-year-old Clinton letter declaring the future candidate's "loathing of the military," Koppel said it came from a "Pentagon source." The source later turned out to be a long-retired general familiar to Koppel as a source on other matters but with no known ties to the current Pentagon or the Bush administration.[21]

Clinton seized on Koppel's hazy citation of a Pentagon source to attack the Bush White House. That day's campaign story on all the networks was accordingly about an alleged Bush negative campaign and only secondarily on the revelations about Clinton's impolitic thoughts in the letter itself. In CBS's first report on the draft issue, five days after it broke, Rather, who has several writers at his disposal, gave it a headline that absolutely no one else could: "Bill Clinton says President Bush's 1988 Willie Horton crowd is smearing him with new campaign dirty tricks." Rather was not pleased by CBS's failure to scoop the world on this, or on Roger Ailes' supposed planting of the Gennifer Flowers story.

On New Hampshire television, unlike the networks, there was no ambivalence about the story of Clinton's ducking the Vietnam draft and trying to conceal it. In one New Hampshire survey, over one weekend, Clinton fell nearly twenty points behind Tsongas. In a way, that poll became an element in Clinton's salvation. On primary night, when the voters pegged Clinton a mere *eight* points back, Clinton took to the network broadcasts with one of the all-time classics of spin control. "I proved I can take a punch," he told NBC's Tom Brokaw. "New Hampshire has made Bill Clinton the Comeback Kid."

Brokaw, no novice at this game, acknowledged only that Clinton had "dodged a bullet." It fell to ABC's Peter Jennings to take the Clinton bait and keep chewing it over and over and over. Three times in the first three minutes of his broadcast Jennings chuckled as he quoted Clinton's (actually consultant Mandy Grunwald's) line about the "Comeback Kid." Then he brought the candidate on live to render it a fourth time himself.[22]

Clinton had indeed dodged a bullet. Harkin and Kerrey never recovered from their also-ran finishes in New Hampshire. Once the campaign left New England, Clinton buried Tsongas—first, to nobody's surprise, on Super Tuesday in Clinton's southern home base, then much more conclusively a week later in Illinois and Michigan. Addressing Tsongas, after this whitewash, Rather was pitiless: "You came to neutral territory. You lost. Isn't it time to throw in the towel? . . . Clinton has 987 delegates. You have 359. Do you really see any way to catch up?"

Clearly CBS News did not. At a staff meeting the next day, with my blessing, CBS concluded that the race for the Democratic nomination was over. We would keep a reporter with Tsongas until he did formally quit (he did so a day later) and for the time being with Jerry Brown.

As it turned out, there was still some life left in the Democratic race. Flat broke and aware that money was pouring into Clinton, Tsongas withdrew a few days before the Connecticut primary, but he still got a lot of votes there. So did Jerry Brown, who won his second and final primary. This lead to a New York contest in which Brown appeared for a short time to have a chance.

That moment did not last long. Brown's big idea for 1992 was a 13 percent income tax, with no deductions, for everyone. It turned out that whoever peddled this idea to Brown failed to mention (or Brown forgot) that to maintain existing revenues would take a 13 percent national sales tax as well. While Brown's economic plan was being reduced to rubble on New York's talk shows and editorial pages, he announced that Jesse Jackson would be his running mate. This did not stop Clinton from winning a majority of the black vote. It certainly had a lot to do with Brown's getting barely 8 percent of the much larger Jewish vote. At the end, Brown trailed not only Clinton, by a wide margin, but Tsongas—whose name was still on the New York ballot—as well.

At that point, of the roughly two thousand delegates needed for the nomination, Clinton had over a thousand. No one else had even a third of that. After a few days' reflection on re-entering the race, Tsongas prudently did not. And so, in mid-April, three months before the convention that was supposed to pick the Democratic nominee for President, the chief business conventions were designed to do had already been done.

1996: FIXING THE SYSTEM AGAIN

By the time Michigan and Illinois reduced the Democratic race to Bill Clinton and the improbable Jerry Brown, less than half the party's voters had had a chance to vote in its primaries or caucuses. By the time New York settled things for good, those who might have voted approached two thirds. Still, if you lived in the country's most populous state, California, or the fourth, seventh or tenth (Pennsylvania, Ohio, New Jersey), the train never reached your station.

Reaction to the 1992 experience brought major changes in the nominating calendar. Fed up with another cycle of irrelevance, California finally discarded its fifty-year tradition of holding the nation's final primary and moved to March, where its huge stash of convention votes could once again become a prize worth fighting for. So too did Ohio, Wisconsin and even New York—aware that, with the stampede of the remaining large states into March, even April might be too late for a primary to matter next time.

As 1996 approached, all these moves together drew the country towards a system often advocated by some political theorists: regional primaries. By the end of March 1996 each of the four quadrants of the country would choose most of their convention delegates in successive weeks: the Northeast in the first week, the South on the second Tuesday, the Midwest on the third Tuesday and California, along with several other Far West states, on the fourth Tuesday.

No advocate of regional primaries, however, ever suggested they be held on successive Tuesdays. Nor was it the intention of the individual legislatures, which acted for the most part on their own, that as a consequence the great majority of convention delegates in both parties would be chosen in just twenty-two days. That, however, is how it worked out. A couple of cycles back, as this process was going forward, somebody gave it a name: "front-loading."

Political sophisticates quickly reached a consensus on what, more than ever, you had to do to run for President in 1996: raise a ton of money and raise it fast. You could not hope to stage an upset in Iowa or New Hampshire and then on the strength of that upset raise money for the big state primaries with their staggeringly expensive media markets. The current primary calendar allowed no time for that.

There were two leading preachers of this consensus. One was the Clinton White House, which announced early in 1995 that it would raise the legal maximum in record time and whose prodigious Clinton-Gore filings at the Federal Election Commission were designed to intimidate any Democrats entertaining rebellious thoughts. It worked. The other preacher was Phil Gramm, the Republican senator from Texas who claimed he actually enjoyed asking people to give him money and who had nearly $10 million to show for it before formally joining the race.

The supposed eight-figure entry fee had an intimidating effect on Republicans as well as Democrats. One after another, citing in most cases the ordeal of raising the required money, some of the likeliest members of a first tier of Republican candidates—Dan Quayle, Dick Cheney, James Baker, Bill Bennett, Jack Kemp—declined to run. In their absence Bob Dole, the party's longtime Senate leader, had the first tier to himself. To his rear, however, there was lots of company. Joined by Gramm and several other senators, the governor of California and five additional contenders, the 1996 Republican campaign tour—despite all the high-profile absentees—comprised the party's largest field of candidates ever.

If 1992 had seen the latest start to a presidential campaign since the 1960s, the 1996 campaign—given the urgency of the money chase—got off to the earliest start ever. With each announcement, the networks routinely presented their two minutes' worth of biographical basics, positioning in the party's ideological spectrum, soundbite from the announcement speech and appraisal of the candidate's prospects by an "analyst." In the early spring of 1995, however, these announcements seemed wildly out of step with the current news of the day.

While every few days some Republican, often quite obscure, would declare his readiness to combat Clinton in the fall of 1996, a freshly-elected Republican Congress could be seen night after night engaging that same Democratic president over the agenda on which the House majority had been elected. As Newt Gingrich's chamber passed nine out of ten of the items in its "Contract with America," you could watch the Senate presided over by presidential front-runner Dole creep along tardily in its wake.

Though overshadowed by the Speaker in the nightly news from the Hill, in the contest for attention with his actual rivals for the nomination, Dole was out of sight. Dole's rivals, of course, faced formidable competition aside from Dole for the attention of our broadcasts. There were, first of all, a bunch of running stories which, on any given day, were apt to have a development to report: O. J. Simpson, Oklahoma City, Bosnia, and, to the extent that politics made the cut, the partisan struggle on the Hill. Gingrich, the dominant figure in that struggle, kept hinting, moreover, that he himself might run for President—which would have rendered Dole's existing rivals even more invisible.

An even greater obstacle to the second, let alone the third tier of candidates was the threatened candidacy of Colin Powell. Unlike Gingrich, whose presidential effort never went beyond his own teasing, Powell had important Republicans preparing a serious campaign while he made up his mind. Powell's poll readings were sky-high. His book tour got far more coverage in the country's major media markets than appearances by any of the declared candidates.[23]

Network coverage of Powell's decision-making surely set some kind of record. Andrew Tyndall, whose logs of the network evening news broadcasts are a standard source, registered more than eighty minutes' worth of Powell stories in 1995, none of them a knock. That was twice as much coverage as the Dole campaign got and almost as much as all the Republican campaigns combined.[24]

As the election year of 1996 began, it was not easy to find a story. Dole led by huge margins both in the national polls and in the closely watched polls of Iowa and New Hampshire. In monthly *CBS News/New York Times* polls of Republicans for the entire year, a fairly steady 40 percent or so favored Dole. None of his rivals ever got more than a third of that.

Nor were a lot of the issues at the top of people's minds being argued by the candidates. Gramm and Dole, both of whom had perfect scorecards with the pro-life movement, seemed to be forever having to convince the movement's leaders that they didn't just vote "right" on the Senate floor—that deep down they really *cared*.

All of the candidates embraced the Republican agenda that was being pursued against Clinton on the Hill and dominating (as it had to) the broader political news of the period. The minor differences among them on issues not currently before the country were hard for the broadcasts to dwell on. There was, to be sure, the curious phenomenon of Pat Buchanan, the lifelong flag-carrier of the Republican right, flirting with positions of the Democratic left on foreign trade and corporate welfare and with those of Clinton himself on preserving Medicare. Only on foreign trade and protectionism, however, did the other candidates engage Buchanan, and that would not come till later.

Finally, to the rescue of those in search of a campaign story, came Steve Forbes—the business-magazine dynast and single-minded advocate of a uniform income tax rate for everyone. With a 400-million-dollar fortune to draw on, Forbes thumbed his nose at federal matching funds and was thus free to spend as much as he liked anywhere he chose.[25] To prevent Dole from running off with the nomination at the outset, Forbes leveled a television strike on the front-runner without precedent in a primary campaign. Forbes did not, however, have to spread his money, vast as it was, across the entire country. Most of it went into fewer than a half dozen relatively small states, in which seven-figure advertising budgets for any office were rare or unheard of.

As the network news finally turned its attention toward the race, there were now at last three solid stories to tell, and Forbes was central to all of them. There was the issue of negative advertising itself, as Dole dipped into his own treasury for a withering round of attack ads against Forbes. There was the flat-tax issue, which came to dominate the dialogue on the stump as all the other candidates ganged up against it. There was Forbes' rise, as a result of all this advertising and attention, to levels of support approaching Dole's in both Iowa and New Hampshire polls. A majority of all the campaign stories in January on the network news broadcasts dealt in one of these ways with Forbes.[26]

Meanwhile, after a year's obsessing over the front-loaded campaign schedule in March, it began to dawn on the wise men of politics and journalism that something radical had happened to February. In yet another try at challenging the "first in the nation" hegemony of Iowa/New Hampshire, quite a number of states had set up competitive events in the weeks just before and after. Ten days before Iowa, Alaska had scheduled a straw vote just like Iowa's at its caucuses. Six days before Iowa, Louisiana would elect outright the first national-convention delegates.

Forbes had chosen Alaska, and Phil Gramm Louisiana, to draw first blood and animate supporters down the road. Dole's campaign had canvassed the party's extremely conservative activists in both states before deciding not to get involved himself. To keep Forbes and Gramm, however, from chalking up cheap early wins, Scott Reed, the Dole campaign manager, ordered lists of likely prospects in both places turned over to Buchanan—who was seen, for the long run, as far less worrisome.[27]

In Alaska, Buchanan delivered as planned—beating Forbes by just 170 votes. None of the networks made a lot of it. Louisiana was something else. Buchanan, who'd been heavily outspent, won thirteen national convention delegates to Gramm's eight. Had thirty votes at one meeting hall gone the other way, Gramm would have won the day with eleven delegates to ten. For the networks, however, it was no squeaker. "If Buchanan got more delegates," Gramm had rashly declared, "it will be a setback for me." A candidate who sets himself up like that (as even Muskie had never done) can expect little mercy. On ABC the next night, Gramm could watch file footage of that statement. Concluded Peter Jennings, "Buchanan won the bragging rights." The CBS verdict, from Rather: "An embarrassing setback in Gramm's own backyard."

Meanwhile, in Iowa, the Dole campaign mischievously turned over 10,000 names of wavering Gramm supporters to Buchanan. Still more mischief: posing as a poll operation, Dole's phone banks called thousands of Forbes supporters and asked, as if taking a poll, how they would feel if they knew Forbes believed that abortion and gay sex should be legal. The message was reinforced by a lethal round of thirty-second television spots.[28]

At the Iowa caucuses, in contrast to the exit polls at primaries and elections, the networks interview voters as they go in. Almost immediately this time, to nobody's surprise, they declared Dole the winner. Almost as good news for Dole: of his two most formidable rivals, Gramm would finish fifth, Forbes a distant fourth. In engineering precisely that outcome, however, Dole had helped to fashion a new hazard for himself. "Biggest story of the night," summed up Rather, "Buchanan's surge into second." "The surprise," echoed Peter Jennings, "is Buchanan." Chimed in [then] NBC's Bryant Gumbel: Buchanan was "the biggest winner." Not only had Dole's three-point win flunked the networks' expectations test, but Buchanan had won an A.

When Buchanan, eight days later, drove that perception coup in Iowa to the real thing in New Hampshire, barely 200,000 Republicans in all had been heard from. Alaska, Louisiana, Iowa and New Hampshire combined were home to less than 3 percent of the party's voters. Dole was still the overwhelming choice of Republicans nationally and would remain so. Nevertheless, the year-long front-runner was in perilous shape.

Dole by then had spent most of the 42-million-dollar war chest accumulated for that twenty-two-day roller-coaster in March. At the rate he was going, mostly to counter Forbes, Dole would hit the spending limit for candidates receiving public funds by early March. For Forbes, who took no public money and had plenty of his own left, there was no such limit.

Three days later, a half million dollars in television ads aimed at 30,000 primary voters in Delaware won Forbes his first victory. The next week, $4 million worth of television as well as mail won him Arizona.[29] When South Carolina held its primary four days later, however, Forbes was in a state that he had not carpet-bombed with ads. Buchanan's penchant for black hats and prancing steeds, his merry calls for an uprising of "peasants with pitchforks" and the daily discovery of extreme cases among his campaign workers cooled much of the fire lit in New Hampshire—though it took a bit longer to cool off ABC News. In South Carolina, even the religious right got behind Dole, undermining Buchanan's only remaining base, and Dole won easily.

With the four Super Tuesdays of March about to happen, Forbes could no longer hope to win cheap victories by pouring a few million dollars into a Delaware or an Arizona. He had already spent more than forty million. That, Forbes would soon conclude, was enough. The race for the Republican nomination for President was over.

And it was still only February. Not only would the Republican convention be a formality, so would all the front-loaded primaries in March, not to mention those afterwards—in states where 95 percent of the country's Republicans vote. Was this any way to nominate a candidate for President? Quite a few Republicans, who historically had scoffed at the Democrats' passion for tampering with the system, wondered if the time had not come for Republicans to tamper.

In the meantime there remained, for both parties and the networks, the formality of the conventions. When television news at mid-century first entered the life of America, these uniquely American events became the supreme test of a network's capacity to cover news. By the close of the century, they had become the pits.

2

FROM GAVEL TO GAVEL
TO TEN TO ELEVEN

(The Twilight of the Conventions)

A S THE PRIMARY SYSTEM SO FONDLY NURTURED BY THE NET-
works grew and flourished, the institution that once defined
television's role in politics faded with every cycle. Before television, politicians struggled with each other for control of the convention. Today they struggle with the networks for control of the broadcast.

When the first nationally televised conventions were held in
1952, the politicians of both parties had other things than television
on their minds. They had come to nominate candidates, write platforms and do a lot of other party business; and, unlike most conventions of the current television era, often no one could be sure how
any of that business would turn out. When approached by ABC, CBS
and NBC the Republican chairman, Guy Gabrielson, suggested they
pay for the broadcast rights—as they would for a World Series, the
Kentucky Derby or a Miss America contest. One of the television
people observed that this would amount to an illegal corporate contribution, and Gabrielson, perhaps with a sigh, dropped the matter.[1]

At the time these negotiations were going on, the cross-country
cable that made network broadcasting possible had only recently
been finished. The national party conventions of 1952 would be the
first major television attractions seen live across the nation. A majority of Americans still did not own television sets, and sales boomed in
the weeks preceding the conventions.

For the pioneer producers of television news, convention coverage was a large step toward the status they would soon take for granted. Don Hewitt, who later reigned over television's most successful broadcast, *60 Minutes*, was then a very junior producer in a very junior medium. Hewitt recalls: "TV had been radio's little brother. Radio could go anywhere. TV was stuck in a studio. Then we said, hey, let's cover a convention. We can stake it out like a football game. We know when it's going to be played, we know where the rostrum is, we know where the delegates are going to sit. For the first time television could flex its muscles and say, 'We can do anything radio can do, and we can do it better.'"[2] When CBS Radio would not surrender Edward R. Murrow or even one of its lesser stars for the television broadcast, the fledgling television unit recruited a young reporter named Walter Cronkite from the network's Washington affiliate.

Westinghouse paid $3 million to sponsor the CBS convention broadcasts in their entirety. To guarantee the sponsor its money's worth of airtime, CBS got a commitment from the internetwork pool sharing the cable to stay in operation "from gavel to gavel." Thus was born a phrase and a practice that for thirty years governed the coverage of at least two networks, CBS and NBC, and more often than not ABC as well. That practice, adopted when program schedules were still fluid and experimental, became the standard for network news after the compelling contests of 1952 and the uninhibited way in which their participants made history before Hewitt's (as well as the other networks') meticulously staked out cameras.[3]

At what turned out to be the last truly brokered convention, the Democrats nominated Adlai Stevenson on a third ballot. It also turned out to be the last presidential nomination to take more than one roll call. As years passed, succeeding generations of network producers and reporters would dream of covering another.

Meanwhile, at network television's first Republican convention, there was only one ballot but an even better story and a livelier show for the broadcasters. While one war hero, Douglas MacArthur, was delivering the keynote speech, another, Dwight Eisenhower, a contender for the nomination, attacked Senator Robert Taft's camp as "cattle rustlers" who had made off with the Texas delegation in the dead of night.[4]

When the convention opened, Taft had a clear lead in delegates. The nomination turned on whether the general could get Taft delegates from Texas and some other states unseated in favor of his own. While Ike delegations on the floor waved standards reading "Thou shalt not steal," a credentials committee controlled by Taft barred television cameras and was on its way behind closed doors to dismissing the Eisenhower challenges.[5]

In doing so, however, the Taft managers had not reckoned on the visual impact of a brand new phenomenon: the television stakeout. In *Out of Thin Air* NBC's Reuven Frank, a major figure in the early years of television news, recalls:

> Television is good at showing closed doors. Whenever a committee member left the room, he was waylaid and asked what was going on. The Taft leadership soon realized how they were "playing" on camera. A Taft representative finally confronted the NBC cameras and insisted it was not Taft who objected to live coverage. It must have been some other fellow. . . . The Eisenhower people smelled blood. They also came to the cameras, proclaiming they favored television, they loved it, they wanted it, and barring it was an outrage, a denial of the American way.[6]

One reporter standing outside those closed doors, however, was in no position to complain. CBS's Walter Cronkite could report everything said inside as though he had the room wired—because he did. A network technician, after hours, had struck a blow for the people's right to know by connecting a line to the committee's own sound system. "He ran a wire," according to Cronkite, "up the outside of the hotel and into a broom closet several floors above. There one of our newspeople listened through earphones and wrote notes that were rushed to me downstairs. The sources of these reports baffled both the Republicans and my broadcast opposition." Sig Mickelson, who as the network's head of television news authorized the bugging, acknowledges, "At this early period in television history, ethical considerations did not deeply disturb us." CBS at the time, to be sure, had been in the news business for a quarter of a century.[7]

The party managers eventually thought of removing the visual stigma of the closed door by opening it—but only to reporters, not to cameras, which might *show* the unsightly brawl inside. NBC, recalls Reuven Frank, promptly rose to that challenge. "Since the committee's debates could not be shown, six Texans were recruited, three from each side, to make their cases in the studio, to claim legitimacy, cry fraud, call each other names, shout when shouted at, and predict victory. Every television program or news bulletin included a prominent statement about the barring of cameras, and each was a blow to Taft's candidacy." The next meeting on credentials was opened to television, and, before a national viewership, Taft was shamed into concessions that ultimately cost him the nomination.[8]

The Republican convention ran five days, the Democratic convention six. There were morning, afternoon and evening sessions. Gavel-to-gavel coverage at both conventions ran between 139 hours (CBS) and 152 hours (NBC).[9] There was blood on the floor at both conventions. None of that blood, however, had much effect on what the voters did in November. The Republicans' struggles were far messier, but the party went on to win the White House by a landslide and to elect what would turn out to be the country's only Republican Congress in nearly two-thirds of the century.

For television news, the 1952 conventions marked the beginning of a new relationship with the men and the occasional women who ran the country. To help likely speakers in their appearances, CBS held a "school for candidates" in Washington—conducted by Cronkite and the bureau chief and attended by, among others, Speaker of the House Sam Rayburn and Congressman John Kennedy. For a one-day course, the instruction took in make-up, dress and diction and other helpful hints; one senator recalled, "Walter Cronkite taught me that getting across in TV is all in the eyes." An NBC advisory to prospective stars of the podium advised against white or yellow shirts ("too violent a contrast") and taffeta for women ("much too audible") and recommended "on polished bald pates a coating of pancake make-up."[10]

A larger lesson was taught by Mickelson, the CBS television news chief, at a joint meeting with Republican and Democratic party chairmen in Chicago. The parties were of one mind, both wanting to hold their conventions at the Chicago Stadium—site of many past conventions. No way, said Mickelson, who was authorized to speak for ABC and NBC as well. The stadium had no space for the equipment and staff they would need for their broadcasts. Sorry.[11]

Mickelson got his answer the next day. The conventions would be held where the networks wanted them, at the Stockyards Amphitheatre—which had 5,000 fewer seats for rewarding contributors but did have the facilities television needed. Years later, Mickelson still recalled it as a famous victory: "The score was now 2 to 0 in television's favor." (The other victory was not having to cut the parties in on the advertisers' huge fees).[12]

In later years the networks would become more circumspect about acknowledging their own clout. The official line became that the parties conducted their business as they chose and the networks would cover that business as *they* chose. Bill Leonard, who oversaw the CBS broadcasts in the 1960s, liked to say that the conventions could be held on an aircraft carrier at sea and CBS would find a way to cover them. This boast went a bit too far, since high and sturdy camera platforms had to be built and enormous amounts of light generated, especially in the early years of color—and neither was very doable on choppy seas at short notice. Nor, at the party planning meetings for the conventions did CBS, any more than NBC or ABC, hesitate to point out electrical or air-conditioning deficiencies or line-of-sight obstructions at the dry-land sites under consideration.[13]

Still, in that relatively innocent era, what Leonard said about the separation of roles was true in spirit—especially with regard to keeping hands off the convention program. The networks in turn felt free to ignore that program whenever, as happened most of the time, they got bored with it or found a better story elsewhere. In the eighty hours or so between the opening and closing gavels, only a handful of scheduled events were guaranteed coverage: the Pledge of Allegiance and the Trooping of the Color, the keynote speech on opening night, the roll call for President and the acceptance speeches for President and Vice President. No camera shots were more carefully planned than the anchormen's positioning of their own hands as they joined the delegates in pledging allegiance to one nation under God. (Less visible members of the team were free, like any Massachusetts schoolchild, to exercise our First Amendment rights—though complaints are still heard, mainly at Republican conventions, about subversive network technicians on the floor.)

In the very second round of convention broadcasts, the issue of who decides what is shown to the country was joined by the Democrats. Hollywood's Dore Schary had produced a thirty-minute party commercial called "The Pursuit of Happiness," cheerfully narrated by a 38-year-old John Kennedy. In calling the 1956 convention's opening night session to order, Chairman Paul Butler declared: "One of our major networks has failed to keep its commitment to present this documentary film to the American people." None of the networks had made any such commitment, but Butler knew that only CBS had decided firmly to pass on the film. He made that clear by publicly thanking ABC and NBC for being good Americans. Reuven Frank, the NBC producer who chose to air the party's "documentary," recalls NBC's floor reporters happily helping to orchestrate the prolonged booing of CBS that followed.[14]

CBS PLUS THIRTY

The power of conventions to create stars in television news, and to fix the ranking of the network news divisions for years to come, was soon apparent. 1952 had been a triumph for CBS and for Cronkite—who was at his best covering an event where, most of the time, neither the final outcome nor the next development was assured.

Four years later, however, neither party had a convention contest. Cronkite's knack for reporting and explaining fast-breaking news made for relatively boring broadcasts when there was far less breaking news, fast or slow, to report and no devious schemes to expose. Over at NBC, Chet Huntley and David Brinkley, as obscure when the 1956 conventions began as Cronkite had been four years earlier, provided what Cronkite could not. Huntley readily kept pace with the CBS anchorman in reporting what little news there was. Brinkley, with a quick wit and a large store of anecdotes about the Washington figures in the hall, easily and entertainingly filled the vast expanse of time between the opening and closing gavels.

After the conventions, Huntley and Brinkley were rewarded with NBC's nightly television news broadcast—then a distantly trailing rival to its CBS counterpart. The viewer appeal they displayed at the conventions traveled well to weekdays at dinnertime. In the spring of 1960, NBC's *Huntley-Brinkley Report* replaced CBS's *Douglas Edwards with the News* as the most widely watched network evening news broadcast, and for much of the 1960s there was little CBS could do about it. ABC, with fewer stations and much tighter budgets, would not for many years become a contender in this game.

———

Two enormous egos were involved in this struggle: those of Robert Kintner, the president of NBC, and William Paley, the chairman of CBS. Kintner was a former newspaper reporter who rose rapidly to the top of first ABC and then NBC; in both places he was an ardent patron of live news coverage. Asked once by a special-events producer how long he should stay on the air, Kintner replied with a legendary edict: "CBS plus thirty."[15]

Under this edict, long after the convention delegates had left the hall and long after most viewers had surrendered and gone to sleep, Huntley and Brinkley, John Chancellor, Sander Vanocur and Robert MacNeil for NBC and Cronkite, Roger Mudd, Mike Wallace and Charles Kuralt for CBS would do round after laborious round of reprise and "analysis" to decide which network could claim the most (literally) exhaustive coverage. In that heady era of a young and expanding industry, with the networks making money hand over fist and their share values doubling every three or four years, the fact that tens of thousands of dollars went out the window with each thirty-minute segment apparently bothered no one.[16]

At CBS, Chairman William Paley's men had dominated broadcast news since World War II. In the early years of television, they had won all the merit badges for ratings, sales, awards and overall prestige. On the eve of the 1960 conventions, however, Paley was furious to find CBS trailing NBC on all four.[17]

There was more to this rivalry, of course, than the vanity of two network bosses. Most of the networks' broadcasts could easily have appeared on any one of them. There is no NBC, ABC or CBS imprint on *ER*, *NYPD Blue* or *Touched by an Angel*, nor was there to their counterparts a generation ago. It was the daily evening news broadcasts and the major events coverage which give the networks their public identity. For sales forces and affiliates, winning the quadrennial battle of convention coverage had a value beyond the effect on newswatching loyalties alone.

At the first of the 1960 conventions, as dismaying to the CBS hierarchs as the ratings gap with NBC was their comparative visibility in the hall itself. Perched high above the floor in television's very first anchor booth were Huntley and Brinkley—the huge NBC logo rivaling the podium itself for attention in the hall. Press photographers, and for that matter the floor cameramen of CBS and ABC, found it hard to keep this glowing projection of another network's power out of their shots.[18]

CBS was outrun by NBC's floor correspondents, its next generation of news-reporting stars, as well as being towered over by those anchor booths—from which Huntley and Brinkley interacted smoothly with both their reporters and the politicians below. Meanwhile, in a studio far from the convention floor, a dour Walter Cronkite and a solemn Edward R. Murrow, sadly miscast as a counter to the glib Brinkley, droned on in splendid isolation both from the convention action and from each other. To the CBS chairman's dismay, most Americans who watched the conventions watched them on NBC.

After the 1960 embarrassments, Paley fired one head of CBS news. On the eve of the next round of conventions, when there had been little change in the evening news ratings, he fired another. After the first 1964 convention, another NBC ratings triumph, Paley even dumped Cronkite from the second. "NBC must be destroyed at all costs," Paley was quoted in one newspaper column.

The quote was formally repudiated, but, whatever the truth of it, it captured the spirit of network news in the middle 1960s. For 1964, CBS created a separate Election Unit with five times the 1960 budget for primaries, conventions and elections. NBC, not to be complacent, spent four times what it had spent before.[19] At a pool meeting for the conventions, CBS producer Don Hewitt found an NBC planning book and made off with it. NBC producer Scott Connal soon noticed both the book and Hewitt missing and tracked Hewitt to his hotel room. Connal got his book back after pleading that it could cost him his job. There also appears to have been some talk—Connal is a large man—about pitching Hewitt—who is not—out the window—ten floors up. Hewitt today says the book was pretty boring.[20]

"COMMITTED TO CBS"

1964 was my first full year at CBS, as an associate producer in the spare-no-expense Election Unit. One way I thought we might get a competitive edge, in reporting the story if not in entertaining the nation, was by tracking convention delegates from the time they were chosen—the same way campaigns did. Until then, reporters had relied mostly on campaign sources, comparing the rival claims and drawing conclusions as best they could. At a time when most delegates were not formally committed, this kind of reporting could make the outcome appear very much in doubt when it was in fact a done deal. In time every network would have its own delegate count, and these would play a large role in reducing conventions to the uncontested rituals they have largely become today.

With a team of junior reporters I did my own research, state by state, sometimes county by county, getting delegate estimates—which turned out to be very accurate—from local party officials who were not used to this kind of attention from national news centers. Soon after Barry Goldwater was widely held to have suffered a crushing defeat in the New Hampshire primary of 1964, CBS delegate trackers found he had quietly done so well in the majority of states then holding caucuses instead of primaries that he had the Republican nomination all but won. By my calculation, if Goldwater won the eighty-six delegates in a winner-take-all California primary, the California bloc would put him "over the top," a phrase normally used to describe what happens at some point in a roll call at the convention.

At CBS, we saw no reason to wait that long. For the night of the California primary, we rented the hall in San Francisco that six weeks later would house the convention. We set up a bank of chairs representing the delegates already won by Goldwater, another bank representing California and a finish line representing the 666 votes required for nomination. When an exit poll in California, while much of the state was still voting, informed us that Goldwater had won, CBS rearranged the chairs on the convention floor and with little qualification asserted that the Republican presidential nomination was his.[21]

For CBS at this point, the actual Republican convention to be held later in the same space was a formality. Thanks to an in-your-face speech to the party's right wing by Nelson Rockefeller, an even more in-your-face speech to the Rockefeller wing by Goldwater and still another by Dwight Eisenhower to the news media, the convention did have its moments. Still, those moments were not enough to make an asset of the CBS edge in reporting breaking news. In the ratings book, it was one more shellacking of CBS by the Huntley-Brinkley talk show.

That would be the last. By the next campaign, CBS's widely-recognized advantage in election night reporting (see Chapter 3), a generally stronger news organization, Walter Cronkite's dominance of the competitively very important space-travel beat and his evolving stature as a national treasure transcending mere journalism finally overcame the zest and wit of Chet and David.[22] In 1967 CBS *Evening News* became the most watched television news broadcast, and it would remain so for nearly a decade after Cronkite's retirement in 1981. On the convention floors and on the air, for nearly a quarter of the century, the CBS anchor booths would prevail.

The CBS delegate count had been a great success in 1964. For 1968, we decided not to rely on a relatively modest canvass of a hundred or so local party officials. We would poll the delegates themselves in the thousands, as they were picked, and poll and poll them again.

At that Republican convention, you needed 667 delegates to win. As the convention opened, Cronkite announced that Richard Nixon had 631, Nelson Rockefeller 244, Ronald Reagan 154. F. Clifton White, who ran Reagan's late-starting campaign, knew that many of Nixon's supporters had originally wanted Reagan and were not legally bound to vote for Nixon. With Reagan now in the race, however, few of those Nixon Now/Reagan Later Delegates, as they were listed in my chart, would budge. One of them, an old friend of White's, said he was sorry but he'd made a commitment. To whom had he made this commitment? White asked. "To CBS," came the reply.[23] When the roll call began, CBS had 689 votes for Nixon. Cronkite, who would give the CBS count for each state just as the state's vote was about to be called for, chuckled at the handful of marginal discrepancies. The actual vote for Nixon was 692.

This would be the last convention at which CBS did not put the nominee over the top before the opening gavel. In later years campaign strategies would be directed at the network delegate counts as they once had been at the conventions themselves. A week before the Republican convention of 1976, when John Sears, Ronald Reagan's campaign manager, realized that CBS was about to award President Ford the nomination, he announced that Reagan—if nominated—would pick Richard Schweiker, a popular Pennsylvania senator, as his running mate. The large Pennsylvania delegation had been, and would remain, solidly for Ford. It would take CBS, however, nearly a week to recanvass that delegation and make sure Ford still had his winning margin in what was an extremely close contest. In the meantime, the Reagan campaign was still alive.

Four years later, ABC (which had raided *Newsweek* to install Hal Bruno as its political director) and CBS combined to terminate the Bush campaign; this time they nominated Reagan two months before the convention did. Soon after the polls in the Michigan primary closed, Bush was declared the winner of the primary by nearly two to one. A few minutes later, however, came the bad news for Bush. Under the primary's proportional rules, Reagan's third of the vote had earned him enough delegates to claim the ABC and CBS nominations.

DONILON'S LAW

At the first nationally televised convention in 1952, the Democrats had had all the best of it on television. It took them three ballots to settle on Adlai Stevenson, but the exercise appeared to have brought them together, and nobody went away mad. The Republicans, on the other hand, held one of the nastiest political brawls of the century.

That the Republicans nevertheless won in November remains a

unique exception to the normal pattern of television-era politics. When the Republicans held another bloodbath among themselves, in 1964, the Democrats won a landslide in November. Four years later, Democratic turmoil inside and outside their convention hall in Chicago helped bring the Republicans back to power, and another Democratic brawl in 1972 helped the Republicans to carry forty-nine states for Nixon. During the period covered by this book, politicians in both parties concluded that conventions in which anything is left to chance, in which struggles of any kind get shown on television, set the nominees up for defeat in November.

Tom Donilon, the Democratic operative, gave this commonly accepted truth a name ("Donilon's Law") and broadened it to cover the entire nomination process: "A party's chance of winning the presidency varies inversely with the length of time it takes its nominee to clinch the nomination." Donilon's Law could easily be restated as an Eleventh Commandment for convention planners: "Thou shalt not make news." There must not only be no doubt about the nomination. There must be no doubt about anything. Since the 1970s, Democrats have settled their entire ticket well before the convention opened, and in both parties the goal of a convention scrubbed free of conflict, passion and news now takes in the content of the party platform as well.

Platform struggles over slavery, the tariff, gold and silver, prohibition, civil rights and the Vietnam war once rivaled fights for the nomination in the intensity of factional feeling on the floor and the level of interest of the public. A party's state and local candidates as well as its national ticket were held to answer for the platform. Whole state delegations walked out of conventions over planks abhorrent to them. In extreme cases, a state party's electors might even bolt in November. But in an era when binding primaries and network delegate counts have virtually ruled out floor fights for the nomination, the greatest peril in the eyes of party managers is a lively airing of issues. Their aim is to suppress disputes about the platform any way they can.

At the 1976 Republican convention, the last convention in either party at which the outcome was to any serious degree in doubt, supporters of Ronald Reagan proposed a "morality in foreign policy" plank. A Reagan-backed minority report thumbed its nose at Gerald Ford on détente with the Soviet Union, nuclear testing, the Panama Canal treaty, and the denial of a White House visit to Russia's most renowned dissident: "We commend that great beacon of human courage and morality, Aleksandr Solzhenitsyn," the plank cuttingly began. Already trailing Jimmy Carter by 30 points in the polls, President Ford was being offered a full night of debate on all three networks on the moral content of his foreign policy, after which he would prevail (if lucky) by at most a handful of votes in a hall full of Republicans.

Ford Campaign Manager James Baker was running the first of his five presidential campaigns—the all-time record for either party in turns at the helm. Baker concluded, in effect, that what wasn't seen on television couldn't hurt you. The Ford campaign notified the Reagan camp that there was no need for a floor fight—the morality-in-foreign-policy plank (full as it was of anti-Administration poison) was fine with Ford. It was promptly buried in a long document adopted by a voice vote, and, while Cronkite at my suggestion found an opportunity to chuckle at the irony of all this, the matter was never heard from again.

At the 1984 Democratic convention, Walter Mondale did pretty much the same thing with that party's platform. He agreed to a Jesse Jackson plank supporting quotas and a Gary Hart plank restricting the use of military force, though both were, to say the least, unwelcome and Mondale had the votes to beat them. But, precisely because there was no debate and no vote, neither of these issues were made much of on the television broadcasts; nor were they noted much in print. As a result, they had little effect on the election.

For 1988, Democratic Party chairman Paul Kirk set out to contrive an entirely news-free convention. The New York primary in early April had left Michael Dukakis with a large edge in delegates and only Jesse Jackson to face in the remaining primaries. Kirk commissioned the shortest platform in convention history, barely three thousand words—none of which, Republicans gleefully pointed out, were "abortion," "taxes," or "God."

There was only one chance of news breaking out, accordingly, in the four nights of prime-time coverage announced by the networks.

That risk lay in whether Jackson would accept the party's gift of virtually its entire Tuesday-night entitlement on network television and in return would forgo a platform fight while the networks were watching. No one really doubted, however, that Jackson would accept this deal. On the Friday night before the convention opened, I came across Kirk and his wife in an Atlanta restaurant. "Did you find any news?" asked Kirk. "None." "Good," said a beaming party chairman, his dream of a successful convention intact.

The Democrats to a high degree, and the Republicans when they choose to work at it, have thus managed to strip conventions of their one-time decisive role in shaping national policy and leadership— the role which brought network television to cover them so lovingly in the first place.

THE WITHERING AWAY OF PRIME-TIME COVERAGE

Much of the pass that convention coverage has come to is due to changes in broadcasting itself. Forty years ago, when all of this began, there was no locked-in prime-time, daytime or late-night schedule to preempt. Advertisers were eager to buy time on convention broadcasts, affiliates were eager to carry them, viewers who did not yet own television sets went out and bought them so they would not miss the making of history. In those early years, especially before color, the production costs for two conventions were not at all bad for eight complete evenings of prime-time programming during a time of year normally given to reruns.

ABC from time to time tried to break the pattern of four full nights of prime-time coverage for both conventions. In 1968 it stuck to its regular schedule until 10:00 P.M. and then presented a summary of what had happened earlier. This broadcast strategy worked reasonably well at that year's Republican convention, where the main element of suspense, a late surge for Ronald Reagan, never got to the floor (though, behind closed doors, it came within a handful of votes of denying Richard Nixon a first-ballot nomination).[24]

At the Democratic convention, however, there was a quite unexpected attempt right out on the floor to draft Ted Kennedy, which had the blessing of the host mayor, Richard Daley of Chicago.[25] That effort, which collapsed when Kennedy ultimately disowned it, took place while antiwar riots were going on in the streets and fistfights were breaking out on the convention floor—some of them involving correspondents for networks which, unlike ABC, were broadcasting throughout the evening. ABC News found itself coming on the air at 10:00 P.M. and trying to broadcast its taped reports of earlier events while important news was breaking in front of it and crying for immediate live coverage.[26]

"I THINK WE'VE GOT A BUNCH OF THUGS IN THERE, DAN"

Not that CBS and NBC, on the air as in the past from gavel to gavel, were especially well prepared for the extraordinary story that erupted at a political event that had seemed initally to have little going for it. Miami Beach had pitted against each other Richard Nixon, Nelson Rockefeller and Ronald Reagan—three Republicans of large stature whose pursuit of power would dominate their party's politics for a third of a century—in a struggle whose outcome was never certain until the night before the roll call. Chicago, on the other hand, was a contest among stand-ins. Of the two men whose ambitions polarized the Democratic Party in the 1960s, Lyndon Johnson was not running and Robert Kennedy was dead. There appeared no way that Johnson's stand-in, Hubert Humphrey, could fail to get the nomination—unless Johnson changed his mind and, after thinking hard about it, he didn't.[27]

At the networks, nobody wanted to leave Miami Beach. The convention center was state of the art, the work space and parking were outstanding, and downtime at the oceanfront hotels was mostly wonderful. In Chicago, all the arrangements sucked. Hope for another month in the sun rose momentarily as a citywide strike in Chicago reached a point of no return for installing network lines, but Mayor Richard Daley knocked some heads together and the lines went in. Microwave stations, however, were not part of the deal. That meant no live coverage outside the hall and delays getting film and videotape through streets often blocked by demonstrations and paramilitary movements.

Fearful, with good reason, of violent antiwar demonstrations, federal, state and local governments had mustered ten thousand police and six thousand national guardsmen to patrol the streets. Wary, for equally good reason, of how all this law enforcement might look on television, police restricted the network mobile units to a handful of locations where demonstrations were least likely to occur. Reuven Frank, who ran NBC's coverage, recalls, "We were convinced this was Daley's doing, or some flunky; helping the boss keep antiwar demonstrators off television. But Daley or his flunky had outsmarted himself. The demonstrators, knowing where the Mayor and the Chicago police had situated the mobile units—there and nowhere else—came to *them*."[28]

Television now had its story. The networks, of course, expected antiwar demonstrations and knew they could get ugly. Still, few in any of the news media were prepared for the state of siege they found on their arrival—or the hostility they themselves encountered. Nearly a quarter of a century later, NBC's Frank made his own sentiments clear:

> The number of students totaled more than ten thousand, yet there was more than one cop for every long-haired kid. . . . Our coverage each night began by showing the barbed wire framing the International Amphitheater; it became the theme, the trademark. Editorial? Of course. But journalists from all media had been injured by police, and in many instances they had been sought out. "I'm from *Newsweek*." "Fuck *Newsweek*," and his glasses were smashed.[29]

A national commission on violence, which later sided with the networks and decreed what happened in Chicago a "police riot," tallied 43 news people struck or maced in the week of the convention.[30] By far the most conspicuous took their lumps live on CBS. On Tuesday evening Dan Rather was crossing the floor toward some insurgent Georgia delegates who had won an upset vote at the credentials committee, when Walter Cronkite observed from the anchor booth:

> It looks like a couple of the sergeants at arms or security people have one of their number by both armpits and are forcing him out. Dan Rather?

Rather: Take your hands off me. Unless you intend to arrest me, don't touch me. Don't push me, please. . . . Walter, as you can see . . .
Cronkite: These are security people around Dan, obviously getting roughed up.
Rather: Walter, we tried to talk to the man and we got bodily pushed out of the way. . . . I'm sorry to be out of breath, but somebody belted me in the stomach during that.

Cronkite then delivered one of those sound bites that get aired again and again for years to come: "I think we've got a bunch of thugs in there, Dan."

The next night, Mike Wallace found a New York delegate in a dispute with a plain clothes security guard over his credentials and being hauled off the floor. "Sergeant at Arms," demanded Wallace, "why are you doing this?" As the guard responded, "Where is his identity?" a half dozen uniformed cops stormed in. Wallace: "Now comes the strong arm. . . . It's a very effective—Oh!" Wallace is down, and Rather is now on the case. "Walter, this is the roughest scene of the convention." As Wallace tells it, he made the mistake of trying charm on a cop. "Flashing a broad smile," Wallace asked, "Officer, what are you so upset about?" and "chucked the man under the chin in an avuncular way." The cop, unamused, slugged Wallace in the jaw and arrested him—though not for long. Over at NBC, observed Reuven Frank, "Unworthy thoughts were uttered that if they were pounding floor reporters, why not ours—so *we* might enjoy the publicity."[31]

The real pounding, to be sure, was going on in the streets, where the police, provoked by calculating radicals among the demonstrators, were striking out at their tormentors (along with many behaving quite peacefully) in front of network mobile units—who were now breaking loose from their assigned stations.

Film and videotape of the violence downtown got to the convention hall during the nominating speeches for Humphrey, and as the totally predictable roll call began, the networks going gavel to gavel rolled out their pictures (via satellite) to the whole world. In one of television's most controversial control room decisions, CBS aired pictures of some of the roughest police action during a floor interview in which Mayor Daley told a fully recovered Dan Rather: "Our police department is the greatest police department in the United States, and the men in there are all family men and decent men who don't respond with any undue violence."

On the final night of the convention, Daley arrived early at the CBS anchor booth and gave the most celebrated television reporter of all time a lesson in delivering a message. "First," said the practiced politician, "let me say you're a constant visitor in the Daley home every evening, and we'll still continue to watch you." Then came a hair-raising account of "terrorist plans" ranging from urban riot to assassinating all three contenders for the presidential nomination. "I would like to say this here and now, this administration and the people of Chicago will never permit a lawless, violent group of terrorists to menace the lives of millions of our people, destroy the purpose of this national political convention and take over the streets of Chicago."

Daley cited reports of schemes "to assault, harrass and torment the police into reacting before the cameras. . . . In the heat of emotion and riot, some policemen may have overreacted," as the networks had shown. But "how is it that you never show on television, Walter, the crowd marching down the street to confront the police? I'd like to have them show the 51 policemen that were injured, some of them severely. I've never seen on television a picture of a wounded policeman lying on the street badly hurt."

CBS, actually, had shown a fair amount of taunting of the cops, and pictures of wounded policeman lying in the street, if you have them, don't wind up in the out-takes. Television news doesn't work that way. Still Daley had delivered an eloquent critique of the networks' coverage, and Cronkite (in what he later described as the worst moment of his career) responded feebly throughout. He had prepared little for the interview, he told me, had simply intended to let the mayor say his piece and, in so doing, "hang himself."

Arguments about the open war at this convention between reporters and the police persist to this day. Though NBC and CBS called most of the shots, Daley and his cops prevailed—in the jargon of the 1990s—on the spin. Viewer mail at CBS, even allowing for the normally negative tilt of such mail, was heavily against the coverage:

11 to 1. A week after the convention, Gallup asked: "Do you approve or disapprove of the way the Chicago police dealt with the people who were registering their protest against the Vietnam War at the time of the Democratic convention?" Even with the poll's benign characterization of the demonstrators, the public, by 2 to 1, backed the cops.[32]

As a television spectacle, Chicago 1968 would remain unique. Four years later, NBC's Reuven Frank, while acknowledging that the 1972 Democratic convention had its moments, found both 1972 conventions for the most part a snore and concluded that the time had passed for traditional convention coverage.

In 1972, this was still a minority view. The Democratic convention had initially thrown out most of the California delegation and thereby came very close to rejecting George McGovern, the year's main primary winner. It then dumped (for good) the Chicago delegation headed by Mayor Daley in favor of an insurgent group headed by Jesse Jackson. It adopted a platform calling for total withdrawal from Vietnam and amnesty for draft evaders but, after a floor fight, rejected planks endorsing unrestricted abortion (this was before the Supreme Court's decision in *Roe v. Wade*), gay rights and a guaranteed annual wage. There followed a prolonged, humiliating search by McGovern for a running mate, and a floor fight over the man he finally found—who would later be replaced when some past episodes of mental illness became known.

Four years later, the Republican convention came within thirty votes of rejecting the party's own incumbent President in a contest that taxed all the resources of the networks to cover it and also drew the largest viewership of any convention of the past thirty years. The 1976 Democratic convention, however, was a four-day coronation of Jimmy Carter in New York, the networks' home town, where the reporters and producers, most of whom lived in the area, could not wait to leave the hall each night after their dreary search for material to fill a whole evening of prime time.

In 1980, there would be one final round of gavel-to-gavel coverage. In terms of sheer sport for television's reporters and producers, the conventions of 1980 had their moments. President Carter arrived at the Democratic convention with a substantial majority of the delegates, but Edward Kennedy, who had won most of the later primaries, was close enough for his side to create doubts about the certainty of Carter's publicly committed votes all being ultimately cast for him. Kennedy, with over 40 percent of the delegates on the floor, could flood the prime-time schedule with minority planks for the platform.

These planks had to be voted on; Kennedy also had the votes to force roll calls, and some of those planks (which repudiated formal Administration policy) actually passed. No one on Carter's side ever thought of following the Ford strategy of 1976 and quietly caving—especially when few of the challenges to Carter's positions had ardent followings among the voting public. The final night of the convention brought one of the classic moments of television news: the *pas de deux* of Kennedy and Carter as the President circled and recircled his defeated rival in pursuit of an embrace which the rival resolutely evaded.

The 1980 Republican convention, where there was not even the pretense of a contest for the nomination, nevertheless produced a glitch—one which convention planners in later years would cite as a horrid example of how news at a convention is almost always bad news for the nominee. In this case it was the unprecedented prospect of a former President taking second place on the Reagan ticket.

Walter Cronkite, in his final appearance as a convention anchor 28 years after his 1952 debut, pried Gerald Ford's availability for Vice President out of him in by far his finest interview. It started with the former President shrugging off rumors to that effect. As Cronkite probed, however, Ford displayed detailed expertise on the constitutional issues involved in such a ticket (he and Ronald Reagan were both residents of California).[33] Mrs. Ford was then drawn into a discussion of how she would decorate the country's new vice-presidential mansion. (There was none when Ford previously held the post.) She had obviously given it some thought already.

Worse still for the architects of a Reagan-Ford ticket was a phrase in a memo I'd sent Cronkite summarizing the deal then being negotiated between the Reagan campaign's Ed Meese and Bill Casey and, representing Ford, Alan Greenspan and Henry Kissinger. "What seems to be under discussion," I wrote, was a "sort of co-presidency." Under it, Ford (with a little help presumably from Kissinger) would have special responsibility for defense and foreign policy. When Cronkite ran that "sort of co-presidency" idea past the former president, Ford took the bait and went on to dictate the terms of such a role. An appalled Reagan, watching CBS in his hotel suite, called Ford and pressed him for an acceptance without conditions and, apparently to his relief, was turned down.[34] It was the best story, and the only sour note, to an otherwise very cheerful convention. It would also be the last Republican convention covered from gavel to gavel.

Four years later, when Dan Rather took Cronkite's place at the 1984 Democratic convention, it was 9:00 P.M., and the session had already been gaveled to order several hours earlier. All of the networks had new corporate managements. Earnings-per-share ratios were being scrutinized by take-over strategists, whose opinions were a popular topic for the *Wall Street Journal* and the financial pages of the *New York Times*. Twenty-million-dollar convention budgets were history, or about to be, and so too was gavel-to-gavel coverage. The networks now uniformly took the air at 9:00 P.M. and struggled to get off again by 11:00, or as soon after that as a clean exit could be made. No longer would network television news tailor its coverage to fit the story. Henceforth the story would have to fit the coverage.

THE CONVENTION SCRIPT (1972–1992): FROM SCOOP TO HANDOUT

The television scoop of the 1972 Republican convention was CBS floor correspondent Dan Rather's capture of David Gergen's top secret, "eyes only . . . full television script of every second, every minute of tonight's proceedings." Anchorman Walter Cronkite introduced Rather's find, saying, a bit darkly, "Tonight's session has been very carefully orchestrated." Rather went on, "Nixon Republicans want the conventions to portray to the American people the idea of discipline, control, orderly process. By looking at this convention as a television studio, they can avoid the chaotic appearance" of George McGovern's nomination a month earlier in the same hall.

There was something tacky, Rather and Cronkite made it clear, about a tightly scripted convention. Twenty years later, however, at both the Democratic and Republican conventions of 1992, it needed no feat of investigative reporting to turn up minute-by-minute scripts for each. Dan Rather, and most importantly Executive Producer Lane Venardos, got them from me. I in turn got them from the convention managers, in the course of making deals about the time and duration of our no-longer gavel-to-gavel coverage. At the other networks, our counterparts were doing the same thing.

In the twenty years since Rather's scoop, tightly scripted conventions had become the only kind. In 1992 both tickets were decided well before their conventions opened. The platforms, too, had already been adopted—and the rules made it easy to suppress debate—without even a vote on the matter. None of the network news divisions could see four full evenings of news to cover. Nor could we argue credibly to the corporate bean counters for the sacrifice of eight nights of prime time (estimated value: $40 million) to an effort, sure to fail, to turn these obsolete events into television that most Americans would choose to watch.

With some variations, the networks announced well ahead of time that they would be on the air for just one hour on the first three nights and two hours for the speeches Thursday night when the candidates would formally "accept" nominations decided, after prodigious efforts, months earlier. NBC, in a radical departure from the norm, put Tom Brokaw and all its floor reporters and technicians at the disposal of Public Broadcasting's *MacNeil-Lehrer Newshour* for the seven hours or so of convention time when NBC itself would be airing sitcoms. CBS skipped the second night entirely in favor of the all-star baseball game, which had been scheduled before the convention dates were known.

All this resulted in very tight negotiations between the networks and the parties to get events worth showing to viewers scheduled within the barely one hour on most of the nights for which coverage was planned. We especially wanted these events over (so we could gracefully exit) by 11:00, when our affiliates would be on our backs to make way for their money-making late-evening schedules.

Both sides to these negotiations were dealing with their own special currency. At the parties and the campaign headquarters, "face time" on television long ago became a form of patronage for paying off debts incurred in gaining the nomination. In 1992, face time came in different grades. One Democratic official recognized three: Ordinary Prime Time, starting at 8:00 P.M., when only Public Television, CNN and C-Span were covering; Super Prime Time, starting at 9:00, 9:30 or most often 10:00 P.M., depending on the night, when the broadcast networks were covering; and, finally, Off Prime Time, before 8:00 P.M., when visibility was confined to the hall itself or C-Span. It was during Off Prime Time that the Democrats allowed supporters of Paul Tsongas to debate the one pro-forma platform issue they had allowed on the convention schedule. It was where Republicans would have held their debate on the abortion plank if those who wanted such a debate had found the votes for it.

Viewing the stream of truly boring "Friends of Bill" assigned Super Prime Time by the Democrats and of Bush loyalists given choice slots by the Republicans, CBS offered deals to both parties. Mario Cuomo, then governor of New York and a speaker CBS News found more interesting than many of the Clinton cronies being offered, was scheduled to place Clinton's name in nomination at about 8:15 on Wednesday night. This was not even close to the scheduled start of major network coverage at 10:00. If the Democrats would meet us halfway, starting Cuomo after 9:00, CBS would go on the air at nine. That deal was made, and NBC, though not ABC, joined us.

Three weeks later, as the Republicans were about to meet in Houston, came the deal, recounted in the Introduction, that made Pat Buchanan the star attraction at George Bush's convention.

At CBS, nothing Executive Producer Lane Venardos negotiated with the convention managements was planned in more loving detail than the massed balloon drops. This, the veteran producer knew, would be the most compelling moment of his broadcast. He was not about to let the party's engineers screw it up. This was the moment on which his expertise and his artistry would be matched in direct competition with those of his colleagues at the other networks. Pride and professionalism both required that on CBS the balloon drop be perfect. Here the politicians on one hand and television on the other were allied in a joint artistic endeavor.

On the other hand, CBS would not have anything to do with a taped life of Clinton prepared by his Hollywood friends and shown at the convention so that television could be pressured into carrying it. While ABC, PBS and CNN aired the Clinton campaign's 14-minute commercial, CBS, following its traditional practice, produced and aired its own life of the nominee. (NBC filled most of the time with talk in the anchor booth).

It could not have been clearer that CBS had rejected the one-sided sales pitch of Clinton's own television pals. Ten minutes before Clinton was to accept the Democratic nomination for President, CBS News, in its balanced synopsis of the nominee's career, included soundbites from the Gennifer Flowers tapes.

Amid all the arm-wrestling over the timetables at both conventions, in 1992 the networks and the parties had arrived at an apparent concordat over the terms of coverage and what seemed like a potentially stable replacement of the once-prevailing norm of gavel to gavel. From the point of view of the parties, the restriction to one hour on the first three nights and two hours on Thursday (90 minutes for NBC) was not all bad. It was as much time as their packagers could usefully fill (more, in fact) and it severely restricted the potential for mischief—whether by prying reporters or by nay-saying minorities on the floor.

What about the public? In reducing convention airtime to barely a fifth of that of 1952 and a third of the coverage given as recently as 1980, of what exactly had the networks deprived their viewers? Certainly, they missed little news. The nominations had long ago been settled. The platforms had been written, and no serious challenge was possible—given party rules designed to thwart any such challenge and the political pressures on delegates not to soil the party's precious moments on television.

At the Republican convention a platform asserting, on behalf of all Republicans, the pro-life positions professed (on most days) by the party's incumbent nominees was adopted on the second night without debate—though half the delegates (and two-thirds of the party's adherents among the public) told CBS News that they would rather skip the whole matter. The governor of Massachusetts was allowed, in a time period not covered by the networks, to express his dissenting views in a single sentence.

This is not to suggest that Bill Weld's authorized murmur of dissent on the party's anti-abortion plank (a position even more categorical than the Pope's) would have rung out to the world if the networks had only devoted more prime time to the conventions.[35] The party managers would simply have arranged for an afternoon or morning session. At the Democratic convention, Jerry Brown appeared likely for a time to get a vote on some unwanted, or, as the side with the votes put it, "divisive" platform issues; Harold Ickes, the Clinton convention manager, told me a likely time for any debate on those issues would be nine o'clock in the morning.

1996: THE TWILIGHT OF THE CONVENTIONS

There was once a reason why conventions took four days. They had work to do.

On Monday the party chairman would call the delegates to order. They would settle disputes over who had a right to be there, adopt rules for the convention and for the next nominating cycle, and hear a "keynote" speech designed to bring the party faithful to their feet and set the tone and the issues of the campaign to come.

On Tuesday the party would adopt its platform, on which there might be some argument. Sometimes bitter, usually spirited and often eloquent, that argument enabled the losers to go back home and tell their supporters they'd at least tried.

On Wednesday came the formal nomination. Even when everyone knew who would get it, there was usually a roll call. It enabled losers to show how much support they'd won and hear some nice things said about them before they rose and called for the nomination to be made unanimous. It was also the occasion until fairly recently for the nominee to announce, or let slip, whom he had picked as his running mate.

Finally, on Thursday, the candidates would each accept their nominations in a sequence of speeches with well-defined responsibilities. The vice-presidential nominee would invite the delegates to join him in denouncing the opposition party and all its deeds. The nominee for President would close things out on a high note by summoning the country to share his vision of greatness yet to come.

Aside from the speeches on Thursday (and even that was about to change), by 1996 nearly all of these traditionally defining functions of the four-day convention no longer mattered. Both nominations had been settled five months (a record) before either convention. The vice-presidential nominations in both parties would also be done deals before the conventions opened. In the past, Republicans had always reserved that one story, if nothing else, for the convention.

Roll calls for the nomination, the main business once assigned to Wednesday night, had either been dumped entirely or banished to day-parts uncovered by the networks. Time-consuming and terminally corny ("The great state of Wyoming, home of————— and—————and—————proudly casts all twelve of its votes for that——————————"), they evoked nothing but smart-alec comment from the anchor booths.

The platforms were now set in concrete (and designed to be left there) before the conventions opened. This took away the business traditionally assigned to Tuesday night. The platform in any case was all but formally declared irrelevant in 1996. At the Republican convention, both the party chairman and the presidential nominee said they hadn't read it and weren't likely to!

What then was there for a conscientious network news organization to cover in those four or five hours which their companies were prepared to set aside to cover the conventions? To the politicians, that was a silly question. The convention *was* the coverage. Those thousands of delegates and alternates who filled the hall night after night, painfully chosen by primaries, caucuses and state conventions, pledged and transported and wined and dined in the convention city, had no real reason to be there aside from being seen and heard on television: to fill up the wide shots; to provide moving, amusing or colorful close-ups for the cutaways; and to applaud and parade on cue.

In San Diego the convention planners became in their own

heads full-time television-show producers. Aside from what the nominees had to say on Thursday, if then, there would be no news to report on *any* night. Those same politicians had made sure of that. It was now their mission to help the network news producers fill up the hours they had so diligently drained of stories.

The Republicans, whose convention came first, had reviewed the networks' convention broadcasts for the past twenty years. Bill Greener and Paul Manafort, convention managers respectively for the Republican National Committee and the Dole campaign, saw themselves as sophisticated collaborators in a coproduction.

"We did our homework," said Manafort. "We know when the anchors interview guests in the booth, when they go to their correspondents on the floor, when they cut away for commercials and station breaks. It comes to about sixteen minutes an hour. We want to make sure you get those sixteen minutes, and we're going to put people or events you can easily cut away from, and cut back to, in places where you want them."

When Manafort and Greener marched their party's beloved former President, Gerald Ford, to the podium in San Diego shortly after the clock struck ten (Eastern Time) on Monday night and none of us put him on the air, media critics chalked up another black mark for network insensitivity and flawed priorities. Not so the convention planners of Ford's own party. They had put the tiresome old man precisely where they wanted him—knowing he would be shown at most momentarily, without getting a chance to drone away and drive viewers to their VCRs. Said a philosophical Greener,

> This notion that at ten o'clock we're going to have the Pope at the podium and you're going to go right to him—that's baloney. What's going to happen is that CBS is going to establish Dan Rather in the anchor booth, then they're going to establish the story line, then they're going to a commercial, then they're going back to Dan Rather and *then*, if you're lucky and you've got something at the podium that interests them, they may go to you.

Self-serving as this might seem for the networks, the party impresarios were happy to oblige. There was no limit to how accommodating the San Diego Republicans were prepared to be about the networks' needs, which they had studied so assiduously in advance. All but the very most important speeches would be limited to five minutes, about right for commercial breaks, or for a detour from the podium to the floor correspondents and an anchor booth dialogue or interview.

What the Republicans running this convention (or the Democrats two weeks later) were *not* about to accommodate was any hankering by television news for dissent or spontaneity. They had had enough of that in Houston four years before. This time, if Pat Buchanan wanted to appear at the convention hall, he could submit a minute, maybe a little over, on video; they would look at it and let him know.

When Dan Quayle submitted his five-minute speech (which Manafort described as "Goldwater '64") they dispatched Ken Duberstein, Ronald Reagan's last chief of staff, to make it kinder, gentler. When reports reached Manafort on Monday night of a possible pro-life walkout during Colin Powell's speech, he had the doors to the hall opened, and the aisles around the suspect delegations were immediately filled. "They were locked in their seats, couldn't move. No walkout. No way, too, you guys could get to them."[36]

As usual, there was a pretaped video introduction for the acceptance speech, and by long tradition CBS News had other plans for the seven minutes, six and a half seconds that the party's commercial would run. This time, instead of an argument, they got total cooperation. Manafort and Greener did not have to be told that CBS would skip the video and needed precise timings to render its alternative in the darkened hall. No problem. They were happy to provide Steve Jacobs, the network's executive producer, with absolutely firm times for the video to start and finish, for Dole to enter the hall ("at the Guam delegation") and for the lights to go on with the nominee at the podium.

> *Jacobs:* "What you're telling me is that you can't go into film early. That what you're telling us? Cash American money?"
> *Greener:* "Cash American money. You can leave it on the table."

Businesslike and sensible as all this accommodation might seem on the surface, it also placed the Republican (and later the Democratic) convention planners in the role essentially of coconspirators with the networks in the creation of something that seemed far removed from journalism. "I feel slightly soiled," Peter Jennings, as though he had just arrived from Mars, told the *Washington Post* after attending a briefing by Greener and Manafort. "They have gone so far as to plan our commercial breaks."[37] The Republican television strategists had in fact blundered. Proud as they were of having crafted, in their own minds, not only the program in the hall but the "real" convention on the air, they blabbed about it shamelessly to all the media.

For something like 10,000 print reporters, who were facing the same dearth of real news as their television counterparts, there turned out to be one story they could pursue which we could only touch on (as we did from time to time): the stroking of the networks. Soon the television trailers and control rooms were awash with print reporters taking notes. Over breakfast each morning, network producers and executives, along with their anchors, could read their own comments daily on the meaningless story which they had hauled hundreds of people and zillions of dollars all the way across the country to report. A computer search of newspaper stories filed at the conventions found over 400 appearances by the top executives of network news— more than half of those by CBS News President Andrew Heyward and his chief deputy, Lane Venardos. The central theme of all those inkbites: Never again.

For ABC's Ted Koppel and his *Nightline*, next time would not be soon enough. "This convention is more infomercial than news event," spouted Koppel midway through San Diego. "Nothing surprising has happened. Nothing surprising is anticipated. So most of us from *Nightline* are going home."[38] On Wednesday night, after ABC's Peter Jennings had finished gushing, like Rather and Brokaw, over Liddy Dole's debut as Oprah Winfrey, *Nightline* devoted its nightly half hour to an update on the TWA 800 crash. There was not, to be sure, much news there either.

For most of television news, however, before any major changes could be made, there was still a Democratic convention to get through and leave behind. In Chicago the networks were not dealing with a team of Washington-based political consultants who'd taken a crash course in television news production. Since 1988 the Democratic conventions had been designed by Gary Smith, a Hollywood producer who specialized in big-hall spectacles like CBS's Tony Awards and Kennedy Center galas. Since 1992 Smith had been joined by the Clintons' own Arkansas-born and -bred sitcom dynasts, Harry Thomason and Linda Bloodworth Thomason.

The Washington crowd who called the shots in San Diego had gone along with the ruse that conventions were news events and that what television was doing there was news coverage. The Hollywood producers engaged by the Democrats to program Chicago came out of prime-time entertainment. To them, there was no ruse. The conventions were plain and simply a four-part miniseries. It was their job to fill each shining prime-time hour with such compelling television that the networks would stop yammering about news.

For opening night Thomason proposed a total embargo on politicians. Instead the country would hear from "real people": a factory worker who'd been able to care for a dying parent thanks to Clinton's signing the Family Leave law, a minority student whose tuition was funded by her Americorps earnings, a severely wounded Chicago cop to represent the men in blue funded by Clinton's crime bill—grabbers like that. Mike Berman, the Democrats' veteran convention programmer, pointed out that this is precisely the kind of drivel that the networks would dump in favor of anchor-booth interviews or whip-arounds among their correspondents on the floor. He also lamented, to no avail, "There are a lot of people out there who want to watch their politicians in action, take their measure. Why should we try to look like what we aren't?"

While politicians remained blackballed on opening night, the Clintonites' search for "real people" was not limited to the obscure. Thomason floated Billy Graham's name, but Hillary worried that he might get off the reservation on abortion. Dick Morris had a poll which showed (fifteen years after the man last anchored the evening news!) that the strongest draw you could get would be Walter Cronkite. Cronkite, however, who over the years had turned down serious overtures to run for the U.S. Senate and Mayor of New York City and who hardly needed more face time at a convention, was not about to cross this particular line at the age of seventy-nine.[39]

It was Morris who seems to have come up with Christopher Reeve. The paraplegic Superman, a symbolic hero fit for Sophocles, had outdrawn everything on prime time but *Seinfeld* and *ER* the week Barbara Walters interviewed him on ABC. As Sam Donaldson (a rare on-air nabob of negativism) would point out on his network's convention broadcast, Reeve had no known connection with the Democrats. But so what? Morris had a poll to prove the people wanted him.

In the world series of tear-jerking that ensued at both conventions, Reeve's eight minutes of prime time (eight more than all of the party's Congressional leaders combined) scored as many cutaways to weepy faces as any of his formidable competitors (six minutes on Dole's war wound during Liddy's *Oprah* gig, Al Gore's ode to a dying sister, Jim Brady's brave, faltering attempt to walk a few steps before Sarah began her Monday-night speech). To establish some connection with the event of which Reeve was the centerpiece, this totem of the "paralyzed community" (as Jennings put it) also got some lines that might have been crafted (by an intern) for Donna Shalala: "Of course we have to balance the budget. . . . We have to be very careful with every dollar we spend. But we've also got to take care of our family and not slash programs that people need. . . . Our scientists can do more . . . that means more funding for research."

Sarah Brady, the other real person featured on that forgettable Monday night, did have a plausible connection with what Clinton and his party stood for. On no single issue was the line so sharply drawn between the parties as it was on gun control, or so aggressively emphasized in so many contests for office. And no politician could have made the Democratic Party's case as effectively as Brady. Any lapse, however, into political relevance was softened by Jim's own heart-clutching appearance in his wheelchair and his brief effort to stand up. One lost count of the close-ups throughout the week of physically challenged delegates.

The cumulative effect of all the brave and touching victims on display in San Diego and Chicago was enough to make a cynic of even the rare Billy Budd in the press corps. CBS producer Steve Jacobs implored his correspondents daily as they planned their work, "Don't be cynical." (At one point Ed Bradley, weary of all this coaching on how to do his job, told Jacobs to knock it off.) In any case, it largely worked. Hardly a discouraging word was heard on any of the networks as the parties vied with one another in plucking at the heartstrings of the country. On ABC, as if not enough pathos had been wrung in Reeve's own ten minutes of airtime, Jennings confided that Reeves had considered "packing it all in" until his wife persuaded him that life was still worth living. On CBS Rather gushed, "Superman was stronger than a locomotive, and he could leap over tall buildings in a single bound. And tonight he moved this United Center with a single speech."

Containing cynicism got much tougher in Chicago on Wednesday night. The embargo on politicians lifted, Al Gore shifted his acceptance speech from the traditional Thursday night to get a show of his own—the better to launch his year 2000 campaign for President. Recalling how at the last convention Gore invited the world to share his feelings about a nearly fatal accident to his son, we were already speculating on what he would do for an encore—when copies of his 1996 speech arrived in the CBS trailer.

And there it was.

> When I was a child, my sister Nancy was older than me . . . and I loved her more than life itself. . . . Years later the cigarettes had taken their toll. . . . [H]er pain was nearly unbearable. . . . All I could say to her, with all the gentleness in my heart, was "I love you." And then I knelt by her . . . and then she breathed her last.

Later that evening, on the monitors around the control room, while the Vice President of the United States was baring his heart and soul, a menu of empathizing faces in the Gore and Clinton family boxes as well as targets of opportunity on the floor challenged the awesome skills of CBS director Eric Shapiro (as similar menus challenged his counterparts at the other networks) to select the most gripping at any moment and lay it over the speech. As Shapiro did so, Andrew Heyward, the veteran broadcast producer who was now the division President, could not contain his admiration for Shapiro's workmanship. When the sequence ended, Heyward pronounced with authority, "You're a fucking genius, Eric." In the anchor booths, of course, the correspondents had to deal not only with the evolving pattern of Gore's (some might call it) exploitation of his family's private trials but with the relationship in real time between Nancy's final breath and the candidate's conversion (as a senator from a tobacco-growing state) to a crusader against cigarettes. In case anyone needed help on the research, Ed Gillespie, the Republican National Committee's flack, went around the news trailers eagerly passing out videos.

All of the network broadcasts duly recalled Gore's track record on heart-stopping family vignettes. The references were not necessarily disparaging. Dan Rather's citation of Gore's prior "strongly told and emotional story about the accident that nearly killed his son" was very much in keeping with his overall assessment of the current speech: "a home run . . . a barn-burner." ABC's (later CNN's) Jeff Greenfield found a unique accolade to bestow: ". . . the most emotional speech any of us have ever heard about the death of a sister." Nobody was so boorish as to point out that six years after Gore knelt at Nancy's deathbed he was still taking contributions from tobacco companies—though NBC's Tim Russert did note that tobacco money remained as welcome as ever at the Democratic National Committee.

If nothing else, Gore's evocation of his sister enabled his Wednesday night performance to eclipse Monday's stricken movie star as the emotional highlight of the 1996 Democratic convention. Frank Luntz, a Republican pollster employed by *Nightline* to measure the impact of convention goings-on upon a roomful of viewers, reported that the highest-scoring performers at the respective conventions were Gore and Elizabeth Dole. At San Diego's barn-burner, too, the normally tough-minded television newsmen covering it were reduced to such gee-whiz cheerleading as, "Wow, gold medal performance, why isn't she on the ticket?" (Brokaw), "Four star . . . brilliant piece of stagecraft" (Jennings), and "Tremendous . . . delivered big time . . . television anchors thanking destiny that Elizabeth Dole went into politics and not television" (Rather).

They were not, of course, wrong. Gore at his sister's bedside and Elizabeth Dole's 22-minute hymn to "the man I love" were undoubtedly the showstoppers of the 1996 conventions. That was the trouble. The intriguing struggles and the uncertain outcomes of the conventions of 1952 had launched a golden age of television coverage of presidential politics. At its very best it brought the country John Kennedy's New Frontier speech, the great exchange on "extremism" between Nelson Rockefeller and Barry Goldwater, the glowing concession speeches of Ronald Reagan in 1976 and Jesse Jackson in 1988. After 1996, the question that lingered with the networks was: does it take 300 news division staffers and $10 million from the news-reporting budget, not to mention ten hours of prime airtime, to cover what passes for news at conventions as we know them today? The answer for the year 2000 at every broadcast network was: No way.

3

FOR WHOM THE NETWORKS CALL

O N NOVEMBER 7, 1916, THE WORLD'S FIRST ELECTION NIGHT broadcast was heard by a small number of ham-radio operators within a few hundred miles of a laboratory in upstate New York. The announcer was Lee DeForest, the principal inventor of the vacuum tube and one of the pioneers of broadcasting itself. DeForest closed by declaring that Charles Evans Hughes had been elected President.[1]

That would not be the last time that radio, and later television, called an election wrong. In 1948 NBC's H. V. Kaltenborn, not otherwise a mythic figure in broadcast news, won immortality in the victory speech of a re-elected Harry Truman. Truman's imitation of Kaltenborn predicting his defeat around midnight of the night before is among the most widely recognized soundbites of all time.

At the time when Kaltenborn took his own place in history, Truman was leading by more than a million votes in the popular vote count and had won or was clearly ahead in states with close to a majority of the electoral vote. Had anything like today's election-calling technology existed then (or, in truth, had Kaltenborn and the experts assisting him exercised better judgment with the data they had) all of the networks, including NBC, would have reported fairly early that Tom Dewey's chances of overtaking Truman were slim.

After 1948, the networks looked for some resource beyond the gut feelings of experienced reporters. In 1952, CBS and NBC each employed one of that era's primitive computers to compare, as the vote from each state came in, the current year's major party vote for President with that of the election just before. The election of 1948 had been a squeaker that could have gone either way. So four years later, when the Republican vote was up by a lot in every early-closing state, it did not take sophisticated circuitry to detect a Republican tide. When CBS and NBC took the air at 9:00 P.M., they proudly displayed "Univac" (CBS) and "Mike Mono-Robot" (NBC). Both of these embryonic devices promptly, flatly and accurately predicted an Eisenhower victory.[2]

By 1956, ABC had a computer too, and this time there was absolutely no way for any reporter or machine to go wrong. The presidential race was a rematch, and wherever you looked as the early returns came in, Eisenhower was leading more decisively than before. When the network broadcasts began, at 8:30, all three promptly predicted the Eisenhower victory that their computers had been signaling for more than an hour.[3]

After that three-way tie, in 1960 the stakes were raised. ABC bragged that it would call the race by six o'clock. CBS promised to do so by seven. Neither met its self-imposed deadline, but ABC won the race to make the first projection. At 6:54, it gave the nod to Nixon— at 10-to-1 odds. CBS finally caught up at 7:16, when its Washington bureau chief Howard K. Smith declared: "The first forecast we can make is, with 1 percent of the precincts reporting, the trend indicates Richard M. Nixon will be elected tonight. . . . Nixon could get as many as 459 electoral votes."[4]

That result, had it actually taken place, would have been at the time the largest Electoral College win in the history of the Republican party. It turned out, of course, that the 1960 presidential contest was the closest since 1880—and the Democrat, John Kennedy, won. Worst of all, from the perspective of CBS management, for the first time far more election night viewers had watched NBC.[5]

RAISING THE STAKES

Thus ended the era when computers called presidential elections from the raw returns reported by the wire services. Among the few virtues of that primitive technology: it was very cheap. The race among the networks to call elections first would now be pursued at a more sophisticated and far more expensive level.

Among the most thoroughly engaged viewers when CBS projected a Nixon landslide was Kennedy's campaign pollster, Lou Harris. "I heard the Senator coming up the stairs, and I turned off the two TV sets. . . . Peter Lawford came in with this stuff just off the wires, and I crumpled it and threw it in the corridor. The Senator immediately sensed that something was wrong, and I said it was nothing to worry about. In 20 seconds flat he got it out of me, stuck his finger under my nose and said, 'Lou, from here on it's you against the machines.' "[6] Harris would beat the machines that time, but by the next election he had joined them.

As it happened, the Kennedy pollster was a neighbor in Riverdale, New York, of Bill Leonard, a CBS producer assigned in 1961 to arrest the network's run of election night pummelings by NBC. There had been a mayoral election that year in New York City, and the NBC station had outstripped its CBS counterpart by hours in calling a race that was not especially close. In both cases the network news divisions had been calling the shots for the local flagship. For CBS, this was not quite so humiliating as the parent network's recent projection of the wrong president, but New York is where the men who run the networks live—and where they watch the local news. Heads rolled again at CBS News, just as they had after the national rout in 1960.[7] To his neighbor Bill Leonard, Lou Harris offered a deal. Americans, he argued, vote in blocs: economic, ethnic, religious, geographic and some others. If you know how the major blocs among a state's voters are tilting and compare it to their normal tilt, you can assert very early with a lot of confidence who has won.

From the polling Harris had done for candidates, he constructed models of the precincts in each state. The precincts included in the model Harris called "cells." The model for any given state might call for so many white or black cells, so many Protestant, Catholic and in some states Jewish cells. So many might be of Irish, Italian, Polish, German ancestry; so many rich, poor or in between; so many urban, suburban or rural. Each of these state demographic models Harris called a "recipe."

To make the recipe work, researchers hunted out precincts occupied as lopsidedly as possible by the targeted voter types. One secondary benefit of the Harris plan was that it enabled correspondents, once the race was called, to characterize the contribution each demographic element had made to the outcome.

Harris originally called the system Precinct Profile Analysis, or PPA, until one member of the planning group pointed out the nursery connotation of the acronym and suggested Voter Profile Analysis, VPA, instead. The cost was huge: extensive field research, computer hardware and programming from IBM, a stiff fee and expenses for Harris. In 1964 the CBS campaign and election budget would be five times what it was in 1960, and the principal new cost was Lou Harris and his recipes. But CBS in 1962, when the deals were cut, was desperate. "We had been so thoroughly whipped by NBC," recalls Leonard's deputy, Bill Eames, "that we had no other choice. We needed something to win with, something big."

In 1962 four big states were electing governors. In each case the Republican candidate, if he won, would automatically be a strong contender for that party's next presidential nomination. In New York, Nelson Rockefeller was running for re-election. In Pennsylvania and Michigan, William Scranton and George Romney were challenging Democratic incumbents. And in California, Richard Nixon (who, given 30,000 votes in the right places two years before would have been President already), was trying to gain a base in Sacramento for another run at the White House.

Theodore White was in the CBS control room as the Harris recipes came to a boil on election night, enabling Walter Cronkite to roam the political battlefield like some Norse divinity, decreeing the victors and the vanquished while the other networks were waiting for more returns to come in over the wires. In a number of cases, CBS would administer its *coup de grâce*, a checkmark for their opponents, to candidates who were actually leading in the vote count. Recalled White years later,

> [CBS Producer Don] Hewitt . . . was like the admiral of an aircraft carrier, surveying his feeds on telescreens, absorbing intelligence from Leonard and Harris below, talking to Cronkite, the anchorman—but

also like an admiral, scrutinizing the enemy, watching the monitors on his two rivals, ABC and NBC. And at this moment, Hewitt struck—Cronkite announced that CBS declared [incumbent Democrat Pat] Brown the winner over Nixon in California.[8]

Unprepared to compete that night with CBS on the main story, NBC News had been filling time with its signature asset, the wry wit of co-anchor David Brinkley. Recalled White in the last of his classic books on presidential politics: "Hewitt swiveled in his chair to watch his monitor on the chief enemy, NBC. Brinkley was on. Obviously NBC was monitoring CBS just as CBS was monitoring them. In Brinkley's ear was the tiny earpiece of all commentators who must keep in touch with production control. Brinkley visibly winced as his earpiece told him of CBS's call. Hewitt chortled, "Wry that, you wry son of a bitch, try and wry that one."

Nixon's defeat in California was the last call of the night, a night of coast-to-coast victories for CBS. Throughout the evening the VPA models had been churning out calls, all of which stood up, and the other networks limped along in the wake of CBS throughout the night.

The language of the call was itself magisterial: CBS as the national umpire, calling, or alternatively, declaring candidates safe, or out, as they dashed for home. In later years, network executives, sensing the arrogance some might perceive in this language, urged correspondents to soften it to "CBS News projects" and, later to "CBS News estimates that . . . ." The correspondents however, while following orders, were thoroughly disdainful of the academic-sounding weasel word. In any event, in the measured organ tones of Walter Cronkite even "estimates that" had the resonance of high authority.

As an example of such an "estimate," two hours after the polls closed in Michigan, George Romney trailed incumbent Democratic governor John Swainson by 100,000 votes. At that point, the VPA model ruled Romney the winner. That Swainson's lead came entirely from heavily Democratic Wayne County was easy enough for the CBS newsmen to grasp. But to declare a candidate flatly the loser while the reported votes were heavily in his favor was not an everyday feat.[9] The word was passed to Cronkite and the graphics producer, and the checkmark went up on the so-far trailing Romney.

One of the most satisfying CBS decisions came on a race in which, even after all the sample precincts reported, VPA could not detect any winner. The race for governor of Massachusetts, in a phrase that soon entered the national idiom, was ruled by CBS "too close to call." All of the CBS calls that night, most especially Massachusetts, stood up. The race ruled too close to call went to a recount, and the winner, by two-tenths of 1 percent of the vote, was not certified until more than a month after the election, and only a few weeks before the swearing-in.

Though NBC was far behind in reporting the news that night, it once again ran away with the ratings: 48 percent of the television sets in use, compared to 35 percent for CBS. Bill McAndrew, who ran NBC News, knew, however, that he could not keep those ratings indefinitely on the twinkle in the eye of David Brinkley—if Huntley and Brinkley could not deliver the news.

"I'LL SEE YOU WHEN I GET BACK FROM DALLAS"

Part of Lou Harris's deal with CBS was that he would no longer work for candidates. So in the fall of of 1963, when the first and, as it turned out, the last strategy meeting for the re-election of John Kennedy was held in the White House, the President's 1960 pollster did not attend. Richard Scammon, then director of the U.S. Census, did. Scammon's eminence as an election-data expert preceded his appointment to the Census post, and he'd devised a formula for cutting back on the South's traditionally inflated share of delegates at future Democratic conventions. No one at the meeting worried much about getting the President himself renominated, but the South had done little for this Kennedy at the 1960 convention and did not figure to be an asset as other Kennedys pursued power in years to come.[10]

President Kennedy dealt quickly with the business at hand and then engaged Scammon in an unscheduled seminar on political science. Did Democrats moving to the suburbs become Republicans by exposure to their new environment, or did their becoming suburbanites reflect their already leaning more Republican? What was the political payoff for Kennedy's administration from the war on poverty? The poor, said Kennedy, don't vote much, and most of them are already, he said, "on our side." If there are any votes for him in the antipoverty program, said Kennedy, it was from well-off white liberals—not from the poor or the black themselves. Scammon felt he and the President were getting on well, and as the meeting closed, Kennedy said he'd like to talk some more about these things as they headed into the next year's campaign. "I'll never forget his closing words," says Scammon, "as I left. 'I'll see you when I get back from Dallas.'"

When John Kennedy did not get back from Dallas, Richard Scammon's brief vision of joining the inner political circle of a President faded. Lyndon Johnson was not interested in any scheme to reduce Southern voting power at conventions, nor did he and Scammon have any prior connection. In 1960, as it happened, Scammon had been an occasional on-air political analyst for NBC. In 1963, NBC, responding to CBS, had created its own Election Unit and picked its Chicago bureau chief, Frank Jordan, to run it. Jordan promptly hired Scammon—to counter Harris and VPA.[11]

BAROS AND SWINGOS AT NBC

Unlike Lou Harris, with his exotic recipes of ethnic, racial, economic and urban/suburban/rural "cells," Richard Scammon sought out precincts with a history of either (1) reflecting the state's overall vote for Republican and Democratic candidates or (2) swinging between the parties from one election to the next in step with the voters. He called the first kind of precincts "barometric," or, in Scammon's lingo, "baros." The second were "swingometric"—or "swingos."

The tough part was finding the baros. They had to be precincts, said Scammon, "within a percentage point of state averages, going back several elections . . . full of middle-of-the-road, middle-class people, who for one reason or another were temperature sensitive. We had to check them out, make sure they were stable areas. You could have a baro precinct that was half black and half white, but you had no way of knowing that it would stay put. In fact, that kind of precinct could change on you very quickly."

Scammon's preferred way of computing the returns from his baros and swingos was in his head (he did that very well) or, when things got a little too close, by punching up the numbers on an old-fashioned adding machine, "the kind with a little roll of paper." At one point Scammon had a supporting team of clerks—"little Jewish guys with *payess* [long, curly sidelocks]," NBC producer Shad Northshield called them—who shared Scammon's prowess with those turn-of-the century antiques.[12]

NBC, however, was then a wholly-owned subsidiary of RCA, an electronics company with a contemporary line of computers, and in 1964 RCA had a new one to promote. Its top-of-the-line Model 301 thus became the designated means by which Scammon's baros and swingos were to be converted into election night calls. The 301's, however, had a way during broadcasts of either breaking down entirely or, perhaps worse, flooding the studio with unmanageable quantities of paper. Throughout 1964, as often as not, they left Scammon with only his adding machines and his little Jewish guys with *payess* to compete with Harris, VPA and IBM.

One effect of the 1960 campaign, with its uniquely young, uniquely Catholic Democratic candidate, had been to focus attention on the demographics of voter support and disaffection. The ethnic, racial and religious cells in VPA readily supplied, for a while, this kind of data. The baros and swingos selected by Scammon did not. So NBC had to collect the vote from still another brand of precincts which Scammon called "tags": precincts largely populated by a group whose overall tilt could make a difference as to who won.

Finding the tags was not easy. "We had to be careful so the poor in our tags didn't wind up all black and the rich didn't end up 35 percent Jewish," recalled Bud Lewis, who ran NBC's election unit for many years. "I remember going through Long Beach, looking for pure blue-collar precincts . . . trying to determine ethnicity by looking for funeral parlors. People like to be buried with their own kind."

All of this needed a name. Some NBC wordsmith came up with Electronic Vote Analysis, obviously conceived with its acronym, EVA, in mind. The first encounter between the fully-armed CBS and NBC Election Units came in the New Hampshire primary of 1964—where CBS and VPA resumed their romp. EVA, however, won handily in Oregon, and a week later, with the Republican nomination about to be decided in California, Leonard and Harris both knew they could not afford another loss to NBC.

Twenty minutes after the polls closed in just two California counties, with only a few thousand votes counted and Nelson Rockefeller leading in those, CBS News announced that Barry Goldwater had won the primary. Rockefeller's lead in the actual vote held up throughout the night and even through the morning news broadcasts. When all the votes were finally counted, Goldwater won by 70 thousand votes (out of 2 million cast), and a number of careers at CBS News returned from the brink.

On election night, CBS ultimately won the year when NBC's RCA computer had its final breakdown. By 9:04 CBS had rung up 271 electoral votes for Lyndon Johnson, and Walter Cronkite declared him returned to office. This was not done, as Univac and Mike Mono-Robot did it in the 1950s, by projections from a handful of early-closing states. The premise then had been, "We have these curious machines, they've turned up some predictions, and when the votes come in we'll see if they're right." The findings of VPA and EVA, on the other hand, were presented as the final word. State by state the race for President was called. When the Johnson total passed 270, a graphic flashed "Johnson Elected" just as the anchorman was saying so. At that moment a proclamation assigned by the founders to the Chief Justice of the United States had been performed, with barely 20 percent of the popular vote counted, by CBS.

The finality with which all the networks were now "declaring" or "calling" winners enormously raised the penalties for being wrong. It also began an argument, still unsettled, about whether presidential calls should be made at all while the polls in any of the fifty states are still open.

HOW WRONG CAN YOU GET?

Over a long evening, CBS's VPA and NBC's computer-challenged EVA called close to a hundred statewide contests—for President, for the U.S. Senate and for governor. For all the chancy calls on election night and in the primaries, only in one Senate race did anyone get stung. That came after a frustrated NBC producer had begged Scammon to call something, anything, before CBS did. Scammon mentally flipped a coin on the closest contest of the night, and it came down wrong. It would not be the last or the most damaging case of Scammon's going against his better judgment under pressure from NBC management.[13]

In the off-year election of 1966, ABC finally entered the lottery with its own sample precinct strategy and the requisite catchy acronym: RSVP (Research Selected Voter Profile). In its very first election, RSVP managed to get the message wrong on the governorships of Oklahoma, Minnesota, Alaska, New Mexico and Arizona and on a Senate race in Wyoming—an election-calling record unchallenged to this day.[14]

CBS went astray the same year when its computer repeatedly rejected returns from some black precincts in Maryland which, against all prior voting history, had gone heavily Republican (for Spiro Agnew). No one had told the computer that Agnew's opponent for governor, George Mahoney, was an obscure segregationist who had won a fluke victory in the Democratic primary, and normally Democratic black voters had been *expected* to take a walk.

The postmortems at all three networks went deep, calling into question the essential premises of all the calling systems. The ethnically pure precincts called for in the Harris recipes, if they hadn't disappeared long ago, were becoming harder than ever to find. So, too, were the precincts that met Scammon's standards for mirroring year after year the statewide vote or the election-to-election swing in the statewide vote.

At CBS, a decision to dump the Harris recipes coincided with the dumping of Harris himself. His services were expensive, and he was dictating further expenses by CBS over which it could exercise little control. Having assumed, moreover, the role of ultimate judge of when and what the people have spoken on Election Day, CBS News executives were uncomfortable with the fact that the actual judgment was being made by an outside consultant.[15]

In 1967, CBS hired Warren Mitofsky, a Census Bureau statistician, to do its election calling. Out went all the paraphernalia of precinct selection based on race, religion or ancestry. In came math.

Mitofsky's plan called for a random sample of the precincts in each state. As the sample precincts reported, the probability of this model's reflecting the actual statewide vote could be calculated with some precision. It was up to us at CBS to decide how often, over time, we could get away with being wrong. Mitofsky would then make the call when the computer said his chances of being right were in that remote range.

NBC was more eclectic. It continued to search out barometric precincts for Scammon's inspection, but it also began to employ random sampling in states of greater importance or where the races figured to be close. It had a model based on the county returns for races that were too close to call from the precinct models, and it did a lot of pre-election polling to provide still another nudge towards early calls.[16]

After 1966, an era of restraint set in at the decision desks. Few mistakes were made in 1968 or the early 1970s. None of the networks was a clear leader at calling things first. ABC sacrificed the natural flow of its broadcast in order to rush calls in nationally unimportant races on the air. A few days later, in trade papers and the *New York Times*, large ABC ads would boast of having called more races first than anybody else. At NBC and CBS, which saw their election units as elite, principled competitors, these claims by ABC's upstart unit and the on-air strategy that supported them evoked both anger and contempt—especially when company executives outside the news division seemed impressed by them.

CARTER AND CBS EKE OUT A WIN IN WISCONSIN

The Wisconsin Democratic primary of 1976 was the kind of media event that media critics, not without reason, deplore. It elected 68 delegates to the Democratic national convention on a day when New York was electing 274. Yet on primary night all of the country's star political reporters were in Milwaukee. New York's problem was that its delegates were elected individually, and there was no way to determine which candidate had won the most delegates in time for the network broadcasts and the morning paper deadlines. Wisconsin, on the other hand, held a flat-out vote for President, exactly what the network models were designed to call. Whoever got the most votes in Wisconsin would therefore be the only winner on the network specials or on Page One of the next day's papers.

Jimmy Carter at this point was on a roll, having won the Iowa caucuses and the New Hampshire, Florida and Illinois primaries. New York, however, with its large Jewish vote, was expected to go to Henry "Scoop" Jackson, Israel's strongest backer in the U.S. Senate. Among the liberal Democratic voters of Wisconsin, Morris Udall, the most liberal candidate in the race, was given his best chance anywhere for a breakthrough.

Half an hour after the polls closed in Wisconsin, ABC's key reporting precincts, mostly urban with machine voting, were solid for Udall. Frank Reynolds, the ABC anchorman, duly declared Udall, who had yet to win a primary, the winner. At NBC, Dick Scammon's baros were tilting slightly to Udall, but he was in no rush to make a call. Working out of a hotel ballroom in Milwaukee, however, Scammon was under tremendous pressure. This came not only from NBC managers aware of what appeared to be a major scoop by ABC but also from a large coterie of print reporters who held the NBC oracle in awe and were waiting for the oracle to speak before filing what would be the lead stories in their papers. At 10:30 Scammon spoke, NBC put its chips down next to ABC's, and across the country scores of newspapers finally went to press with Udall the victor in Wisconsin. Among those who would find themselves burned by this call was the *Washington Post's* David Broder, the most influential political reporter of his time.[17]

Meanwhile, at CBS, no matter how you totaled up the vote from its sample precincts, and VPA had four different ways of doing this, the Carter/Udall vote came out dead even. At 11:00 P.M., when all the sample precincts had reported, and no winner was apparent, Cronkite pronounced the race too close to call. As he did so, NBC and ABC were covering a victory party at which Udall crooned over and over again, "How sweet it is."

By 1:00 A.M., however, most of the votes coming in were from paper ballots in rural counties, and this vote was decidedly for Carter. By 1:23, with 97 percent of the vote counted, Carter led by 3,000 votes. That was enough, and Cronkite declared Carter the winner.

(No one reported till a day later that Scoop Jackson had defeated both Carter and Udall in New York—and thus had won twice as many delegates as both of them combined had won in Wisconsin.)

What NBC did in Wisconsin in April 1976 did not approach its midnight declaration that Tom Dewey had been elected president in 1948. But Carter and CBS publicists, not to mention Mitofsky, did everything possible to draw that parallel. Carter and Mitofsky were both seen in the press the next day holding up copies of the *Chicago Tribune*'s "Dewey Defeats Truman" headline at the time of the earlier miscall. Scammon, the dean of American political pundits, took much of the heat. Broder acknowledged that he had always used the NBC sage as a "security blanket." Mitofsky, still a relatively young man but possessed of a fully matured ego, gloated in the *Washington Post* and *Newsweek* about the rival technologies: "Scammon is still holding his finger to the wind, and what they do at ABC makes no sense at all."[18]

Unlike that springtime triumph in Wisconsin, in November Mitofsky's super-caution earned him no profiles in the national weeklies. Mississippi, the state Carter needed to go over the top, elects its seven electors individually. NBC and ABC gave Carter all seven when his first elector was declared a winner. Mitofsky took another fifteen minutes making sure Carter had the four electors he needed. Result: one more November election, the third in a row, in which CBS watched another network proclaim a president first. By far the most humbling CBS election night, however, was yet to come.

1980—EXIT POLLING, THE NEW BALLGAME

A few minutes after 8:00 P.M. on election night in 1980, Warren Mitofsky watched, helpless, as NBC called one state after another for Ronald Reagan in places where the polls had just closed. At 8:15, NBC announced that Ronald Reagan had won twenty-two states with a combined total of 270 electoral votes and would be the next president of the United States. It would be more than two hours later before CBS, trailing ABC as well, could make the same announcement.

Particularly galling to CBS, as it took this unprecedented shellacking, was that NBC had done it with a device pioneered by CBS. In order to make that spunky Goldwater call in 1964, Lou Harris had secretly surveyed a statewide sample of voters leaving the polls in California.[19] Three years later, Mitofsky, unaware of what Lou Harris had done before him, tested a similar strategy of interviewing voters in our VPA precincts. It turned out to be pretty dependable, at least in races that weren't close. During the primary season of 1968 and on election night, it enabled our evening news broadcasts to report on the "trend" thus far in voting that was often still going on.

In the 1970s, however, CBS used its exit polls more for explaining elections than for calling them. For the first time, you could talk about elements of the population that do not congregate heavily in certain precincts: young people and old people, men and women, registered Republicans and Democrats, blacks who do not live in inner cities. You could also ask voters their opinions on campaign issues and how that affected their vote. All of this enriched the late-evening discussions on our election broadcasts and became a valuable database for academic research.

On Election Day 1980 all the networks had national exit polls, and by early afternoon it was obvious that, in contrast to what their pre-election surveys had indicated, Reagan was headed for a blowout. CBS opened its prime-time broadcast dropping broad hints: "All the signs point to good news for Ronald Reagan at this point, stormy seas for President Carter," declared Walter Cronkite at the outset, and then turned to Bruce Morton, who had been studying the exit poll and "has the story." Morton's "story" was about how late deciders, union members, blue-collar workers, women and Catholics voted, but neither he nor Cronkite ever came right out with the bottom line: a solid popular vote margin for Reagan.

While Morton and Cronkite were parsing the blue-collars and late deciders, over at NBC Chancellor and Brinkley kept racking up those electoral votes from Florida, Michigan, Ohio and Texas—using exit polls systematically for the first time to make an early call on the Electoral College. It was more than two hours after NBC's exit polls called the race before CBS, relying on real votes, could do the same. Cronkite thereupon closed out his career at certifying presidents by declaring, more than a half hour after Carter (on the basis of the NBC calls) had conceded, that "Ronald Reagan will become the next President of the United States."

Bill Leonard, who created the CBS Election Unit and was now the news division president, was also closing out a career. In a post-election memo to his senior staff, Leonard was not a happy camper: "For years we dominated election night. . . . About ten years ago, that began to change. We shrugged off the fact that we were calling the races more slowly and boasted that we were calling them more accurately. That is not quite true. NBC was calling them faster and just as accurately."

Brushing past the state exit polls, which enabled NBC to chalk up an electoral-vote majority for Reagan hours before CBS could, Leonard asked why we had not just gone with our own projection of the popular vote: "From the time I got a call at four-thirty in the afternoon until we called the race at ten-thirty, we sat there *knowing* that Reagan had been elected. Why," he asked himself, "didn't I say to you, 'Listen, we've got to say what is obvious—not simply that it looks like Reagan, but that it *is* Reagan? . . . I do know that I felt like a damn fool when the President of the United States gets on television and congratulates the next President and we are still droning along implying that the election has not been decided."

VOTE EARLY OR MOVE

Four years later, in 1984, when the country next elected a president and the networks again went toe to toe, Bill Leonard had retired, and it was probably just as well. Far from stiffening its backbone, CBS was even more circumspect in reporting a much bigger landslide. By early afternoon, Mitofsky and his counterparts at the other networks had national exit polls showing Ronald Reagan roughly twenty points ahead of Walter Mondale. But there was no midafternoon interrupt reporting a "trend," or, in the current term of art, "characterizing" the outcome. On *CBS Evening News*, Dan Rather, now the anchorman and looking at data suggesting a Reagan landslide of possibly record proportions, employed a possibly record number of qualifiers in reporting, "*Indications* of a substantial win for Ronald Reagan *may* be borne out *if* voting trends don't change by the time *all* the polls have closed." [Emphasis mine]

Rather's lame, labored, tentative speculation about an assured fact reflected four years of hounding of the networks by Pacific Time Zone politicians, congressional committees, academic gurus and journalists of other media. And it all stemmed from one network's early call of 1980—which had given NBC its grandest victory in all the election night wars and had humiliated CBS.

That 1980 NBC call at 8:15 Eastern Time appeared in the Pacific Time Zone at 5:15—nearly three hours before the polls closed there. A few days after that call, California's Secretary of State March Fong Eu claimed, that "Would-be voters suddenly became nonvoters after the media projections. . . . Election volunteers did not show up and voter information phones stopped ringing during a time when they are usually all tied up." According to *Congressional Quarterly*, the Bible of Capitol Hill, "When word reached the lines outside the polling place, many voters simply went home—prompting several West Coast candidates to blame NBC for their defeats."[20] Far West Democratic losses charged to television included the chairmen of the House Public Works and Ways and Means Committees and the Senate Foreign Relations Committee. All had been known to be in trouble and all lost by narrow margins. However, no one ever explained why, among voters already at the polls when they heard of NBC's call, there should have been more Democrats than Republicans deciding that their vote "no longer counted." "It's a little like the rain," observed Richard Scammon, "which falls impartially on Democrats and Republicans."[21]

But was any of this supposed rain on voters of either party real? CBS News tried with little success to document those reports of lines at the polling places melting away after the NBC call—or after President Carter's concession speech an hour and a half later. Some of us who give speeches on the West Coast would ask if anyone in the audience had ever decided not to bother voting because of a network call, or could tell us of someone else, or actually saw people on line at polling places leaving in disgust. No verifiable example has ever turned up. Newspaper reporters who wrote of such happenings were queried as to the time and place. Again, no luck. They had only heard from someone else, or read somewhere, that it had happened somewhere.

There are shelves full of survey research archives arguing both sides of this issue. One thing the surveys show conclusively, however, is that most voters in the West believe that other voters (not, of course, themselves) are likely to change their mind about voting when they learn that a network has called the race for President. After the 1980 election, network crews covering other stories in California ran into some hostility over the issue. On one such occasion a CBS producer, in an aside to a colleague, muttered, "Vote early or move."

As it happened, when this dispute came to a boil in the mid-1980s, the chairman and the ranking Republican of the House Subcommittee on Elections were both members from states in the Pacific Time Zone. As one network president after another, coached by their News Division heads and congressional lobbyists, trooped before the subcommittee, they solemnly pledged to absolutely never call a race in any state until all or most of its polls had closed. And there would be no more "characterizing" of the "trend" of the voting in their national exit polls. In other words, for the first time, network chiefs were pledging their reporters to suppress information in their possession while professing on the air to be reporting the news. As a result of this corporate commitment, network correspondents were routinely seen implying an uncertainty about who won which simply did not exist. It made some of us, to say the least, uncomfortable.

Not all the country was kept in the dark. The same lawmakers who dictated the blackout created their own back-channels to the networks to get the embargoed information. An underground commerce in this journalistic contraband grew from one election to the next. The lips of the network news divisions may have been sealed to the public, but our beat reporters (not to mention election unit executives like myself) spent much of Election Day supplying the information we could not share with the public to politicians across the country. For network reporters, this was a recognized form of payback to sources who, most of the time, supply *them* with information. So too was the day-long stream of election data from network lobbyists to their contacts on Capitol Hill and at the White House.

———

Tim Wirth, a Colorado senator who headed the Senate's telecommunications subcommittee in the 1980s, was one of those who demanded that the networks suppress calls in the East, even after the polls there had closed, until the polls closed in the West. Compliance with this demand would in effect ban election night broadcasts altogether until most viewers in the East had gone to bed. Though Wirth induced the congressional leaders of both parties to press this demand on Election Day in 1984, nobody complied, and it was not followed up.

In 1986, however, Wirth faced a tough challenge for his Senate seat. Starting at noon, Mitofsky got hourly queries from the Senator's chief aide on what our exit polls showed on his own race. As it happened, we couldn't help him much. The race was too close to call and would stay that way until well after the polls closed.

Meanwhile, as corporate heads of the networks were caving in to demands for "voluntary" restrictions on the airing of exit poll information, the arms race among their election units grew if anything more intense. Acting on Leonard's severe rebuke over the licking CBS took in 1980, Mitofsky easily got the money (it was a lot) for coast-to-coast exit polling in the next election. At ABC, Roone Arledge, with, apparently, a blank check to compete on every front, matched NBC and CBS dollar for dollar. At all three networks, however, the feeling grew that those dollars were getting out of hand.

CEASE-FIRE AT THE EXITS

Everything conspired in the late 1980s to force a truce in the election-calling wars. When the wars began, election coverage had been seen as an audience booster for the network news divisions and hence for the networks overall. By the end of the 1980s, however, election night viewership for all the networks combined had shrunk to less than half the households watching television. In the week of an election, the three least watched prime-time broadcasts were normally the NBC, CBS and ABC election specials. The most watched broadcast of the week in any given market was normally an undistinguished movie that ran on election night on an independent station.

Not surprisingly, with budget-cutters in full cry at all the networks, the election units with their eight-figure budgets were shining targets. The unit cost of recruiting, training and paying several interviewers for a full day of work at each precinct was a large multiple of what we used to pay for a simple reading of the totals when the polls closed. The projected CBS Election Unit budget for 1989–92 was $21 million—several times what it was before exit polls in nearly every state became the rule.

In relatively wide-open general elections, moreover, like those of 1984 and 1988, all that money bought you relatively little. In those years, results in most states were called when the polls closed, virtually simultaneously by CBS and ABC. In the late 1980s NBC News, which spent as much as anybody, was doomed to come in dead last most of the time, hampered by a quixotic edict from its president, Michael Gartner, that it could not declare a winner from the exit-poll interviews alone. NBC therefore had to feign ignorance (even after the polls closed) until real votes came in.[22]

In 1984 and again in 1988, CBS News under Warren Mitofsky finally called a presidential race first. But ABC was barely a few moments behind. In 1988, the last election before the truce was called, CBS put George Bush over the top at 9:17 P.M. ABC did the same at 9:21. The combined cost of the units involved for this election cycle was in the neighborhood of thirty million dollars.

Most frustrating of all, the networks had to sit on the product of all their labor and expense for hours before sharing it with the public. With each election, too, more extravagant embargoes were urged on us. In the off-year election of 1986, for example, when the major question of the night was whether Democrats would regain control of the Senate, David Broder, the perennial scourge of television news, called on the networks to withhold reporting on Senate party switching until the polls closed in California. The usual suspects in Congress promptly called on the networks to follow Broder's advice, but this time no one buckled. Well before the polls closed in the Pacific time zone, we made it clear that the Democrats were on a roll—and to this day no one has turned up a single West Coast voter who left the polls in disgust because his Senate vote could no longer affect whether Bob Dole remained leader.

Between the cost and the hassle involved in competitive election calling, CBS and ABC began thinking seriously about a pool—something that NBC had been urging since the 1970s. After the 1988 election, NBC folded its Election Unit and announced that it would join one or more of the other networks in a cost-sharing venture. CNN, which had never done its own projections, offered to join as well.

The question then became which of the two standing Election Units would become the nucleus of a four-network pool. On the recent record in calling races, CBS could claim a modest edge. It had called the last two presidential elections first, but by only a handful of minutes in each case. Since the early 1980s, CBS and ABC had each called all but one race correctly. The director of ABC's election unit was approaching retirement, but CBS's Mitofsky at fifty-three was still in his prime and was the recognized leader in his field. When that year's CBS News president, David Burke, offered to guarantee that the pool would cost no more than a million dollars a year per member, the matter was settled. ABC disbanded its Election Unit and the CBS Election Unit, which had been the first, became under a new name the last.

The four-network board of directors called their new baby Voter Research and Surveys (VRS). It got off to a rocky start in the off-year election of 1990. A communication failure between the exit-poll contractor (an ABC subsidiary) and the VRS mainframe (under lease from CBS) kept the national exit poll out of reach for most of the network evening broadcasts as well as such finicky nonmember subscribers as the New York Times and the Washington Post. The state exit polls, however, worked fine, all the calls were on the money, and the pool went into the 1992 campaign right on budget—a budget that saved the members an average of $10 million each.

On February 18, 1992, VRS made its debut in presidential politics. By early afternoon on the computer screens of the member networks, history seemed to be in the making. In the New Hampshire Republican primary, George Bush led Pat Buchanan by a puny 48 to 42 percent. (For some of us with long memories, those numbers seemed spookily familiar. Six New Hampshire primaries back, Lyndon Johnson had edged out Eugene McCarthy by 49 to 42, and a few weeks later Johnson abandoned his bid for re-election.) Those early Bush-Buchanan numbers were never broadcast, but they circulated throughout the day among the coterie of politicians and reporters with access to news unsafe for public consumption. As it turned out, the public in this instance was well served by the embargo. When the real votes came in, Bush had won not by a piddling six but by a solid sixteen percentage points.

This was the first appearance of the "Buchanan bias" in exit-poll responses for which Mitofsky in later primaries would try to make adjustments. (In polling usage, it should be noted, the term *bias* has nothing to do with the politics of the pollster. Survey experts define *bias* as error—unlike sampling error, which can be plus or minus— that errs in only one direction. When you find it, it's not always easy to explain. Mitofsky's best guess is that Buchanan's voters were prouder of what they'd done and, hence, more prone to respond, than Bush's were.) Although Buchanan got a third or so of the vote in several more primaries—certainly a profound warning of the incumbent's vulnerability—he himself was going nowhere. Asked in the exit poll why they had voted for him, few of Buchanan's supporters in the primaries said they wanted the man to be President.

Some of the most telling commentary of the primary season in both parties kept turning up in the exit polls. Bill Clinton won most of the Democratic contests and easily won the party's nomination, but the exit polls suggested that his party's primary voters were anything but pleased with their handiwork. It was in the New York primary, for example, that Clinton dispatched his last remaining opponents, Jerry Brown and Paul Tsongas. But as the Democratic primary voters left the polls, only half of them thought Clinton was honest enough to be President! Though 41 percent had voted for him, only a third of those did so without reservations. A majority wished there had been other candidates from which to choose.

In Pennsylvania, the next major primary, Clinton no longer had active opposition, but it was too late for VRS to call off its exit poll. Largely because of that, Clinton conducted a full-scale campaign not to win the primary but to better his score in the exit poll. Half a million dollars' worth of campaign commercials later, cheers went up at Clinton headquarters when three out of five of Pennsylvania's *Democratic* voters found their nominee honest enough to be President. Both the original Clinton problem and the means of dealing with it would prove prophetic for his presidency.

By the final day of the primary season, the nominations in both parties had long been settled, and neither Bush nor Clinton was in danger in any of the day's events—not even in California, whose last Democratic governor, Jerry Brown, was still on the ballot. When the VRS members met to draw up questionnaires for the final day of primaries, CBS proposed a way to turn these slam-dunk events into contests. By then, national surveys showed Ross Perot running very competitively as an independent against both Bush and Clinton. CBS suggested we ask both Democratic and Republican voters in the final primaries how they would have voted if Perot had been on the ballot.

Once again, the exit polls were a better story than the primaries themselves. On the official California ballots, Bush easily disposed of Buchanan, and Clinton dispatched Brown with a little more difficulty. But, on the VRS ballots that included Ross Perot, Perot whipped Bush in the Republican primary and tied Clinton in the Democratic primary. Perot also beat Clinton and lost narrowly to Bush in the networks' wholly-owned Ohio primary. Had the primary voters of both parties in both states been voting that day on a three-way race between Bush (R), Clinton (D) and Perot (I), VRS indicated that Perot might have carried both of them.[23]

"Anyone who doubts that this is a three-man race for the presidency," declared Tom Brokaw on NBC's primary night broadcast, "should talk to voters in presidential primaries from New Jersey to California tonight." "The big story tonight" echoed Rather, "is Ross Perot." No independent had ever enjoyed such a launching—certified as on a par with the major party nominees by the most powerful forces shaping American public opinion. Had a man less deeply flawed than Perot (and just as rich) received such a send-off, the 140-year reign of America's two-party system might have been over.

———

After its shaky start in New Hampshire, VRS had settled down for the rest of the 1992 primary season. On election night, all of the VRS calls stood up, as did Mitofsky's original budget projections, and a side business in marketing exit-poll data to newspapers and local television stations produced a nice Christmas bonus for the members. NBC News and CNN, however, were under heavy pressure from their managements to get the cost of voter research even lower. One cost-cutting proposal that all members supported in principle was to merge VRS with News Election Service (NES), the pool that counted real votes for the same four networks as well as for the Associated Press. Merger negotiations stalled repeatedly over who should head the merged organization—Warren Mitofsky or Robert Flaherty, the longtime director of NES. The issue was decided when Mitofsky and the board could not agree on money. Mitofsky's deputy at VRS, Murray Edelman, and Flaherty eventually shared responsibility for the combined election pool, and still another name for it was found: Voter News Service (VNS).

In Edelman's new role as chief election caller for network television and the main U.S. wire service, he got abundant counsel from the members to be, above all, cautious in calling the off-year elections of 1994. Only on election night did the rest of us find out that ABC's Roone Arledge had given orders to make independent calls from the VNS data. For this, ABC called on John Blyden-burgh, a political scientist who used to make the calls for their own election unit. The gamble paid off in a few ABC calls made well before VNS and hence well before CBS, NBC and CNN. These coups included the three hot stories of the night: Mario Cuomo's defeat for a fourth term as governor of New York, Oliver North's loss of a Senate bid in Virginia and the defeat of Jeb Bush for governor of Florida.

The post-mortems at the other networks were severe. ABC's aggression could not go unpunished. Under the VNS agreement, all of the members had a right to make their own, unilateral calls based on the pool data. Others, including CBS, had thought about it but concluded they could not beat Mitofsky, or later Edelman, at their own game. Edelman insisted that ABC would not have scored against him in 1994 had he known there would be a contest. How right he was would soon be apparent.

THE WAR RESUMES

Having unilaterally disarmed, CBS and NBC were easy prey to ABC's sneak attack in a handful of contests. In an arms race, however, among alert and fully prepared members of the internetwork pool, there could easily be no winners.

The majority of elections are not close and are easily called from exit-poll interviews when the polls close. For races that cannot be called from the interviews alone, the next opportunity comes with the actual vote returns from the exit-poll and other precincts that form a model of the state's voters. Picking a winner from these models at any time is subject to a mathematically definable risk: 20 to 1, 50 to 1, 100 to 1 and so on.

Historically, the standard applied by the CBS Election Unit and, after the merger, by VNS has been one chance in 200 of being wrong. Counting presidential, senatorial and gubernatorial contests, presidential primaries and some other things of national interest, over two hundred calls are made in every four-year cycle. This does *not* mean that every four years or so a bad call gets made. Only a relatively small number of the contests are close enough to present any risk. Over seventeen elections held between 1962 and 1994, CBS/VNS had been forced to eat only seven of their calls.

Now that competitive calls were back, CBS went to the obvious place for help: Warren Mitofsky, who had developed a nice consulting business on election night projections around the world (e.g., Mexico, Russia, South Korea). Mitofsky pointed out that the only prudent way, on a systematic basis, to beat VNS and, more importantly, to beat an aggressively calling ABC was to improve the odds. That meant staffing more precincts as well as finding a way to integrate the augmented samples with those of VNS.

The starting price for such a strategy was a million dollars. The principal beneficiaries of this entire exercise, moreover, assuming it worked, would be the egos of the news executives; hardly anyone in the greater world, even in the world of media and politics, knew, let alone cared, about this rat race among the networks. CBS News President Eric Ober gagged at the prospect of explaining to the company's famously tight CEO, Laurence Tisch, what spending this million dollars would do for the shareholders. There was also doubt (based, in part, on some investigative reporting) whether ABC's Arledge, whose 1994 coup could have been paid for out of petty cash, would spring for big money in 1996.

For CBS, being king of the hill again on calling elections was never the goal. The goal was simply not to let anyone else, especially ABC, take that hill. For a lot less than a million dollars, therefore, CBS hired Mitofsky as a consultant for 1996—to match wits with ABC's man in looking at the same VNS material and picking winners—hopefully first but above all not last. Concerned only about averting another rout by ABC, CBS shaved the cost even further by sharing Mitofsky's services with CNN. As Mitofsky himself pointed out at the beginning, this would have to be a war not only of brains but of nerve. Beating VNS with any frequency would require some relaxing of that 200-to-1 standard of certainty, and beating ABC could require shaving points on whatever risk level ABC adopted.

To help fray nerves further all around, the first battles of the new war would be fought not in general elections, where past Republican/Democratic voting patterns give some stability to the precinct models, but in the presidential primaries—where there is no such foundation. The first of these was Louisiana's newly-created firehouse primary, where, as seen in Chapter 1, Pat Buchanan upset Phil Gramm and left dying what had once been regarded as a formidable Gramm campaign. Here it was Murray Edelman, after his fastidious election night in 1994, who turned out to be the cowboy. With both ABC and the CBS/CNN consortium unwilling to touch it, Edelman early and boldly called Buchanan the winner. Hours later, in the final count, Buchanan did emerge on top—but by a margin of barely thirty votes in one voting district.

The Iowa caucuses were next. In a close three-way race, ABC and Mitofsky both blinked, VNS called Dole the winner promptly from its entrance poll, and there was no chance for any of the networks to claim victory over the others.

In New Hampshire, Edelman finally got cautious. New Hampshire was the state where the networks' model four years before had been off the mark by ten points! This time the exit poll showed what looked like a clear Buchanan win, but everyone was leery of the "Buchanan bias" we had seen so much of in 1992. Soon after eight o'clock, however, when some real votes were in, Pat Buchanan's lead looked solid. Mitofsky signaled the call and Rather made it—along with somebody at CNN. Ten minutes later ABC followed suit.

NBC, which also had a calling team of its own, stuck with VNS, where Edelman saw little space between Buchanan and Dole. Two hours later, with 80 percent of the vote counted, Buchanan's lead had shrunk to less than 1 percent—where it held, precariously, to the end.

Picking the wrong winner in a New Hampshire primary, which the three networks came uncomfortably close to doing, would have rivaled the NBC/ABC humiliations in Wisconsin twenty years before, but ABC, CBS and CNN dodged that bullet this time. A week later, their luck ran out. By Tuesday, February 27, the credentialed front-runner, Dole, had been defeated once again—this time by a half-million-dollar aerial campaign by Forbes in an otherwise little-contested Delaware. There were three primaries on February 27, two of them in North and South Dakota, which had been largely conceded to the Kansan in the race. VNS was expected to call Dole the winner in both Dakotas as soon as the polls closed, and it did.

The third primary, in Arizona, was therefore the designated playing field—not just for Dole, Forbes, Buchanan and Alexander but for the network calling teams. Once again, the Arizona television spectrum had been carpet-bombed by Forbes, and Dole (with those Dakota wins in his pocket) could probably have gotten a pass for the day with a second place in Arizona. But that, of course, would have been a pretty boring story.

In the early exit poll and vote returns, Mitofsky and his ABC rival discerned a more interesting, if less obvious one. When the polls closed at 9:00 P.M., the exit polling showed a close race between Forbes and Buchanan, with Dole trailing both of them—though not by much. Arizona had never held a presidential primary before. Edelman had therefore drawn his sample with no voting history to rely on, and was therefore inclined to be extremely cautious. Mitofsky too was in no hurry to pick a winner, but it sure looked to him as though Dole would finish third. He so advised his clients, and around 9:30 CNN's Judy Woodruff announced, "Bob Dole will come in third." Minutes later, ABC interrupted *Home Improvement* so that Peter Jennings could put a little spin on his network's call: "Some will say an embarrassing third."

At CBS none of us felt obliged to interrupt the prime-time movie to report, without knowing the winner, who would finish third in a winner-take-all primary. As eleven o'clock approached, however, Dan Rather was due to present a two-minute summary of the day's primaries for use on the late-evening broadcasts of our affiliates. With the decision desk still clinging to that third-place call in Arizona, CBS, not belatedly enough, made the call.

Nobody is perfect, of course, and among the stories that television news has blown over the years, getting third place wrong in a primary would not ordinarily be ranked among the all-time hall-of-fame blunders. It took all the massive pundit power of ABC News to accomplish that. "It is still too early to be drafting a funeral oration for Bob Dole's presidential ambitions," declared Ted Koppel as he took to the air on *Nightline*. Koppel then launched a half-hour ceremony that was little else. "Yes, [Dole] won North and South Dakota tonight," but "The prize was Arizona. . . . Dole did not win Arizona. He came in third." Jeff Greenfield, the network's prime political sage (currently at CNN) was then called on to explain how Dole's coming in first in two primaries and third in the other, while Pat Buchanan placed second in all three, had reshaped the political landscape. "All year," said Greenfield, "we've assumed this battle was going to come down to a fight between Bob Dole and one of his potential rivals. Now the assumption is the fight is between Buchanan and a field of rivals fighting to battle *him*."

By that time (approaching midnight) VNS had determined that Forbes had won Arizona. Among the three top contenders, only Buchanan this day had clearly won *nothing*. Still, said Koppel, summing up, "The most electrifying candidate of the night is Pat Buchanan." The electricity at *Nightline* was not confined to one hemisphere. "Buchanan shock waves," reported Koppel, "are being felt around the world." From London, the foreign editor of the BBC was called on (at 5:00 A.M. local time) for a read on how Brits were reacting: "They are mystified, because they think . . . 'The Americans are quite sensible. How can they do this to themselves?' "

The Americans, as it happened, were not doing anything special to themselves. Dole did not finish an embarrassing third in Arizona. The electrifying Pat Buchanan did. Among the networks that got the story wrong that night, CBS was blessed by having only two minutes, seen on a handful of stations, in which to embarrass itself. Still, on his evening news broadcast the next day, Dan Rather on behalf of CBS made a wholly unqualified confession of error.

ABC, on the other hand, whose *Nightline* broadcast of February 27, 1996, could serve as a party gag reel of political analysis gone mad, began the February 28 broadcast with a broad-based *mea culpa* on behalf of "a lot of us in the news business." Soundbites from all the networks were aired at the top to show how "many of us" had blown it the night before. Koppel then gave a mistakes-were-made explanation worthy of the Clinton White House: "The media do not ordinarily get their information from the same single source, but in the case of election or primary-night data like exit polls, we do, which accounts for why so many of us were wrong." That single source, Koppel failed to say, had never told *Nightline* or anybody else that Dole would finish third.

Among the mistakes which had been made and the *mea culpas* tendered, there were some, not least at ABC, who groaned privately about Roone Arledge's original decision to reactivate the calling wars—and the certainty that the rest of us would rise to that bait. For the daring gamble that won them a ten-minute edge in New Hampshire, CBS/CNN did not get a single pat on the back outside their own inner sanctums. The Arizona blunder, on the other hand, gave election reporting on television its worst black eye in twenty years.

Four days later, Dole won the South Carolina primary by so wide a margin that VNS called the contest for everyone as soon as the polls were closed—as it did for all of the year's remaining primaries. The competing network decision teams had gotten through the primary season without any winners and, in one memorable night, a lot of losers. There would not be another chance to go wrong until November.

LAST CALL FOR '96

As the network decision desks crammed for their final test of the year, they had more to contend with than sampling error and the smarts of their rivals at the other desks. First they had to contend with the Pledge. In homage to the myth about lines at the polls van-ishing once a presidential race has been called, before each election the network news chiefs make a formal commitment not to even hint, before the polls close, at what their exit polls have to say about the outcome.

Four years before, Eric Ober, the CBS News president who signed that year's pledges to congressional-committee chairmen, had taken a very activist view of their enforcement. A veteran television-station manager, Ober told the network's correspondents and producers he wanted no winks or nods, he was onto all their tricks, he would not stand for any of them.

When the network evening news broadcasts aired that election night, both the national and state exit polls already pointed to a fairly easy win for Clinton. Nobody apparently told NBC it couldn't drop hints, so Tom Brokaw did little else: "Long lines everywhere . . . If a big turnout means big change, this is going to be a long night for Pres-ident Bush. . . . With the polls closed in the first two states . . . omi-nous signs for the President." From NBC Kennebunkport, we heard that "the Bush camp is resigned to what lies ahead." From Little Rock, we heard, Clinton's "welcome home felt like a victory celebra-tion." That sort of thing.

On CBS *Evening News*, however, faithful to the network's news president du jour, hardly a clue. Reporting that the race is relatively close in Dan Quayle's normally Republican home state of Indiana, Dan Rather does venture, "If it's that close in Indiana, what is that going to tell us about the rest of the night?" Though Dan failed to an-swer his rhetorical question (on NBC, Brokaw did) Ober told the control room he should cut it out.

———

By election night 1996, the revolving presidential door at CBS News had delivered a fresh taker of the Pledge. Andrew Heyward, a veteran producer and no neophyte on this issue, agreed with the rest of us that we did not have to shield our viewers from what was going on in the world. Rather, Schieffer and the rest were now free, like Jennings and Brokaw, to speculate about the winner, so long as we could find something apart from the embargoed exit polls to hang it on.

At 7:00 P.M., with the polls closed in just eight states and barely 1 percent of the popular vote counted, an unleashed Dan Rather was still not allowed to say that the exit polls already showed nearly 300 electoral votes leaning decisively for Clinton and his re-election therefore all but certain. But he could say that Clinton had carried Florida, where the polls had closed, and the last Democrat to do this, Jimmy Carter, was the last Democrat beside himself elected President.

A few minutes later, from Little Rock (where the Clinton folks knew everything there was to know about the exit polls), Rita Braver was able to report that "the victory party is already started." On the whole, however, Rather was still playing what he really knew close to his vest: "It's still far too early to say whether [Clinton] is going to win." That is, far too early to say it on CBS.

Over at ABC, *World News Tonight* at 6:30 Eastern had toyed with the implications of a relatively close race in normally Republican Indiana. Its correspondents with the candidates reported that Dole was working hard on his concession speech and that Clinton's victory speech was just about done. All that it would report from the exit polls, however, was that most Americans thought the country was on the right track, the economy was dandy, and cutting the deficit was more important than cutting taxes. All of this, to be sure, put Clinton (and not Dole) in step with the voters.

Perhaps the best example, however, of the networks playing cat and mouse (under duress and reluctantly, to be sure) with the public came at the close of *NBC Nightly News*. Until now, NBC had been uncharacteristically reticent about the outcome. *Its* White House correspondent reported that Clinton was working on what he only "hoped" would be his victory speech. Clinton, of course, along with NBC, had more than hope to go on.

At the close of the nightly broadcast, with fresh poll closings coming up, Brokaw asked Tim Russert what viewers should "look for" in the state results coming. "Florida, Georgia, Ohio," said Russert, are crucial states. "If Florida goes for Clinton, there may be no stopping him." No Republican, Russert points out, has ever been elected President without carrying Ohio. So watch what happens in Florida and Ohio. While this conversation was being aired, Brokaw and Russert already *knew* how Florida and, almost surely, Ohio would go. VNS, on its internal screens had already called Florida and was about to call Ohio. Candor would suggest that NBC tell you this, just as candor would suggest that, when Rather says "it's far too early to say who is going to win," he make it clear that the reason it's too early is that his lips are sealed—not that he doesn't know.

Not surprisingly, there are intelligent people outside the network control rooms who suspect that a more self-serving motive underlies this lack of candor on the part of the networks. In the post-election issue of *The New Yorker*, Louis Menand wrote: "Beside voter turnout, the nets have another, less high-minded election night concern— viewer turnout. The worry is that viewers who learn at seven o'clock that it's all over will hit the remote and start cruising for *Seinfeld* reruns."[24]

The worry inferred by Menand was surely there (and borne out by the lowest election night ratings on record). But no one who was in one of the network control rooms around, say, 8:40 P.M. on election night would have dreamed they were willfully holding anything back. Each of the networks had its own state-of-the-art best-ever graphic declaring "Clinton Re-Elected," ready to launch—with copy, analysis, remotes and marquee-name interviews to follow when they returned from their station breaks at nine o'clock. At that point Clinton had 218 electoral votes. Among the states where polls would close at 9:00, 49 more votes were ready to be announced for Clinton at the stroke of nine. That made 267. It took 270, three more. The only immediate prospect for those three needed votes was Kentucky, which had been too close to call for hours. Not since Arizona had there been such an opportunity for a network to get stuck out on a limb. Absolutely no one was rooting against a Kentucky call out of concern over viewer tune-out. Everyone, in fact, was relieved when VNS made the call in time for all of our "Clinton Re-Elected" graphics to go up at nine.

On the main call of the election, therefore, there was a five-way tie among the networks (Fox had joined the pool) and anyone else with an AP wire. In spite of the legions of consultants massed by the competing networks, the main calls of the night, including the Republicans' retaining the House of Representatives, were made by the pool. There were no grounds for any individual network to order in champagne or take out full-page ads claiming victory.

VNS finally made one bad call (a Senate race in New Hampshire) after making four hundred, in four elections, that stood up. ABC got a Senate race wrong all by itself when it declared a Democrat elected in Oregon and the Republican won.

Bill Clinton had, oddly enough, created an extra-constitutional hurdle for himself, a "mandate"-empowering 50 percent of the popular vote. CBS's Dan Rather kept urging people to get out there and vote on that mandate while the polls were still open—even after we declared the contest prescribed by the founding fathers over. CBS put some extra effort into tracking the icing on Clinton's cake. Shortly after midnight we indicated that the President, in his quest for a 50-percent mandate, was a loser. It was the one clear beat of the night, but no one sent out for Dom Perignon over that.

4

MASTERS OF ALL THEY SURVEY

"THE PEOPLE HAVE SPOKEN—THE BASTARDS!" WORDS SPO-
ken from the heart by Dick Tuck, the legendary Democratic mischief-maker, when Los Angeles voters rejected
his bid to represent them in the California legislature. That nothing is
decided until the voters speak their mind on Election Day is a tenet of
the democratic faith which not only politicians but those who cover
them ignore at their peril.

In the early years of network polling, public opinion surveys were
limited to national policy and lifestyle issues. It was only after great
hesitation that the networks finally took the plunge into polling's
most treacherous waters: elections. Robert Chandler, who headed the
CBS News election unit in the late 1960s and early 1970s, recalls
three years of polling exclusively on issues, because CBS initially "decided to eschew attempts to predict the outcome" of elections.[1] Political reporting was burdened, then as now, by an academic posse bent
on frustrating the natural curiosity of most Americans about how
their candidates are doing.

CBS was not alone in responding to the qualms, as Chandler put
it, of "political scientists who claim that predictive polling . . . erodes
the democratic process." NBC, in those years and well into the
1970s, polled extensively, both in primary states and in the major
states during general elections and unlike CBS, it did ask how its respondents were inclined to vote. "In order not to confuse voters,"

however, Bud Lewis, then head of NBC's election unit, kept his "horse race" findings off the air and used them only to help in his election night calls.[2]

In the networks' pious effort, at the beginning, to shield the public from information that might not be good for it, they had equally high-minded allies in other media. When the *New York Times* polled New Yorkers on the 1970 race for governor and the country in 1972 on the race for President, it too eschewed reporting on how its respondents planned to vote.[3]

THE "SCIENCE" OF POLLING

There were to be sure, sound reasons to be wary about polling on the presidential horse race, aside from placating the academic bluenoses. Even the most careful survey research has risks. The research gets its validity from the mathematical laws of probability, one of whose provisions is that every now and then you're going to be relatively wrong even if you do everything right. What the laws say is that, if you ask a perfectly random sample of so many people for their opinion on anything, what you get will reflect, within so many percentage points, what you would hear from the entire population—*nineteen times out of twenty*.

This is the familiar "error due to sampling" that is ritually affirmed somewhere in most poll reports—though that 1-in-20 chance of erring beyond the advertised limit is seldom mentioned. However, a polling unit that does, say, 40 polls a year is likely to go off the reservation twice during that year. The immutable laws of mathematics, however, do not tell you *which two* of your 40 polls will be the turkeys.

To get a genuinely random sample, moreover, of, say, a thousand grown-ups in a telephone survey, the respondents should be the first thousand persons targeted at the first thousand randomly dialed home numbers. Of that thousand persons, however, some may never be at home no matter how often you call, and of those you reach, about one out of three is likely to stiff the most persistent interviewer. And, of course, about 7 percent of the population has no household telephone.[4] All of these things can add to the potential error due to sampling.

If your question has to do with welfare for legal immigrants or ground troops in Bosnia, there will never be an objective test of the final numbers that emerge from your computer. Since different polling organizations seldom ask questions on such issues in exactly the same way, disparate results do not necessarily call into question the precision of the respective polls—though they may raise questions about the judgment or the objectivity of one or more of the pollsters. When you ask people how they plan to vote, however, the questions are pretty well standardized: "If the election were held today and the candidates were————,————, and————, how would you vote?" When different polls taken at the same time get significantly different answers to this question, people get suspicious of the lot of them. They get even more so when the answers recorded on Election Day tell still another story.

It was just such a calamity in 1936 for the country's then-reigning oracle of election outcomes that paved the way for today's "scientific" polling of artfully selected samples. The *Literary Digest* was then the country's most widely read weekly magazine. In all presidential election years since 1924, it had mailed up to 20 million sample ballots to its subscribers and to names found in telephone directories and state driver's license lists.[5] For three elections in a row, the lists had served *Literary Digest* well. The respondents, millions of them, had picked Coolidge, Hoover and Franklin Roosevelt in that order and in the first FDR election had come close to hitting his actual percentage of the vote on the nose. In 1936, the *Digest* mailed out over 10 million ballots and got back over 2 million; 57 percent of them supported the Republican candidate, Alf Landon, and 41 percent backed the President. Yet on Election Day Landon got 37 percent of the vote, Roosevelt 62 percent—the highest popular vote percentage, at the time, ever recorded in a presidential contest. Not only the poll, but the *Literary Digest* as well, were soon extinct.

While the *Digest* was predicting its Landon landslide, three different pioneers of public-opinion research—George Gallup, Elmo Roper and Archibald Crossley—had been conducting surveys of a few thousand voters each. These were not the random samples generally in use today but "quota" samples, which aimed at proportions of designated groups (e.g., men and women, whites and blacks, age and income) that matched those in the population. That method had its flaws, but in 1936 it beat mailbacks from *Literary Digest* readers, car owners and telephone subscribers (then a relatively upscale third of the population) at predicting the election. All three of the early pioneers of "scientific" polling got the landslide right.[6]

Gallup, whose newspaper column, "America Speaks," was widely syndicated, became the dominant pollster of that era—even though his poll in the watershed year of 1936 had been furthest from the mark, 13 points off on FDR's 24-point margin over Landon. In 1940, Gallup predicted a relatively narrow 52–48 win for Roosevelt over Wendell Willkie. It turned out to be a quite comfortable 55–45. Four years after that, in 1944, Gallup foresaw Roosevelt in a 51/49 cliffhanger over Thomas E. Dewey. Once again, on Election Day Roosevelt won relatively easily, 54–46.

Despite such close calls on relatively clear-cut races, Gallup and his fellow pollsters by 1948 had little doubt of their craft. When a Gallup survey in mid-October showed a five-point margin for Tom Dewey (greater than Gallup had shown for FDR in 1940 and 1944), he decided that no further polling was necessary. With breathtaking self-confidence, he declared, "Next Tuesday the whole world will be able to see down to the last percentage point how good we are."[7]

Gallup's competitive bravado stood up in at least one respect on Election Day. He was far closer to reality than Roper and Crossley. In an edition of *Fortune* magazine that went to press in early September, Roper reported a 25-point margin for Dewey and shut down his campaign polling six weeks before Gallup. In doing so, Roper made even Gallup seem tentative: "Dewey will pile up a popular majority only slightly less than that accorded Mr. Roosevelt when he swept the boards against Alf Landon."[8]

The campaign was not, of course, over. No one can ever know whether Dewey would have been elected if the election of 1948 had been held in mid-October, let alone early September. But on November 2, Truman defeated Dewey by 50 percent to 45 percent. Since then Gallup has polled through the final Saturday of every campaign and put the winner first all but once.

That once was in 1976, when Gallup's final survey put Ford ahead by one point and Carter won by two. No apologies were called for. The founding Gallup described himself with obvious pride as the "scorekeeper of the political world."[9] Still, some of the later entries in the field were not so sure they wanted the risks attached to that.

CBS NEWS AND THE *NEW YORK TIMES* JOIN HANDS

In 1972 and 1974, Warren Mitofsky, who succeeded Chandler as head of the CBS Election Unit, dealt extensively on election nights with David Jones, the national editor of the *New York Times*. The CBS exit polls and sample precincts, says Jones, "revolutionized the way we organized our first editions. In the old days we had only the political instincts of our reporters to go on, and we'd lead with something like, 'Voters went to the polls under cloudy skies today.' Now, by five o'clock in the afternoon, we knew who was going to win, and our reporters could start writing about why."[10]

Both CBS and the *Times* wanted to report more deeply and more continuously on what Americans were thinking, and they each had only so much money to spend. In the summer of 1975, Jones and Mitofsky proposed to their own organizations a multimedia partnership, which soon became a model for most of the public-opinion polling done in the United States.

The economic efficiencies of this alliance were great. The *New York Times* circulation department has a large telemarketing force, with long-distance phone lines at fixed monthly rates used mainly in the daytime. Public-opinion surveys are done mainly at night. The *Times* could make these facilities available for the joint operation at relatively little extra cost. CBS News supplied the technical expertise of Mitofsky and his election staff as well as the data-processing equipment and software, much of which was already in place for its election broadcasts.

One of the driving forces behind the *Times*' desire for a polling unit was that past reliance on the expertise and "instincts" of its political reporters had sometimes left it painfully unprepared for the outcomes of the races it cared about most. The *Times*' David Jones recalled the New York Senate race of 1970, in which a minor-party candidate, the Conservatives' Jim Buckley, received decidedly secondary coverage in the *Times* until a poll by an outside firm showed

Buckley in the lead—as he remained through the final count on Election Day.

Though most of the poll findings that, years later, stick out in anybody's mind involve the horse race, these two great news organizations, then the most highly regarded in their respective media, took a joint vow of abstinence. Part of the formal agreement between them was that they would not report their actual numbers on voter preference in political campaigns. At their respective home offices, in fact, the numbers would be closely held within the two polling units.

Both organizations were allowed to report by exactly what margins likely Republican primary voters had good or not-so-good opinions of President Ford and his rival in the primaries, Ronald Reagan: highly favorable by virtually identical margins. But they could only report broadly, no numbers please, that overall these Republicans favored the president. During the fall campaign, CBS would flash numbers on the television screen and the *New York Times* printed graphics showing how independents or adherents of each party planned to vote, or Catholics, or some age group. But they could not report the bottom line on the total public's current choice among the candidates.

All this secrecy about the one finding in a poll that normal people expect to hear first "drove everybody crazy," Mitofsky recalls. Pollsters at the presidential campaigns used to take the numbers that CBS and the *Times* did report regarding elements of the voting population, calculate from them what the bottom line should be and then flaunt their numbers to the CBS and *Times* political reporters—who were not allowed by their own pollsters to know. At the newspaper, a frustrated Johnny Apple, Jr., simply tacked the most recent horse-race finding from the Gallup poll onto stories otherwise based on a fresh CBS News/*New York Times* survey.

CBS correspondents invariably went by the book. This did not, to be sure, prevent Walter Cronkite from reporting in mid-October: "Jimmy Carter has widened his lead over President Ford . . . the survey puts Carter ahead by about five to four." Nor did it stop him the Friday before the election from reporting that the final pre-election poll "shows a thin, thin edge for Carter in a race too close to call."

Such "characterizations" were allowed under the Mitofsky-Jones deal. Only the numbers were not.

Given the 50-percent-to-48-percent margin by which Carter ultimately prevailed, CBS News and the *New York Times* may have gotten this one exactly on the nose. Since they never published their numbers before the election, however, there was no way to take bows afterwards. As for the lofty abstinence of the two news organizations from reporting the horse race numbers, Mitofsky sighed in a post-election memo that no one had praised them for their restraint.

DÉJÀ VU IN 1980

By 1980, to everyone's relief, the horse race was alive and well at all the networks. NBC had formed a partnership with the Associated Press. ABC was temporarily going it alone but would eventually find a partner in the *Washington Post*. All of these intermedia alliances followed the pattern set by CBS News/*New York Times*. The television networks would report each poll on an agreed-upon evening news broadcast. The newspaper or wire service partner would then release its own report in the next morning edition or for morning editions of its subscribers—which usually hit local newsstands a couple of hours later. The partners would jointly write the questionnaires, but when the results came in they would write their reports without consulting one another. There were often major differences in which findings of the polls were reported, or emphasized, by the respective partners and in the interpretations that they placed on them. When the embargo on the horse-race numbers was finally lifted, there were even differences in the numbers posted. CBS, in reporting voter preference for candidates, included not only respondents who said their minds were made up but those who said they merely "leaned" toward one candidate or another. The *Times* included only the solid supporters.

All of these proud news organizations (the *Wall Street Journal* would soon replace AP as NBC's partner) would now have their reputations on the line when they reported their final survey on the eve of the 1980 election. In the polls leading up to it, they would refine their strategies for dealing with the fact that barely half of those old enough to vote will do so. The pollsters know, too, that if their survey is limited to those who are registered to vote, one in five even of those won't vote either.

With the combined backing of CBS and the *New York Times*, both of which were having good years, Mitofsky found himself at the head of the most handsomely endowed survey operation in the business. At a time when most polling organizations, including the most famous of them, were cutting corners to save money, CBS News/*New York Times* went to extraordinary lengths to reach and interview the specific individuals targeted in their random sampling—calling back at least four times.

In placing their bets on where the real votes are in their final survey, most pollsters have their own criteria for identifying "likely voters." The stricter the criteria, the fewer people there will be in your sample and therefore the higher your sampling error. Moreover, if you restrict your likely voters to the very most likely, you eliminate a fair number of people who will in fact vote. Mitofsky devised a formula for including all registered voters—but classifying them according to their comparative likelihood of voting and weighting each category accordingly.

To avoid the fate of the pollsters of 1948, Mitofsky polled through the Saturday night before the election. In theory, and in later years in practice, you could have polled Sunday and Monday night as well, but no other public poll had ever done this. The same individuals, moreover, who did the CBS News/*New York Times* poll had responsibilities to an election night broadcast on Tuesday. They had lots to do over that final pre-election weekend besides another night of polling.

When the final numbers came out of the CBS News computer on that Sunday morning in 1980, Reagan and Carter were in a virtual tie: Reagan 44 percent/Carter 43 percent/John Anderson 8 percent. To some low-tech political junkies, this came as something of a surprise. In the CBS/*New York Times* poll just a few days before, Carter had been ahead—though just barely. There had then come the only Carter–Reagan debate of the campaign, in which most of us (along with the viewers reached in a post-debate CBS/*Times* poll) thought Reagan had done the better job. The final polls in a number of big states had shown Reagan moving ahead. Still, at both CBS and the *Times*, no one doubted the poll's finding of a very close race.

———

On Election Day, of course, Reagan defeated Carter by a healthy ten percentage points. Though CBS did have the right man on top, the one-point margin was well within its sampling error. The discrepancy between the CBS poll and the election returns was about the same as Gallup's thirty-two years earlier when he forecast Dewey defeating Truman.

Like Gallup in 1948, CBS News/*New York Times* in 1980 had company. Gallup's own final poll in 1980 had Reagan up by only three points. The *Washington Post* had two late polls, one of which had Reagan up by 4 percent, the other down by 4 percent. An ABC poll done by Lou Harris had Reagan up by 5 percent. By far the closest to the actual result was an NBC/AP poll done ten days before the election, which had Reagan up by 7 percent.

How could CBS News/*New York Times* in particular have been so far off—in a poll done so close to Election Day? There is no generally accepted explanation. Post-mortems among the pollsters went on for years. Primary exhibits in these inquiries were polls done for the Carter and Reagan campaigns respectively by Patrick Caddell and Richard Wirthlin. Both of these campaign pollsters had been tracking voters, night after night, from two weeks before the election. And both had informed their candidates and others in their campaigns, that, based on polling through Sunday night, Reagan would win by about 10 percentage points.[11]

There was one big difference between the campaign pollsters. Caddell had Carter and Reagan virtually even all week long—until Sunday night, when he contends support for Carter dropped precipitously, and all of Reagan's 10-point gain (representing ten million votes!) occurred. Wirthlin contends that Reagan was ahead by five points or so right after the Tuesday debate and gaining about a point a day until the election.[12]

If Caddell was right, then CBS/*New York Times* and Gallup were also right at the time of their final polls. Mitofsky's only mistake, he believes to this day, was failing to poll on Sunday night. If Wirthlin is

right, then ABC and NBC, neither of which were ever especially de-
fensive about the outcome, were reasonably close to the mark. Whatever the reason, the credibility of polling had its closest call in more
than thirty years.

The main lessons everybody drew were twofold:

1. The horse race matters. Nothing else a pollster does matters
   nearly as much. Every four years you get one chance to establish the credibility of everything you do for the next four.
   You'd better be reasonably close to the mark.
2. At all costs you cannot stint on the resources thrown into the
   final survey or conclude it any sooner than you must to air the
   results.

RIGHT TRACK, WRONG TRACK

For network polling, the consequences of 1980 were immense. In the
final weeks of future campaigns, nightly tracking polls were adopted
as an insurance policy against election night surprises. The costs were
large, and so was the risk of being surprised anyway. The driving force
behind this escalation was ABC and the head of its then third-rank-
ing news division, Roone Arledge. In the early 1980s, Arledge saw
competitive election coverage as a means of overtaking the television
news leader, CBS—just as his counterparts at CBS in the 1960s did
in overtaking the then-reigning NBC.

Until 1984, nobody had ever thought of doing tracking polls before
a New Hampshire primary—partly because of the expense and partly
because of the notorious changeability of primary electorates. In 1984,
the week before the primary, Walter Mondale had defeated Gary Hart
by three to one in the Iowa caucuses. Hart's finishing second in a
crowded field, however, surprised a lot of people and gave his New
Hampshire campaign a considerable lift. A CBS News/New York Times
national poll done just before the New Hampshire primary placed Mondale 35 points ahead of Hart. This was the largest margin I could find in
any contested presidential primary ever, and was so reported on CBS the
night before the primary. That same night, based on a tracking poll,
ABC news reported Mondale and Hart dead even in New Hampshire.

The next day, in one of the all-time upsets of presidential politics, Hart defeated Mondale by 37 percent to 28 percent. ABC was the only news organization which had suggested before the fact that this race was even close. Instead of getting credit for that, however, the network got mostly sneers for having predicted a mere tie.

Thus burned, ABC four years later flinched at tracking primaries. Burned even worse by having had no clue in 1984 that Mondale was in any trouble in New Hampshire, CBS and Gallup in 1988 did not flinch. CBS tracked New Hampshire voters right through Primary Eve and correctly reported George Bush ahead as voters were heading for the polls. Gallup, which stopped polling on Sunday (some people never learn), gave the lead to Bob Dole. For the CBS News Election Unit, as for Bush, it was a timely win.

ABC's main innovation in 1988 was far more spectacular. On October 12, the eve of the second debate between Bush and Dukakis, *World News Tonight* presented a fifty-state "Super Poll" for which 12,000 Americans were interviewed over a two-week period. It was one of the largest samples ever polled in a single telephone survey. The statistical margin of error on such a sample is less than 1 percent.

The national findings in the poll were not particularly bad news for Michael Dukakis. It had him trailing Bush by five percentage points—less than in the most recent CBS or NBC polls and half the margin by which Dukakis would ultimately lose on Election Day.

ABC, however, had not spent a hundred thousand dollars or so and turned over most of its evening news broadcast merely to report a modest prospective edge for Bush in the popular vote for President. The national sample was also broken down state by state for the purpose of projecting winners ("If the election were held today . . .") in each one. The individual state samples were all relatively small, and the error margins were accordingly huge. Samples of barely 150 (with error margins of plus or minus eight percentage points) in states like Connecticut and Colorado were nevertheless used to assign their electoral votes to Bush or Dukakis.

Some of the state projections from ABC's Super Poll made no political sense at all. New York, for example, normally a Democratic state in presidential elections, was found to be more Republican than Florida—which is normally Republican!

Adding up what it found in its fifty state samples, ABC declared Bush in the lead with 400 electoral votes, Dukakis with just 89. "A landslide in the making," declared Peter Jennings as he summed up a *World News Tonight* broadcast more than half of which had been devoted to the "Super Poll."

At the *Washington Post*, ABC's polling partner, seasoned reporters Paul Taylor, David Broder and Tom Edsall smelled more than one rat as they looked over the state-by-state findings and the huge electoral-vote margin for Bush when the same poll showed a mere 51/46 margin in the national popular vote. The *Post* accordingly backed off from any landslide talk and, based on state polling data from other sources, reassigned a fair number of the electoral votes allocated by their co-owned Super Poll.[13]

ABC's political director, Hal Bruno, shared the *Post* reporters' queasiness about the hyping of his company's poll ("a flagrant abuse of polling," Broder later called it), but in that network's table of organization, the Washington-based Bruno and the New York-based polling unit are separate fiefdoms that only rarely interact. Not until a storm erupted over ABC's premature and ill-founded projection of a "landslide" did Bruno get called on—and then only to defend it! Bruno's appearance that night on the network's late evening broadcast, *Nightline*, he recalled as "the worst experience of my entire professional career."[14]

WALL-TO-WALL POLLING IN 1992

By 1992, CNN had joined the traditional broadcast networks in election-year polling—as often as twice a month during the primaries, weekly through August and September and then tracking daily from some point in October through Election Day. Anyone who missed the findings of any of these network polls could get them the following morning in the *New York Times* (CBS), the *Washington Post* (ABC), the *Wall Street Journal* (NBC) and *Time*, *Newsweek* or *USA*

Today—depending on who was sharing the bills with CNN in any particular week.

An even simpler source, used by virtually everyone engaged in serious campaign coverage, or in any of the campaigns themselves, was the daily newsletter, "Hotline," distributed on-line to its subscribers every weekday at noon. Around Labor Day, moreover, "Hotline" added a tracking poll of its own, providing still another stream of horse-race numbers throughout the fall.

In June of 1992, this unprecedented glut of national polling produced its first round of utter confusion. Within a week of each other, CBS, ABC, CNN and *Newsweek* reported four separate polls of a hypothetical three-way race. CBS had George Bush leading Bill Clinton and Ross Perot, in that order. ABC had Perot leading the other two by a narrow margin. CNN had Perot leading them by a lot. *Newsweek*, in a poll done for it by Gallup, had Perot leading Bush by a hair and Clinton by a mile.

Which, if any, of these thoroughly professional scientific polls was right? Since the election wasn't held in June, no one will ever know. CBS News's polling director, Kathleen Frankovic, who produced the odd-man-out poll showing Perot third, took a stab at answering the question on the Op-Ed page of the *Times*. It came down, in her view, to the different order in which the respective polling organizations asked their questions:

> Before asking respondents their choice for President, for example, CBS News/*New York Times* asks respondents to give an opinion of each candidate or say they don't know enough about him. Perot at this point was the least known of the candidates. Those who said they didn't know enough about him to have an opinion may have been inhibited from picking him—even though they might otherwise have done so.
>
> CNN/*Time* regularly reports the least support for President Bush. A likely reason: before asking about preference, the survey asks: "How well do you think things are going in the country these days?" This may deter voters who say things are not going well from backing the man in office.[15]

There are cases to be made for each of the different procedures adopted by the respective polling organizations. On occasion, however, they can yield sharply different outcomes—and raise a fair number of eyebrows.

That of course is about as much as could be said in June of 1992, when the only yardstick that the network pollsters had to measure against was one another. As they approached Election Day, however, and the voters' verdict on their work, there was no way to shrug off differences between their tracking numbers on the horse race.

By then the differences in question strategy cited by CBS's Kathy Frankovic had lost much of their effect. Most voters knew as much as they would ever know about the candidates. Bragging rights for the next four years would go to the network that did the best job of contacting its designated sample and weighting its respondents for likely turnout—and that then lucked out when the lords of chance made their final distribution of sampling error.

In 1992, when Clinton defeated Bush by a little under 6 percent of the popular vote, bows among the pollsters were widely shared. ABC's final poll had put the Clinton lead at seven points; NBC and CBS had it at eight. Four years earlier, the final network polls had been a point or two high on the Bush margin over Dukakis. It doesn't get much better than that. The six major national polls in both years were on average within three points of the actual spreads.

———

By the start of 1996, the ranks of the nationally reported U.S. surveys had grown to nine. As many as six different scorings of the presidential horse race might be read on the same day in "Hotline," and the rest within another day or so. And then the cycle would start all over again.

As in the past, given sampling error and some other imperfections to which even scientific polls are subject, these simultaneously conducted polls from time to time produced readings that, to a layman who didn't know any better, would suggest that something was badly wrong with at least one of them. From the time in March, however, when Bob Dole secured the Republican nomination for President, there was one thing on which the nine were never out of step: Clinton was always well ahead in all of them.

Among the more skeptical readers of polls, in that or any other year, was the putative Republican nominee. Within his own party, Bob Dole had always been a dangerous man to poll for. In his 1988 run he fired the party's senior practitioner, Richard Wirthlin, for giving bad advice on New Hampshire, publicly denouncing him as "Dr. Worthless." Early in 1996 Dole just as peremptorily fired another leading Republican firm, claiming it misled him on crucial Delaware.

In late spring of 1996 the Dole pollster of the moment (another was in the wings) was a relatively junior figure in the Republican polling hierarchy, Tony Fabrizio. Since Fabrizio's ascension, Dole's daily numbers in "Hotline" had been a nightmare. During the early weeks of June, Fabrizio (along with the rest of the world) had seen a Clinton lead of thirteen points in *U.S. News* and a 16-point lead registered by CNN. And that, for Dole, was the good news. A CBS/*Times* poll during the same period had the Clinton lead at 19 points, and ABC/*Washington Post* put it at 20.

Most campaigns, confronted with one poll showing them behind by 16 points and another by 19, would not embrace the marginally lower number in order to dispute the higher one, but Tony Fabrizio on Bob Dole's behalf did exactly that. In an extraordinary memo to CBS's Kathy Frankovic and Jeff Alderman, ABC's polling director, Fabrizio cited the discrepancies among the polls and demanded an explanation "in writing" of the CBS and ABC survey methodologies. When Frankovic obliged, the Dole pollster challenged CBS's weighting of its raw survey findings to census figures on age, sex and race of the voting population—a fairly standard practice in survey research. He also offered some kindly professional guidance on weighting for party preference (frowned on by most public pollsters) and screening for likely voters (done by almost no one in June).

There were some, to be sure, in the Dole campaign working on other strategies for winning the election besides getting the network polls to change their methodologies. First their candidate, to show how serious he was about wanting to be President, resigned from his beloved Senate. That had little effect on even the polls the campaign professed to like. Then Dole proposed his 15-percent across-the-board tax cut, and the polls showed that most voters were more concerned about the deficit. Finally, Jack Kemp joined the ticket, and four nights of relatively warm and friendly television in San Diego did bring the Clinton margins down. Soon after, however, the Democrats had their own four nights of (mostly) empathy in Chicago. All nine public polls (as well as, it was later learned, Fabrizio's own polls) once again showed Clinton leads in the landslide range.

By early October it was the CNN poll, whose findings the Dole campaign had blessed in June, which it now found wanting. On a Saturday in early October, CNN had first delighted the Doles by reporting a mere nine-point spread in its tracking poll. "The race nationwide is tightening," declared CNN White House correspondent Wolf Blitzer. "This single-digit lead is half what it was earlier this month."

The following Tuesday, however, that same network's Judy Woodruff announced that the Clinton–Dole gap had ballooned to 25 points! Nothing anyone could think of had happened between Saturday and Tuesday that might have moved seven or eight million voters from Dole to Clinton. "It's a disservice, and it's wrong," Dole's campaign manager, Scott Reed, exploded in the New York Times. "This is a low-double-digit race and everybody knows that and it's irresponsible for [CNN] to run those."[16]

In the campaign's final month, it was the New York Times and its polling partner, CBS, that posted the most steadily enormous margins for the President. In over six different October surveys Clinton averaged 19 percentage points better than Dole among voters who said their minds were made up. If you also included those who said they "leaned" towards one candidate or another, the Clinton lead averaged 21 points. This is an area in which CBS and the Times have traditionally gone separate ways—CBS including the leaners and hence, in 1996, raising by far the highest expectations in the land for Clinton.

In the last week of the campaign, something finally happened that figured to turn a few real votes Dole's way. Since mid-October the only real news in the campaign had been one story after another about huge donations to the Democratic Party by overnight guests in the White House, along with $400,000 from an Indonesian immigrant who tended gardens for a living and large amounts from Buddhist monks sworn to a life of poverty and from a native American tribal council which had raised it by looting the welfare fund.

On the Tuesday before the election, all of these stories came together as a prime-time scandal when the Democratic National Committee announced it would not file the legally required report on where it got its last-minute money. With no ceiling now to the speculation on what Clinton and his party might be hiding, all the network evening broadcasts led with it—and kept on leading.

By week's end, as pollsters were wrapping up their final surveys, the polls on which they would stake their credibility for the next four years, Clinton's margin was obviously falling. On Election Day, voters who had made up their minds only in that final week would mainly tell exit pollers they voted for Dole.

———

CBS, with a final margin for Clinton of 18 points, was the first to stop polling; there was obviously no way this race could turn around, or even get close by Election Day (as indeed turned out to be the case). In making this decision, with which I readily concurred, CBS's Kathy Frankovic faced the same dilemma that Warren Mitofsky had faced in 1980. The staff that did the poll was also deeply involved in the rapidly approaching election night broadcast—which badly needed their full attention. In 1980, moreover, when CBS/*Times* stopped polling it had no clue about the winner. This time there was no doubt.

Still, when Clinton's margin on Election Day came in at 8.6 percent, CBS found itself a bit lonely out at 18. Most of the established polls (NBC/*Wall Street Journal*, ABC/*Washington Post*, CNN-Gallup, Louis Harris, Pew Center) put the final margin between 11 and 14 points. To the exasperation of the polling establishment, it was a relative newcomer, John Zogby, with a breezy disregard for many of scientific polling's most cherished practices, whose final poll hit the 1996 popular vote for President on the nose.

The bulk of the country's senior pollsters seemed reasonably serene about their quadrennial reality check. Andrew Kohut, whose Pew Center for the People and the Press had posted a final Clinton margin of 13 points, said, "I would give the polls a grade of B. Most were within the margin of sampling error."[17] At the close of what was surely public polling's most strenuous campaign year, some of Kohut's peers caught up on housekeeping chores—like shipping off their year's survey data to be archived at the University of Connecticut's Roper Center for Public Opinion Research.

Two weeks after the election, an article in the *Wall Street Journal* ("The Pollsters' Waterloo") put an end to serenity. The writer was Everett Ladd, head of that same Roper Center where the deeply "flawed" polls skewered in the article are stored for posterity. "Election polling," wrote Ladd, "had a terrible year in 1996." Nor was 1996 just an aberration. The polls "in recent years," wrote Ladd, have made a practice of "overestimating the Democrats' share of the vote." The "Waterloo" in Ladd's title was an explicit reference to the British pollsters whose surveys, just before the Tory victory in 1993, had shown Labour winning.[18]

Ladd was just warming up. He reached a half century back and compared the polls of 1996 to George Gallup's legendary forecast of a Dewey win in 1948. Though the current pack all got the winner right, in Ladd's view apparently a minor matter, the polls of '96 were *worse* than those of '48. By comparison, wrote Ladd, "the 1948 record seems closer to triumph than disaster."

Ladd's sweeping brushstrokes made an easy target for rebuttal. The comparison to 1948 just didn't work. Gallup's final poll that year was 10 points off on the Truman/Dewey margin. Two other public polls were as far off—or farther. Of the nine polls of 1996 attacked collectively by Ladd, however, eight were off the mark by no more than 5 points. As for the pollsters' tendency "in recent years," to favor the Republicans, in 1996 and 1992 the major polls did err overall on the Democratic side. In 1988, the tilt was Republican. In 1984 there was little tilt either way. It was hard to discern much of a pattern here.[19]

The pollsters under attack by Ladd might have contented themselves with pointing out the defective scholarship on which that attack was based. That was not good enough, however, for the National Council of Public Polls, which represents the interests of media pollsters. "After extensive analysis" of Ladd's case, the Council concluded not merely that its members' polls the past year were no disgrace, but that, said Sheldon Gawiser, the Council president, "1996 should be remembered as one of the better years for the nation's polls." All but one of the nine polls, it insisted, were within their scientifically determined sampling error—as accurate, so to speak, as you can ask any poll to be.[20]

Some of those polls, however, that had been found to be within sampling error had been as much as 5 points off on the Clinton/Dole margin. The sampling error specified for nearly all the final polls had been 3 percent. A naïve viewer or reader might wonder how those polls could have been within the advertised margin of error.

Easy, say the mandarins of scientific polling. That error, they point out, is not on the *margin* between the candidates but on the *percentages* for each. In other words, the *difference* between the two could be off by *six* points and the poll is still a sweetheart. In many of the polls done during most of the year, when no Election Day reckoning is nigh, the sampling error is often *four* percentage points, and the potential error on the spread between the candidates is therefore *eight* points.[21]

Where, however, in most of the poll reports viewed on television or read in newspapers in 1996 (or any other year) did one ever see it hinted to viewers or readers that a six-point, let alone an eight-point lead for a candidate might actually represent no lead at all? CNN's *Inside Politics*, for example, a daily half-hour of political reporting that was as religiously watched by journalists and politicians as "Hotline" was read, reported fresh tracking numbers several times a week. In those reports, a five-point shift in the Clinton–Dole gap, sometimes less, was apt to prompt a serious inquiry into what campaign developments might account for it.

———

One did not see much of this on CBS or in the *New York Times*. Michael Kagay, the *Times* polling director, Frankovic at CBS and Mitofsky before her have always nagged their correspondents against making something of changes in poll numbers that may not mean a lot. The 1996 campaign cycle, however, during which CBS and the *Times* celebrated the twentieth anniversary of their polling union, was not one over which to take bows. When the National Council on Public Polls asserted that "eight out of nine" major polls "had errors within the 3 percent margin of error expected for samples of their size," the ninth was CBS/*Times*. How did the pioneer among the country's major media polling partnerships achieve this distinction?

Some part of it was surely due to the early end to interviewing at a time when Dole was probably gaining on the President. Beyond that, the CBS model for weighting poll respondents by likelihood of voting, which had served it well in the past, in 1996 did nothing to improve the poll's showing on the margin. Other polls, which screened out far more unlikely voters than did CBS/*Times*, got closer to the actual results by doing so.

Other practices that had helped CBS/*Times* to achieve precision in the past seemed to work the other way in 1996. Persistent callbacks to reach targeted respondents, random dialing to reach unlisted numbers, repeated efforts to persuade targeted respondents who at first refuse to participate: all of these are recognized as "best practices" in all the codes of survey research standards. All of them, ironically, contributed to the bloated estimate for Clinton over Dole in the final CBS News/*New York Times* survey.

"ROTTEN . . . WORTHLESS . . . USELESS . . . MISLEADING . . . REALLY TERRIBLE"

Those are some of the comments of polling scholars and media professionals (at AP, NBC and the University of Chicago respectively) when the topic of call-in surveys on television comes up. All of the surveys thus far under discussion, including those which gave the country President Dewey, and in a few cases projected a landslide (as opposed to a cakewalk) for President Clinton, were done under the standards prevailing in their time for "scientific" polling. Not all the polling, however, done for television news bears the proud imprimatur of Science. There is also, for the less finicky, "nonscientific" polling.

A classic case is what ABC's Ted Koppel reported on the *Nightline* broadcast of October 28, 1980. ABC viewers of the Carter–Reagan debate earlier that evening had been given two 900 numbers (charge to the caller: 50 cents). They could call one of the numbers to declare Carter the winner, the other to pick Reagan. By the time *Nightline* aired, over 700,000 calls had been logged, and two out of three, reported Koppel, had picked Reagan.[22] For television broadcasters, getting 700,000 audience responses on anything (especially with the viewer paying a surcharge for the call and no prizes offered) was an astonishing achievement. Evidence like this of audience involvement is something network salesmen can gush over to their customers. At *Nightline*, a broadcast then still in its infancy, Ted Koppel promptly made it an audience-building staple—something that gave his audience, if they chose to exercise it, a voice in how the country's affairs ought to be conducted.

From the high priesthood of the polling profession, at the National Council of Public Polls and the American Association for Public Opinion Research (AAPOR) came a steady stream of complaints about the unscientific nature of these self-confessed "nonscientific" polls. If they're not scientific, said the priesthood, you can't call them polls. ABC finally began doing real, scientific polls prior to the call-ins on *Nightline* and then comparing the results. In one memorable case, Koppel had the country's then Ambassador to the United Nations, Jeane Kirkpatrick, stand by while 186,000 viewers made their 50-cent calls and voted 2 to 1 in favor of leaving that organization. Asked for her reaction, Kirkpatrick inquired first what ABC's standard poll of the country showed. It turned out that a poll not limited to viewers willing to pay fifty cents was nearly 3 to 1 in favor of *remaining* in the United Nations.[23]

Nowhere among ABC's polling rivals had disdain for the *Nightline* call-ins been more profound than at CBS. In the fall of 1991, Kathy Frankovic was the incoming president of the American Association for Public Opinion Research (AAPOR)—the guardian agency of professional standards in polling. Called to the office of CBS News President Eric Ober, she found Andrew Lack, then a CBS executive producer who would later become President of NBC News.

Lack had recently toured the facilities in Omaha, Nebraska, of a company called Call-Interactive, which had the capacity to process millions of phone calls in a very few minutes. Suppose, Lack suggested, that after President Bush's State of the Union message in late January we ask our viewers to respond to a series of questions related to the speech? To keep the broadcast from getting too boring (it would follow an hour of George Bush and a half hour of Senate Democratic leader George Mitchell's response) Lack proposed to illustrate the issues being put to the viewers with emotion-grabbing vignettes of real people affected by what government does or doesn't do about those issues.

Frankovic was relieved to hear Ober himself say it was no go unless CBS did a real national poll at the same time that Call-Interactive was tallying its millions of viewer responses. The call-in tallies would be identified as that and nothing more—a demonstration of the network's ability to get millions of viewers to express their opinions. To find out what the American people really felt about these issues, Dan Rather, Connie Chung and Charles Kuralt would report on Frankovic's scientific poll of 1,500 or so randomly chosen Americans.

In its original mission, the broadcast was an unqualified success. Some 25 million attempts were made by viewers trying to respond to the call-in invitation. Some 315 thousand responses were actually tallied and the totals reported on the broadcast. As an inquiry into what was on viewers' minds, however, the CBS broadcast had its flaws. Dan Rather, no fan of any kind of polls, correctly did little to suggest that the tally of viewer calls reflected anything more than the opinions of the particular callers. At the same time, he ascribed little more significance to the more authentic survey: "We have to keep in mind that polls of all kinds have a short shelf life."

Chung and Kuralt, moreover, were thoroughly confused by the two separate streams of data. Still more confusion was sown by Lack's heart-tugging vignettes of women and children victimized by the government policies viewers were being asked to judge: "This was the year my children did not go to the circus or the museum or the movies or McDonald's, the year their only new clothes came from charity, the year my toddler cried from hunger . . ."

Altogether, it was one of the most incoherent broadcasts ever aired. Most of the criticism it justifiably received was directed at the viewer call-in feature. While the on-air disclaimers were designed to ease professional qualms, they raised common-sense questions as to why the call-ins were being done at all. Equally persuasive to CBS News management was a seven-figure telephone bill. For subsequent State of the Union broadcasts Frankovic would continue to conduct quickie polls, but the viewer call-ins would, happily, be history.

Well, not quite. In the spring of 1994, the producer of a brand-new magazine show, *America Tonight*, was allowed to conduct an "interactive" something-or-other in which viewers, after watching one segment of the broadcast, would be asked a question about it. After replaying the famous tape of Nicole Simpson's phone call to 911 ("My ex-husband, or husband, just broke into my house, and he's ranting and raving"), co-host Deborah Norville said, "Get a pen and paper ready and be prepared to make a phone call. . . . In a moment we'll ask you to make a life-or-death decision." After some more file footage, co-host Dana King popped the question: "If O. J. Simpson is convicted, do you think the prosecutors should pursue the death penalty?" At that point in time Simpson had not even been indicted. A graphic then showed:

Yes Death Penalty   1-900-220-2200
No   1-900-220-2211

Callers to the 2200 number carried the day—51 percent to 49 percent for execution. As for *America Tonight*, its fate was already sealed by the low ratings which had inspired the viewer call-in feature in the first place. Call-ins (and reviews) the next day about the "life-or-death" question were no kinder to the broadcast than callers during airtime were to O. J.

THE ONE-HORSE RACE

Even when there is no general election, primary, or even a straw vote in the offing, through the magic of polling, sitting presidents can be made to run a race against themselves. "Do you approve or disapprove of the way ————— is handling his job as President?" When George Gallup first asked this in the 1940s, the President in question was Franklin Roosevelt. Properly adjusted for turnover in the White House, it is now the oldest, most continuously asked question in the history of polling.

Gallup used to run his race between Approve and Disapprove once a month. Today, with at least ten newsmedia polls in the field an average of twice a month, there is a fresh approval (or disapproval) rating for the President every few days. Strung together, these approval ratings become an *ad hoc* tracking poll of presidential success or failure—even when there is no real-world contest in sight. "We have," writes CBS's Frankovic, "as one researcher predicted nearly 50 years ago, a 'continuous ballot box.' Our measures have replaced reality. To much of America, our research is the reality."[24]

The ways of reporting this research-based horse race between a president's shifting bands of supporters and detractors are many and varied. His current "negatives" (Disapprove the way President X is doing his job) can be weighed against his "positives" (Approve the way President X is doing his job). His current positives can be compared to what they were a month ago, or six months ago, or what the analyst predicts they will be if the President is sustained on a veto or can pull off an invasion bloodlessly. One poll just before the Gulf War asked how many dead Americans respondents could accept as the price of ejecting Saddam Hussein from Kuwait!

A popular pastime on the widely distributed Washington talk show, *The McLaughlin Group*, is predicting what the President's job approval score will be at some future date. The polls in effect become events on the political calendar reflecting no reality but themselves. On CNN's "Inside Politics," for example, during the 1996 campaign, presidential candidate Lamar Alexander tries to make his case to the network's Judy Woodruff: "It would take a real Republican, from outside Washington, with the kind of background I have and the kind of message I have, to beat Bill Clinton." Replies Woodruff, in a brisk, case-closed manner, "Why is this message not pushing your numbers up?"

Or consider this Sunday morning exchange from ABC's *This Week*:

Cokie Roberts: Bob Dole has fallen in the polls . . . so has every Republican contender. . . . What's going on here?
George Will: It's a marvel of political physics that this body can fall, and no other body rises.
Roberts: Well, the "Don't know" goes up.
Will: That's right.
Roberts: "Don't know" keeps going up.
Will: Dole's 52 percent was an artificial lead. . . . No one has been that far ahead and failed to get the nomination.

Roberts: Do we start hearing, "Newt, Newt?"
Will: No, no, no. . . . [Newt Gingrich's] negatives are 42 percent—and rising.[25]

Speaker Newt, himself, was no slouch at this kind of poll-induced gibberish. Here's Gingrich on still another weekend talk show, CNN's *Evans and Novak Report:* "Any time this President hides for a while, his poll ratings go up. . . . He'll be back in the mid-forties in another few months."

Crystal-gazing into the future popularity of presidents is not a calling for the fainthearted. George Bush's approval ratings, for example, soon after his bombs started falling on Iraq were found (by me) to rival Winston Churchill's when Hitler's bombs were falling on Britain. A year later, by the time Bush threw up on the Finance Minister of Japan, with the U.S. economy in the tank, this phenomenal spike of approval had vanished.

HOW MUCH IS ENOUGH?

When a Speaker of the House places bets on the approval rating of the President several months hence; when the President himself, according to his own pollster, "can recite minute details about survey data, including his own popularity ratings, off the top of his head," and even camps out in a tent on a mountainside when a poll suggests swing voters will be pleased,[26] when the weekend sages of television stop predicting elections and run instead a weekly futures market in approval ratings, when an impeached President stakes his survival on those ratings, something important in the politics of the country may be getting out of hand. No one has put this issue better than E. J. Dionne, the columnist and author of *Why Americans Hate Politics.* For a collection of essays on polling, Dionne wrote:

> The problem . . . was that the normal curiosity about who would win an election had become an obsession of such proportions that it threatened to overwhelm any meaningful discussion of the problems that actually engaged voters. Voters were no longer the subjects of

politics, democratic citizens deciding the fate of their country. They were objects to be counted, studied and counted again. The proliferation of polls had allowed almost any newspaper or television station in the nation to measure the feelings of any population. Measurement, not democratic debate, was becoming the stuff of American politics.[27]

Mischievous or simply silly, however, as some examples given here of polling overkill may be, it is hard to see polls as a barrier to "meaningful discussion" or "democratic debate" in television or the press. The poll reports on television are seldom long enough to crowd much out. When they are, it is usually because the report goes beyond the horse-race findings and deals with problems that, serious thinkers like Dionne would argue, actually engage voters.

The reason anything new about the likely outcome of a presidential race tends to dominate the day's report is not that broadcasters are obsessed with it. It is that this is the first thing most people want to know about the race when they pick up the paper or turn on the evening news. This is especially true for the 80 percent or so of American voters who have generally made up their minds by the close of the party conventions. For these four out of five voters, the campaign has indeed become a horse race, in which they have already picked (and may even have laid money on) their horse.

This is not to discount entirely the genuine distraction that polling, as Dionne suggests, poses to "democratic debate." Nowhere has that been more apparent than in the reporting of the formal debates between presidential candidates—a political institution that owes its existence to television.

5

THE LESS THAN GREAT DEBATES

O N JULY 24, 1858, ABRAHAM LINCOLN, THE REPUBLICAN CHOICE for a U.S. Senate seat if the party won control of the Illinois legislature, wrote to incumbent Senator Stephen Douglas, who would get a third term if Democrats remained in control. "Will it be agreeable to you," asked Lincoln, "to make an arrangement to di-vide time between you and me and address the same audiences during the present canvass?"[1]

The ensuing seven "joint discussions" (as Lincoln called them) would become the gold standard for political debate for generations of Americans to come, but the format of 1858 called for a hardy breed of both candidates and audiences. The Lincoln–Douglas joint discussions ran three hours without a break. One candidate led off with a 60-minute speech. The other then spoke for 90 minutes. The candidate who spoke first then got 30 minutes more. For the entire series of debates, there was just one topic: extending slavery to the territories. There was no moderator, no reporters asking questions—though in their speeches candidates might pose "interrogatories" for the other to answer in theirs. No polls were taken afterwards, but Lincoln won handily in the history books. Republicans did gain a few seats in the legislature, which might be one measure, but not enough to turn over Douglas's Senate seat to Lincoln.

Two years later, when the same men ran for President, there were no joint discussions. A sizable segment of the voters of Illinois might have made their way to a debate site in 1858, but there was no way in 1860 that a meaningful portion of the national electorate could see or hear a debate for President.

In the twentieth century, long before there was television, network radio offered the means for presidential candidates to match wits and argue their positions before a large share of the country's voters. Throughout virtually the entire heyday of radio, however, none did. In 1940 Wendell Willkie, the Republican nominee, issued just such a challenge to President Franklin Roosevelt. A very secure FDR predictably ignored it.[2]

Eight years later, in radio's final year as the country's primary mass news medium, Thomas E. Dewey debated Harold Stassen, his chief rival for the Republican nomination, on the eve of the Oregon primary. Though only one hour long, not three, the Oregon debate bore some resemblance to the Lincoln–Douglas model. Each man delivered a 20-minute speech and an 8-minute rebuttal. There was no moderator, no reporters asking questions, and just one topic: "Should the Communist Party be outlawed?"[3]

This debate was carried by the NBC, ABC and Mutual radio networks. News accounts of the time report an audience of 40 to 80 million, a suspiciously broad range. In any event, it was certainly large. Listeners were not polled as viewers are today, but, in the curious role of champion for the civil rights of communists, Dewey apparently trounced Stassen in radio's first and final presidential debate. That, at least, was a widely held view in news reports of the time, and it is a plausible conclusion from a reading (a half-century later) of the transcript. Dewey won the primary four days later (though not by much) and after that the nomination. There is no record of any thought being given to a general-election debate with President Harry Truman.

In 1952, the year television news went national, CBS and NBC both put the notion of general-election debates on the table. On a CBS News broadcast, Blair Moody, a Senator close to Adlai Stevenson, the Democratic nominee, had urged the network to "put on General Eisenhower and Governor Stevenson and let them debate. . . . Let's see who really has the stuff . . . it would be a wonderful way to use television."[4]

Frank Stanton, President of CBS, could not have agreed more. There was just one problem, he wrote Moody: Section 315 ("equal time") of the rules of the Federal Communications Commission. Under 315, wrote Stanton, to hold a presidential debate CBS would either have to invite the nominees of "the Socialist, Socialist Labor, Progressive, Vegetarian, Prohibitionist Parties" or produce separate programs "in which each of these other candidates would be given the same amount of time and the same facilities." Neither of those options, needless to say, had any appeal to the network. Stanton nevertheless did sound out the Eisenhower camp, as did Robert Sarnoff, the president of NBC. Eisenhower, comfortably on track for election, shrugged off the network overtures. Four years later, when those overtures were repeated, there was little interest in either camp.[5]

When Stanton and Sarnoff renewed their quest for candidate debates in 1960, there was a good deal more urgency to it. Both their networks had been caught in a stunning breach of faith with the public over quiz shows flaunting apparently astounding powers of recall by their contestants. The broadcasts were eventually exposed as being scripted and rehearsed from beginning to end, and there were calls on both Capitol Hill and Wall Street for heads to roll. There were, accordingly, sound business reasons at this particular time for the network managements to display some citizenship.

One suggestion had come from Stevenson. "Let's get television under control before it runs away with the election process," he wrote in a *New York Herald-Tribune* article. Noting that $7 million (about $40 million in 1999 dollars) was spent on television in the 1956 presidential race, Stevenson called on the networks to provide "free time as a public service, either voluntarily or be required by law to do so."[6]

By the spring of 1960, the Senate Commerce Committee had drawn up a bill which, as Stanton huffily put it, would "commandeer from each broadcaster two hours of prime time for eight weeks" for use as "their campaign managers and television advisers see fit." Why not instead, said Stanton, lift the equal-time barrier and clear the way for the first debates between major party nominees for president?[7]

As it happened, that year's nominees in both parties were more than willing. In Richard Nixon's first campaign for office, he had upset an incumbent Democratic congressman after what *Newsweek* described as "five Lincoln–Douglas debates."[8] He never tired of bragging about both that triumph and the "kitchen debate" in which he and Soviet leader Nikita Khrushchev disputed, among other things, the comparative pungency of horse and pig manure.[9] Jack Kennedy, in turn, had done very well debating Henry Cabot Lodge in the campaign that won him Lodge's Senate seat, as well as Hubert Humphrey and Lyndon Johnson on his way to the Democratic presidential nomination.

Nixon credited the Khrushchev debate with having made him "probably the best known political figure after Eisenhower." Most of Nixon's advisers (including Eisenhower) urged him not to jeopardize that advantage by debating Kennedy. But, going into the Republican convention, Nixon's own polling showed Kennedy ten points ahead. Nixon feared that if he ducked, "Kennedy and the media would turn my refusal into a central campaign issue."[10]

On the night of Nixon's nomination, NBC's Robert Sarnoff wired both candidates, offering eight hours of prime time on his network, four of them devoted to "The Great Debates," contingent on Congress lifting the equal-time requirement for 1960. Letters accepting the NBC proposal were returned the same day—to the great "consternation of CBS over the NBC coup," recalls then CBS News president Sig Mickelson. Frank Stanton's similar proposal had been delivered to both candidates months earlier. A renewed CBS invitation was accepted the day after NBC's.[11]

Three days later, Congress enacted a one-year suspension of 315, and Eisenhower, who thought Nixon was making a mistake, nevertheless signed it. It was now up to the three television/radio networks and the Mutual Radio Network to design a political event for which there was no obvious model or precedent.

THE BURNING ISSUE: FORMAT

After years of associating their proposed debates with Lincoln, Douglas and greatness, the networks came down on the side of "real debates"—long opening statements by the candidates, on one issue, followed by rebuttals. No moderator, no questioners. The "Oregon" model.[12]

On this proposed format Kennedy and Nixon totally agreed— they both hated it. There was no single issue in 1960, like extending slavery in 1858, which could be stated as a resolution and debated for an hour or more. There were, instead, a good many issues, foreign and domestic, which the liberal Democratic nominee and the moderate Republican were prepared to argue if asked about them in a series of broadcasts.[13]

The "traditional" debate format, moreover, had just as little appeal for both candidates. Neither man wanted direct confrontation with the other. "Combative" was not the image either wanted to project. Kennedy and Nixon representatives both insisted on a moderator and a panel of reporters asking questions in the manner of a news conference, and the networks reluctantly agreed. The moderator would be chosen by the host network (the three television networks rotated as host). Two of the reporters posing questions would represent the other networks. Two more were chosen by lot from the print reporters traveling with the candidates. The debates were held in television studios—with no one but the candidates and production people present.[14]

The first Kennedy–Nixon debate remains to this day, for those who saw it as it happened, the most memorable political event of the television era. Its ground-breaking character was obvious and had been heavily promoted by the networks. Viewership broke all records for the medium. (The seventh game of the 1959 World Series held the previous record.) Both men understood that they were engaged in an historic exercise and stated their positions with great care, seriousness and clarity. The debate was limited to domestic issues, although the context of a competition with the Soviet Union for domestic achievements was referred to repeatedly by both candidates.

In this and later debates, there was a remarkable amount of agreement on domestic goals. Both men backed medical aid for the aged: Nixon through government subsidies for health insurance, Kennedy through the social security payroll tax (today's Medicare). Kennedy's federal aid to schools would have boosted teachers' salaries, Nixon's would go for construction. Both were expansive in supporting racial equality under the law and equal opportunity for jobs. Nearly all of the cheap shots, all the digressions from serious discussion of issues came from the reporters and, by the standards of later years, there was relatively little of that.

In the competition for high-mindedness, Nixon (who later said he had been warned by his running mate, Henry Cabot Lodge, to work on his "assassin image") perhaps overdid it. An out-of-character wimpishness can be detected in such Nixon pleas as

> Let us understand throughout this campaign that [Kennedy's] motives and mine are sincere . . . I know Senator Kennedy feels as deeply about these problems as I do. . . . I do believe he would agree that I am just as sincere . . . my proposals for health care are just as sincerely held as his. . . . This is what I deeply believe. I'm sure he believes just as deeply. . . . I suggest, however, that in the interest of fairness he could give me the benefit of also believing . . .

All of this emerges from a reading of the transcripts. There was much more, of course, than the spoken words to the experience enjoyed by 60 million viewers, give or take a few, on September 26, 1960. In the opening eight minutes they encountered one of the most formidable political advocates and one of the most engaging television personalities of that or any other time. Kennedy's still somewhat shrill style of speaking on the stump was replaced by an earnest, cool delivery in the studio. It set the tone for a whole generation of political contestants in the television era.

The contrasting shock of Nixon's appearance is now legendary. The man who went into the debate concerned about a killer image looked pale, sweaty, frail, wary. A self-applied over the counter make-up accentuated the stubble grown since early morning; for an evening debate, Nixon had, incredibly, not even taken a fresh shave. An obsessively tight travel schedule had left him ten pounds underweight, his shirt collar hanging loosely around his neck. "After the program," Nixon recalled, "callers, including my own mother, wanted to know if anything was wrong, because I did not look well."[15]

There was more. Nixon's light-grey suit blended totally (on black-

and-white television) into the light-blue background (Kennedy wore dark blue) at a CBS studio in Chicago. Whereas Kennedy had been schooled carefully on how to address the camera and on composing his own features when the other man spoke, Nixon seemed unaware that his reactions to Kennedy might appear on camera, and some of these also became the stuff of legend. CBS, for neither the first nor the last time, would find itself fending off sabotage charges from outraged Republicans, even though the culpability of Nixon's own staff in this instance is well recorded.[16]

There were three more debates, and Nixon did not suffer the same embarrassments twice. A diet enriched with four milkshakes a day had filled out his shirt collar by the second debate. He wore a dark suit, got a fresh shave and professional make-up, and practiced looking straight ahead with a calm, relaxed expression. Nixon was still Nixon and Kennedy was still Kennedy, but their debate was on issues which were classical between their parties. Those issues were exceptionally well stated on both sides in all four debates (the later ones had viewership comparable to the celebrated first), and it is hard to find evidence that Kennedy's superior skills on television moved a lot of votes. (Years later among scholars there is still an ongoing dispute, with very thin data to go on, as to whether radio listeners to the first debate gave Nixon higher marks than did television viewers).[17] A Gallup poll conducted just before the first debate had Kennedy ahead by 1 percent in the popular vote. After four debates (and, of course, some other things as well) Kennedy won the election by one-sixth of 1 percent.

There is ample polling evidence that most viewers, asked to score the debates, picked Kennedy. After the first debate in particular, this was true even for viewers supporting Nixon—most of whom continued to do so. As Sam Lubell, a public-opinion analyst whose insights came from extensive personal interviewing around the country rather than statistical sampling, observed: "The evidence is overwhelming that Kennedy emerged the 'winner' in the sight of the vast majority of viewers. Why then, if the impact of the TV debates was anywhere near as dramatic as is claimed, did not Kennedy win by a landslide?"[18]

The answer surely lies to some degree in the content of the debates, as opposed to the eye appeal of the debaters—which has since engaged so much of the attention of journalist and academic seers alike. For four hours altogether, the great majority of voters had seen Nixon embrace the record and the policies of a Republican administration that had twice been elected by landslides. Kennedy, in turn, had embraced the largely liberal positions of one faction of his own party. On the issues, which were thoroughly explored in the debates, it figured to be an uphill struggle for even so personally attractive a Democrat. All of this, moreover, stood apart from the by no means clear effect of Kennedy's Catholic faith—a topic studiously avoided by both candidates, though not by the reporters, throughout the debates.

By the most obvious measures, the joint appearances were a great success. Close to a hundred million people watched at least some of them. The average was perhaps two thirds of that. About a thousand times as many people, in other words, watched Kennedy–Nixon, many several times, as watched Lincoln–Douglas once.[19]

Not all the reviews, however, were enthusiastic. The debates had spawned a whole new field of political-science research—and with it a horde of certified experts. One pioneer of this academic specialty estimates that more studies have been done of this one political phenomenon than of any other in history. Among the complaints:

- They were not "real" debates.
- They were more about candidate "image" than issues.
- From a television professional, CBS's Don Hewitt, who produced the first of the 1960 debates, came a complaint about his own role. As a news producer, said Hewitt, he would rather that someone else create the event and that CBS cover it as it covers a convention, an inauguration or any other happening. Hewitt would get his wish.

THE SIXTEEN-YEAR GAP

Whatever the shortcomings of the 1960 debates, the public, by lopsided margins when polled, wanted more of them. As President, Jack Kennedy said he would debate again when he ran for re-election—much against the wishes of his more pragmatic brother and campaign manager, Robert. The President himself sponsored legislation to suspend the equal-time rule again for 1964. It passed both houses in slightly different form just before Kennedy died.

Had Kennedy, as an incumbent President in 1964, put his office on the line in another round of debates, presidential debates might have become a permanent part of the election process then and there. When the bill suspending 315 came out of conference, however, in the spring of 1964, Lyndon Johnson was heading for a likely landslide over Barry Goldwater and saw no reason to complicate matters. In a heavily Democratic Senate, the bill was quietly tabled.

Four years later it was the Democratic nominee, Hubert Humphrey, who was trailing in the polls as the debating season approached. A Democratic Congress was prepared to suspend equal time, and Lyndon Johnson would have signed the bill. Nixon, however, burned once and sitting on what seemed like a solid lead, wanted no part of it. The issue was complicated by the fact that the minor-party candidates that year included George Wallace, who was trailing Humphrey by only ten percentage points in the national polls and who was running ahead of both Nixon and Humphrey in six or seven states. In early October, the House voted to suspend the equal-time requirement to allow a debate among all three of them. That settled it for Nixon, who saw Wallace as taking votes primarily from him. Senate Republicans threatened a filibuster, the bill never came to a vote, and once again there were no debates.

In 1970, Congress passed a federal campaign act which, among other things, would have permanently suspended the equal-time requirement for presidential debates. Nixon, now the incumbent and fearing another independent Wallace run, promptly vetoed it. A year later essentially the same bill, but without the provision for debates, was presented to Nixon, and this time he signed it. A third presidential campaign since the Great Debates of 1960 passed without an encore.

THE "SPOT NEWS" RUSE

When the next presidential cycle came around, in 1976, Stanton and Sarnoff had retired, and a new generation of network chiefs resumed the quadrennial trek to Capitol Hill in quest of an equal-time waiver.

Once again, their mission was going nowhere—when an FCC staffer fresh out of law school had a bright idea. Existing communications law allowed broadcasters to cover "spot news" events involving candidates without regard to the equal-time requirement. Suppose a sponsor unconnected with the networks were to stage a debate between the major party nominees for President—why couldn't broadcasters simply cover that as news?[20]

Colorado's Aspen Institute got wind of this reasoning, filed a formal petition with the FCC and got the desired ruling. That meant there had to be a sponsor other than the networks. The League of Women Voters was an obvious candidate. It had been holding "forums" for candidates at the local as well as the national levels for generations, and had in fact held a number of them in early 1976 among the Democratic primary candidates. The League was ready to provide the networks with their spot news event. All that was needed for presidential debates to resume, after a sixteen-year hiatus, were the debaters.[21]

Jimmy Carter, a national figure for scarcely six months, was a given. Gerald Ford, the sitting president, hardly needed the exposure. But Ford had never run in a national race before, even for Vice President; his pardon of the man who'd put him in line for the job was very unpopular; he'd won his party's nomination by the narrowest margin of any incumbent in history; and he was trailing Carter by more than twenty points in the polls when his own convention opened. This incumbent's situation did not warrant cockiness. In Ford's closing speech at the convention, he accordingly accepted both the Republican nomination and the League's invitation to debate.

It was now the League's turn to deal with all the conditions that have vexed these televised events before and since. The "real" debate format (also known as "true" or "pure" or, most reverently of all, "Lincoln–Douglas") was quickly dismissed, as it had been in 1960. For the three 90-minute meetings between the presidential nominees and (a League innovation) one between the nominees for vice president, it made more sense to have the candidates contrast their positions on a variety of issues instead of just one.[22]

With the passage of years, moreover, the 1960 model had acquired a legitimacy of its own. For most Americans in the mid-1970s, what "presidential debates" brought to mind was Kennedy, Nixon and reporters asking questions—not whatever Abe Lincoln and a fellow named Douglas had done in a Senate race more than a century before.

The new arrangement might appear to have been just what producer Don Hewitt had called for after the 1960 debates, but giving network producers free rein to cover the debates as news was not quite what the League or the candidates had in mind. The networks were not allowed to have their own cameras on site; there was to be just one pool feed for everyone. Though the debates were held in theaters or auditoriums before live audiences (an absolute necessity in order to maintain the fiction that this was a true, freestanding event), the networks were not allowed to show those audiences at all.[23]

Unlike 1960, when they had provided the moderators and most of the questioners, the networks had no say this time in the choice of either. The candidates each submitted lists of journalists they liked to the League, which also had a list of its own. Before each debate, the League would then submit a proposed panel to the candidates before announcing it. This was widely interpreted as giving the candidates a veto over reporters who might ask tough questions, as of course (though the League vigorously denied this) it did. Richard Salant, who was then president of CBS News, denounced the arrangement as one calling for designated pushovers. Thus, when several CBS News correspondents turned up on the lists, Salant made sure they turned their invitations down.[24] There were plenty of news organizations (notably ABC) and plenty of reporters who were not so fussy. Over the years, a fair number of print journalists would advance their careers by appearing in the televised debates. Often their questioning was more adversarial than any of the exchanges between the candidates for President.

At the final Carter–Ford debate, for example, the Washington columnist Joseph Kraft cited some recent economic indices and then addressed the President of the United States: "Isn't that a really rotten record?" For a number of minutes in the second debate, Max Frankel, the Sunday editor (and later executive editor) of the *New York Times*, engaged Gerald Ford in a man-to-man duel that eclipsed any exchange in the entire campaign between the duly nominated candidates. A year earlier the Ford administration had signed the Helsinki Accords, which among other things gave formal recognition to the borders imposed on Eastern Europe at Yalta. Henry Kissinger, who negotiated the Accords, argued that they merely acknowledged a fact that no one had any power to change. But, as he ruefully recalled, "President Ford was accused of an historic sellout."[25]

Ford in fact had had a bellyful of that charge all year long from Ronald Reagan and the Republican Right—for whose revolt against his nomination Helsinki had been a major provocation. So the President should certainly have been prepared when Frankel, in a detailed inventory of recent communist gains around the globe, observed, "We've virtually signed, in Helsinki, an agreement that the Russians have dominance in Eastern Europe." Incredibly, the best response the President could come up with was that the Pope, no softy on Communists, had signed the same treaty. Then Ford (Kissinger not being there to kick him under the table) categorically denied Frankel's premise. "There is no Soviet domination of Eastern Europe," he said, "and there never will be under a Ford administration."

At this point Pauline Frederick, the moderator, turned to Ford's formal adversary, Carter, for comment. But the *New York Times* was not about to yield the floor. "I'm sorry," Frankel interrupted, "could I just follow [up], did I understand you to say, Sir, that the Russians are not using Eastern Europe as their own sphere of influence in occupying most of the countries there?" Deftly, at first, Ford cited Rumania and Yugoslavia, more or less accurately, as Eastern European countries that were not entirely under the Soviet heel. Kissinger, wherever he was, may momentarily have smiled. And then the President stepped into an open pit: "I don't believe," said Ford, "that the Poles consider themselves dominated by the Soviet Union."

No sooner was this debate over than television's wise men picked up where Frankel of the *Times* had left off on Ford's denial of Soviet clout in Eastern Europe. "It'll come as a great surprise, certainly, to the people of Poland," sniffed CBS State Department correspondent Marvin Kalb. "Terribly extreme . . . astounded me," thundered Eric Sevareid. "Major blunder . . . he kissed off the Polish vote," said Bob Schieffer—going, as always, straight to the point.

On the other networks, Ford took similar hits. By the time CBS got to poll the public on who won the debate, the vote was 3 to 1 for Carter. Ford's own pollster at the time, Fred Steeper, insists that a survey taken immediately after the debate found only a modest plurality for Carter.[26]

It did not take the campaigns long to figure out there was now a new playing field. It was no longer enough to win the 90 minutes of confrontation with the other candidate. There was also the 30 minutes afterwards in which the networks decreed a winner. From the very first debate, prominent figures in both campaigns cruised the newsrooms set up at the debate sites by the League of Women Voters, in search of network cameras to offer honest-to-God candid appraisals of how well their own man had performed and how miserably the other fellow had done. Spin doctoring was born.

Five different polling organizations scored the 1976 debates. Viewers gave Carter the edge in three out of four debates. Yet Carter's lead over Ford, more than ten percentage points in most polls before the first debate, had slipped to barely two points on Election Day. "There will never be a way of knowing," Jimmy Carter wrote later, "which of us gained more."[27]

By 1980, as a candidate for re-election, Carter was not inclined to gamble. During the primaries he refused to debate Edward Kennedy, and until close to the end he rejected a debate with Ronald Reagan on terms the sponsoring League of Women Voters would accept. In most prior years, incumbent Presidents or any other nominees who thought debating their opponents unwise did not have to take any heat over refusing to do so. Their allies in Congress would just see to it that suspension of the equal-time rule never got to a vote. Under the "spot news" loophole, however, and the League's *de facto* role as debate sponsor, it was hard for a candidate to avoid debates without appearing to be running from a fight.

For Carter, the concern was not so much about losing a debate to Ronald Reagan. Hamilton Jordan, who ran the Carter campaign, recalled later, "I never . . . questioned how the President would fare against an elderly former actor."[28] The Democrats' concern, instead, was John Anderson, an independent candidate who had run earlier in the Republican primaries and was now getting significant support in public-opinion surveys. Carter's pollster, Pat Caddell, saw Anderson as a magnet for moderates of both parties who were otherwise more likely to vote for Carter. He wanted no part of a debate that elevated Anderson to parity.

After a very troubled meeting of its board, the League set a threshold of 15-percent support in five designated polls for a candidate's inclusion in the debate. In early September, four days before the invitations were to go out, Anderson cleared that bar with just over 17 percent; he was in the first debate. At the appointed time CBS and NBC were there, but the President was not. With an empty chair for the absentee incumbent, Reagan and Anderson spent much of their hour congratulating one another on being there and chiding Carter for his failure to join them in informing the voters.

Reagan and Anderson both got a temporary boost from their debate, but by mid-October Anderson's support had slipped well below the League's 15-percent threshold in all the polls. The League, accordingly, at last gave Carter his one-on-one debate with Reagan. Reagan turned out to be anything but the aging airhead that Jordan and some others in the Carter camp had envisioned. He engaged the President with confidence on social security, arms control and the budget and left it to Carter to commit the blunder everyone would talk about—invoking his daughter Amy as an adviser on nuclear policy. Reagan's trademarked grin and his crushing rhetorical question to the viewers, "Are you better off than you were four years ago?" completed the rout—a rout second only to Kennedy–Nixon I (and perhaps Clinton–Dole II) among all the presidential debates.

Surveys over the next few days all ruled Reagan the winner. On Election Day, Reagan won by over 8 million votes. If the overall effect on the horse race of the multiple debates in 1960 and 1976 had been difficult to gauge, the single general-election debate of 1980 may have been one, finally, which made a provable difference.

————

By the next presidential cycle, the Federal Communications Commission had reversed twenty years of prior rulings and allowed broadcasters to produce their own debates—instead of waiting for someone else to do it so they could cover the event as breaking news.[29] The networks' first chance to do this came during the Democratic primaries of 1984.

Initially there were eight arguably serious Democrats in the race. None of us in broadcasting wanted to impose a free-for-all among so large a mob on our viewers. By mid-March, however, the Democrats' original field of eight was down to Walter Mondale, Gary Hart and Jesse Jackson.

At that point, CBS proposed a debate moderated by a single reporter—Dan Rather in his first presidential season as son and heir to Walter Cronkite, the network's now-retired national treasure. Instead of standing at podiums, the candidates would sit around a table with the anchorman. When the candidates agreed, CBS left little to chance. Joan Richman, the producer, called in the correspondents traveling with each candidate so that Rather could bone up for his role as moderator with surrogates for the men they covered daily. As a broadcast, the real debate got rave reviews. The single moderator and the round table encouraged spirited exchanges between the candidates, that were seldom seen in standup encounters with panels of reporters. NBC liked the format so much that two months later, just before the California primary, Tom Brokaw (another anchor debutant) presided over a similar debate around a similar table.

If the informality of the round table and the single-moderator format, the heated back-and-forth between the candidates, was a hit with the media critics, the Reagan White House wanted no part of it. When the Mondale side (whose man had thoroughly trounced Gary Hart across the CBS table) not surprisingly proposed it, Frank Donatelli, one of the Reagan negotiators, recalls, "We rejected it out of hand. And, when you're twenty points ahead in the polls, as we were, you generally get what you want."[30] The reporter panels and the podiums stayed. So did the League of Women Voters; James Baker, the White House chief of staff, had dealt with them before with no problems.

In 1976 and 1980, the League had quietly allowed the candidates to veto press panelists while insisting publicly that the League had the final say. In 1984, however, this subterfuge collapsed. On the day before the first debate, there still was no panel. Dorothy Ridings, the League president, held a news conference and declared that, out of more than a hundred names submitted to the Reagan and Mondale camps, all but three had been struck by one or both of them.

One of those not struck was Diane Sawyer, then at CBS—the network whose reporters in the past had refused to submit to candidate approval. Since the press panel would otherwise have been reduced to two, Sawyer and CBS agreed to her participation. Ed Joyce, who was that year's president of CBS News, said, however, that CBS News correspondents would decline to appear in any future debates in which the candidates decided who could ask them questions.

In 1984, unlike the prior years when televised debates were held, the race was never close. Ronald Reagan had taken office from a Democratic administration on whose watch the economy had stumbled into a recession and runaway inflation at the same time. Now Reagan was running for re-election during an expanding economy with stable prices, while his opponent, Walter Mondale, was the designated heir of the administration Reagan had displaced. Going into the first debate, Reagan already seemed headed for a landslide.

As it turned out, this would not be one of Reagan's better nights. Had Mondale closed the gap? asked Dan Rather on CBS as soon as the debate ended. After a little hedging and deference to a CBS poll then in progress, Reporter Bruce Morton allowed, "Mr. Reagan, it seemed to me, floundered more than usual, seemed nervous, uncomfortable, ill at ease with the information he was trying to get across."

Still, the CBS News survey being done as Morton spoke would show something short of a sweeping win for the Democrat. Although 43 percent of the viewers polled thought Mondale had done the better job, 34 percent picked Reagan. ABC, which asked viewers who had won, found them about evenly divided. None of the commentary on the night of the debate, or the next day, said anything about Reagan's age. Nor had there been any shift among the viewers polled on who they planned to vote for.

A day later, however, the *Wall Street Journal* lit a fuse. "Is Oldest U.S. President Showing His Age?" was the headline of the lead story. Right near the top it offered this diagnosis from a Eugene Jennings of Michigan State University: "As a psychologist I am very concerned about [Reagan's] inability to think on his feet, the disjointedness of his sentences and his use of the security blanket of redundancy. I'd be concerned to put him in a corporate presidency. I'd be all the more concerned to put him in the U.S. presidency."[31]

That evening, inevitably, the psychologist from Michigan State was the lead story on all three networks. Verifying examples of presidential disjointedness and redundancy were supplied from tape of the debate. An old soundbite of Mike Deaver joking about Reagan nodding at cabinet meetings made the ABC piece—as did a shot of Reagan apparently drifting off during an audience with the Pope. Peter Jennings, always disposed towards a global view of things, introduced the piece by noting the high current incidence of doddering leaders among other great powers (e.g., the USSR's Chernenko, China's Deng Xiaoping). Still another evening news piece featured Nancy Reagan whispering in the President's ear when he appeared stumped by a reporter's question. Reagan's eyes promptly lit up as he repeated exactly the words his wife was seen mouthing.

A day later, CBS and ABC had new surveys. Mondale had now won the debate by 4 to 1, and Reagan's margin in the horse race had been cut in half. It was no breakthrough, however. A week later, in the final debate, Reagan pulled himself together, turned the tables on Mondale with a celebrated quip ("I will not, for political purposes, exploit my opponent's youth and inexperience") and went on to win his previously ordained 49-state landslide.

ONE COMMISSION LEADS TO ANOTHER

With the 1984 election, broadcast debates appeared to have achieved a permanent, recognized place in the country's presidential campaigns. After Reagan's example, and the final removal of all legal obstacles, it would be hard for any future nominee to avoid debating without handing his opponent a powerful issue.

The League of Women Voters, too, appeared to have staked out a claim to permanence—as the presumptive sponsor. It had produced the only general-election debates for three elections in a row. Nevertheless, the League's *de facto* franchise was about to end, in a wholly unforeseen way.

Throughout the 1980s there was growing dissatisfaction over the country's presidential politics. Complaints about the duration and cost of campaigns, the disproportionate role of Iowa and New Hampshire, the charade of party conventions, early network calls, negative advertising, special-interest money, declining voter turnout and so on came to a head in 1985 with the creation of a bipartisan Commission on National Elections to fix all of these things.

Robert Strauss, the most celebrated party official of his time, was the Democratic cochairman of this commission. His cochairman: Melvin Laird, a one-time Republican power in Congress and Richard Nixon's Secretary of Defense. Among some forty others on the panel were the chairmen of the Republican and Democratic National Committees, the Senate Finance Committee and the FCC, and the presidents of the AFL-CIO, the *Washington Post*, NBC News and ABC News, and a recent former president of CBS News.

The Commission held the usual hearings and funded the usual studies and after a year of deliberation issued an 80-page report which concluded, overall, that presidential politics in America wasn't so badly done after all and that not a lot needed fixing. In search, perhaps, of at least one specific remedy for something, the commission floated one on presidential debates. "They should not," the commission argued, "be left to the vagaries and uncertainty of each presidential election."[32] To fix that, the commission called on "the two political parties to assume direct responsibility for sponsoring the joint appearances." In a joint statement issued with the commission's report, Paul Kirk, the Democratic Party chairman, and Frank Fahrenkopf, the Republican chairman, eagerly embraced the proposal: "Future joint appearances," they declared, "should be jointly sponsored and conducted by the Republican and Democratic National Committees."[33]

Lawyers and fund-raisers for the two parties soon pointed out a problem, from the IRS point of view, with direct sponsorship by the national committees: donations to the national committees are not tax-deductible. There soon came into being, accordingly, a tax-exempt "Section 501C3" corporation called the Commission on Presidential Debates—donations to which would indeed be tax-deductible. Otherwise, however, the party chairmen of the day remained in full control. Kirk and Fahrenkopf were designated co-chairmen of a ten-person board of directors, and each of them named four of the others.

In the fall of 1987, citing their mandate from the Straus-Laird Commission on National Elections, Kirk and Fahrenkopf announced that the national committees would together sponsor the 1988 debates, and that the Commission on Presidential Debates was their vehicle for doing so. They also announced four dates, in September and October of the following year, on which the debates would be held. Most important of all, Fahrenkopf told a news conference that all the major candidates in both parties had agreed, if nominated, to appear in its debates.[34]

Michael Dukakis, whose ties with the Democratic chairman were close, would never make a liar out of Kirk. George Bush, on the other hand, had no such qualms about Fahrenkopf. When the time came to discuss the specifics of debates, James Baker, who ran the Bush campaign, insisted that no promises had ever been made. It was up to the Bush and Dukakis campaigns, said Baker, to decide the numbers, dates, places and terms of the debates and to pick the sponsors. The Bush campaign, moreover, had enough trouble with women voters. It would not stiff the League. The League would have to be offered at least one of the debates. When the two campaigns, however, handed both the commission and the League detailed terms for their debates on a take-it-or-leave-it basis, the League threw up its hands and walked away. The commission, now being tendered the entire franchise, happily signed on the dotted line.

Once again the network news divisions were bystanders as third and fourth parties fashioned arguably the most important broadcasts they would air in the presidential campaign. The commission, sensitive to this, suggested that the network anchors be invited as panelists. This was a tough sell to the Bush campaign in the case of CBS's Rather, but that invitation did go out.

Dan Rather had for many years been a persistent, some might say compulsive critic on and off the air of the press-panel format, and he emphasized that in declining to appear. An equally good reason would have been his explosive encounter with Bush earlier that year on the CBS *Evening News*. There was no way Rather could be just an-other member of the reporters' panel popping questions on the deficit and Gorbachev. The CBS newsman, who would have found himself under as much scrutiny as the candidates, prudently took a pass.

The reporters' panel, indeed the whole process of conducting the debates, would find itself scrutinized in the aftermath of 1988 as they never had been in the past. Never was there so much probing by the reporter panels of the psyches of the candidates, most especially the psyche of Dukakis. "Governor," asserted Peter Jennings early in the first debate, "one theme that keeps coming up about the way you gov-ern is passionless, technocratic—the smartest clerk in the world. Can you give us an example of where you have had that passion and lead-ership that sometimes a president needs?"

In the final debate, PBS's Margaret Warner took over from Jen-nings the search for that something missing in Dukakis: "Governor, you won the first debate on intellect, and yet you lost it on heart. . . . The American people . . . didn't seem to like you very much." Grop-ing her way at last to a question, did Dukakis, she concluded, think it important to be likable? Yes and no, said Dukakis, and then Bush, for two and a half truly dreary minutes.

Most famously of all, to be sure, CNN's Bernard Shaw wanted to know whether, If Kitty Dukakis were raped and murdered, the gover-nor would support a death penalty for the killer. Dukakis had spent much of the first debate arguing his lifelong view that capital punish-ment should not be applied to anyone. So it's not clear what answer Dukakis might have given other than the one he did give—"No, I don't"—when asked, in effect, whether he thought there ought to be a special statute covering crimes against his spouse.

Dukakis's failure to transform himself on the spot into a diehard avenger has nonetheless been widely judged to have imposed a death sentence on his campaign. Just how many viewers, however, were ac-tually stunned at the time, how many votes irretrievably lost, when Dukakis flunked the ultimate passion test of the reporters is not alto-gether clear. At no point in the 30-minute post-debate broadcasts on CBS or NBC did Dan Rather, Tom Brokaw or anybody else even mention what Jack Germond and Jules Witcover called Shaw's "killer question"—or Dukakis's fatally "legalistic" reply.[35]

Connie Chung, then at NBC, had been watching the debate in Spokane, Washington with about a hundred "undecided voters," who had been given hand-held meters on which to register their reactions. "Connie," asked Brokaw, "did that little green marker ever go off the chart at any point?" Only once, said Chung, on an abortion question. In a CBS News survey of over five hundred viewers the night of the debate, not one mentioned Dukakis on his wife's rape-murder when asked what in the debate had stuck in their minds.

The shortcomings, however, of the 1988 debates had stuck in many minds. Questioning by the reporter panels had often turned the broadcasts into something more like *Rivera Live* or *Crossfire* than Kennedy–Nixon, let alone Lincoln–Douglas. Both compaigns had seeded the audience rows with cheering (and groaning) claques who responded to cues and generally ignored the pleas of the moderators to please shut up. What had now come to be called "the traditional format" was ripe for change.[36] For the television networks, moreover, the late spur-of-the-moment selection of dates and time of night for the debates laid waste to their prime-time schedules—at a time of year when those networks were already wrestling with the unpredictabilities of baseball play-offs, the Olympics and night football. In a lot of quarters the feeling grew that next time would have to be different.

ENTER (AND EXIT) THE NETWORKS

After the election, when Kirk and Fahrenkopf left their posts as party chiefs, they took the chairmanship of the Commission on Presidential Debates with them. Early in 1991, they called on the heads of the television networks, hoping to sign *them* on to the commission's plans for a 1992 round of presidential debates. The day they were meeting in New York with Laurence Tisch, the chairman of CBS, I was having lunch in Washington with Tom Hannon, the political director of CNN. Kirk and Fahrenkopf had already met with Hannon's boss. The television networks themselves, I remarked, had produced the 1960 debates, and thirty years later these remained the best. There were no longer any legal obstacles to doing it again. Why not?

After meeting with our counterparts at ABC and NBC, with the blessings of our respective managements, we drew up a plan for three presidential and one vice-presidential debates. We checked out our respective Sports divisions on the Olympic (NBC), football (ABC) and baseball (CBS) schedules in September and October. We picked out four dates, including each of the four most watched weekday nights. The debates would be held in network studios in New York, Atlanta, Chicago and Los Angeles respectively. Each network would produce one. Lots would be drawn to decide who did which. Harking back to the CBS/NBC formats in the 1984 primaries, each debate would have a single moderator, supplied by the host network, and no panel of reporters. There would be no one in the studio but the candidates, the moderator and technicians.[37]

When the lots were drawn, to the horror of CBS News president Eric Ober, ABC, whose *World News Tonight* had for the first time in a quarter of a century displaced *CBS Evening News* as the top-rated news broadcast, drew the first presidential debate. Still worse, CBS drew the vice presidential—always the least watched—debate. "You mean," exploded Ober, "that these debates start out with Peter Jennings getting ninety minutes of prime time on CBS?" Exactly, he was told. And a deal, sadly, was a deal!

In September of 1991, Ober and the presidents of ABC News, CBS News, NBC News and CNN sent a joint letter outlining our proposal to President Bush and to all the major candidates for the Democratic nomination.[38] The Commission at this point was busily seeking bids for its own debates. To enter the auction required a hall with at least 17,000 square feet of floor space, a weeklong commitment of 2,500 hotel rooms, 200 of them suites, and a half million dollars towards the commission's operating budget.[39]

Faced with a network proposal that would eliminate the need for all that cash, floor space, hotel rooms and perhaps the commission itself, Kirk and Fahrenkopf struck back on the Op-Ed page of the *Washington Post*. The networks, they argued, were "parts of giant corporate conglomerates with many legislative and regulatory interests." How could they "act impartially and objectively as debate sponsors?" Besides, argued the commission in other venues, the networks are supposed to report the news, not make it.[40]

After exchanging a few more shots, the two sides—"them" and

"us"—tried for some months to agree on a role for each. We got close. The co-chairmen were receptive in principle to our dates, to a single moderator for part of each debate and, initially, to our anchors as moderators. We agreed to a panel for the other part; the commission could pick it. They agreed to studio debates without a live audience—so long as there was a hall next to the studio where their contributors could watch television screens and feel involved.

After six months of negotiations, however, Roone Arledge, the president of ABC News, abruptly backed off. Arledge, we were told, had been reminded (by Kirk and/or Fahrenkopf, we all assumed) that he had been part of that mid-1980s study group from which the debates commission claimed its origin. Just as suddenly, on the very same day, the commission told us it would go its own way. ABC having bailed out, the rest of us had no choice but to drop the matter.

THE COMMISSION, CLINTON AND ROSS PEROT

By dividing and then facing down the networks, after already disposing of the League of Women Voters, the commission could now claim to be the only game in town. All it needed was some respect. Four years before, the Bush campaign had negotiated all the terms of the debates with the Dukakis campaign and then allowed the commission to secure the space, hire the help and pay the bills.

This time, in June, the commission announced a plan of its own, adopting a fair bit of the network proposal: four debates, single moderator, 90 minutes. This was all that the challenger of an incumbent president could hope for, and the single-moderator format was one in which Clinton figured to shine.

Acting as though the "Commission on Presidential Debates" was indeed the official body that its name suggested, Clinton's campaign chairman Mickey Kantor heartily embraced every bit of its proposal and then attacked the Bush campaign when it failed to do the same. Soon Clinton volunteers in feathered outfits were showing up at Bush rallies waving "Chicken George" signs for the television cameras. Two thirds of the voters in a CBS News/*New York Times* poll said Bush was ducking the debates.

Finally, at the end of September, Bush proposed four debates in October. Clinton having milked the "debate about debates" for every possible advantage, the two camps quickly came to terms. The first debate would have what, ironically, was now referred to as the "traditional" format—a press panel! The vice presidential debate would have a single moderator. The final presidential debate would be half "traditional," half single-moderator.

The most original format was proposed by the Clinton campaign for the second presidential debate. Held in Richmond, it included about a hundred local residents, chosen by the Gallup polling firm and made up of roughly equal numbers of Republicans, Democrats and Independents. These people asked all the questions and won a good deal of praise for the serious, unpretentious (i.e., unreporter-like) quality of their questioning. Not surprisingly, given the format's source, Clinton would be thoroughly at home in it, Bush a 90-minute study in unease.

The most important decision by the major party campaigns was to invite, for the very first time, a third participant. To cope with cynics who assume that the commission's five Republicans and five Democrats have a common bias towards the major party nominees, Kirk and Fahrenkopf had recruited a panel of political scientists headed by Harvard scholar Richard Neustadt to advise the commission on whether any candidate beside the Republican and Democrat had a "realistic" chance of being elected. Applying an abstruse formula, the advisers concluded that Ross Perot's prospects were good enough to get him into one debate. As it happened, the major party nominees both wanted Perot (and his running mate) in all the debates. As always, the candidates won.[41]

With only a few days' notice, shoehorning four 90-minute debates (plus another 30 minutes of post-debate analysis) into four closely-bunched nights of prime-time television full of major sports events took genuine effort by all parties. The campaigns themselves did not want to offend baseball and football fans by interfering with these once-a-year events. To avoid that, several debates were held at 7:00 P.M., Eastern time, which meant they were seen during afternoon hours (with fewer viewers normally at home) in the West. The first debate, on a Sunday, was to follow a baseball playoff game on CBS that started at 4:00 P.M. in the East. As luck would have it, the game went into six extra innings and ended at about the same time as the debate. CBS, of course, stuck with the game.

Perot's participation turned out to be the distinguishing feature of this round of debates. Asked in the first for the most important issue of the campaign, Bush predictably responded, "Well, I think one thing that distinguishes is experience." "They've got a point," countered Perot. "I don't have any experience in running up a ten-trillion-dollar debt."

When Bush attacked Clinton's protests while at Oxford against the U.S. role in Vietnam, Perot cannily preempted Clinton's reply, saying: "It's important to measure when and where things occurred. When you're a senior official in the federal government spending billions of dollars of taxpayers' money and you're a mature individual and you make a mistake, then that was on our ticket. If you make it as a young man, time passes."

Perot's stock fell steeply in the next debate, when his running mate, Admiral James Stockdale, proved sadly but hilariously out of touch ("Who am I? Why am I here?"). Nevertheless, after the final debate (a Clinton–Perot tie in the surveys), Perot's support had climbed to 20 percent—about where it would be on Election Day. This would be the largest demonstrable gain for any candidate in the history of presidential debates. In the competition that really mattered, however, the debates made little difference. Clinton had gone into the debates well ahead of Bush. Bush needed to prove himself convincingly to be the better man, and that did not happen.

Meanwhile, the network news divisions, whose companies conveyed the debates to their megamillion viewers, had once again been passive onlookers until the debates were over. In their fifth go at crafting epilogues to some less than great debates, the networks were badly in need of new ideas. Though the hordes of spin doctors at the debate sites were generally recognized as a farce, the networks nevertheless, if only to ridicule them, kept putting them on the air.

Declaring winners and losers had once been a proud prerogative of the network analysts. Their verdicts—it was widely believed, and there was survey data to back it up—would replace in viewers' minds what their own eyes and ears had told them by the time the pollsters got to them the next day. But now the viewers were being polled the moment the debates were over, or even a little sooner, before anybody else could tell them what to think. Some time after 11:00 P.M. the viewer surveys would be aired, and it was a rare network sage who would go out on a limb when the verdict of the polls was imminent.

In 1992, the CBS News survey unit finally ended all reason for anyone's ever going out on a limb. It secured the verdict of the viewers themselves just a few minutes after the debate was over. For two days in advance, we polled a random sample of over 1,400 voters and asked them to watch the second debate. Those who did so were told to call a tabulation center directly afterwards and, using their Touch–Tone pads, answer "Who won, or did the best job?" and how their own opinions of each candidate had changed, if they had. Fifteen minutes after the debate ended, 85 percent of the original 1,400 had punched in their answers. Bob Schieffer could then report, without going out on any limb, that Bill Clinton had won by roughly two to one over both the President and Ross Perot and that two out of five viewers had improved opinions of Clinton and Perot, but only one in five thought better of Bush.

With an unusual grant from the Markle Foundation, CNN pushed the technological frontier of post-debate analysis still further by recruiting a national sample of five hundred voters to watch the debates and to register their reactions from moment to moment by pressing keys on their Touch–Tone phones. A computer transformed the collective output of those five hundred keypads into a rising and falling graph line recorded (though not broadcast) simultaneously with the exchanges that evoked it. The more dramatic and revealing of these moments were then broadcast during CNN's post-debate commentary.[42]

For years the campaign pollsters of both parties, who do this kind of research for strategic purposes, have been trying to sell the networks on superimposing these viewer-response graphics in real time over the debate broadcasts themselves. I myself turned down two such proposals for CBS News. Were any of us to bite, it would naturally become the ultimate horror tale of media license: displaying to debate viewers a purported consensus reaction to what they were viewing at the same time they are presumably forming their own conclusions. By 1996, NBC was also employing this technique for its post-debate broadcasts, but, so far, imposing it in real time on the debate itself remains off limits.

In deference to the academic watchdogs clocking network minutes on issues and the horse race, and because it might also be helpful to our viewers, CBS in the 1980s had begun a different post-debate feature exploring not only who won but, on some of the disputed facts, who was right. David Martin, who covered the State Department and the Pentagon, and Robert Krulwich, our economic correspondent, got this assignment. For example, in the final debate of 1992, when Ross Perot accused the Bush State Department of withholding a disputed cable to the U.S. Ambassador in Iraq, Martin made a phone call and reported, "I talked to the staff director of the Senate Foreign Relations Committee, and he said those instructions were turned over to the committee last year, along with the cables [the Ambassador] sent back." As for Bush's claim that no U.S. technology had been used in Iraq's nuclear-weapons program, Martin identified "at least three instances in which American technology was given export licenses . . . to factories which we know were working on the bomb."

"The record in Arkansas," said Bush in the debate, "I mean look at it, and that's what we're asking America to have. . . . He talks about all the jobs he's created in one or two years. Over the last ten years, since he's been governor, they're 30 percent behind, 30 percent of the national average." "What's the truth?" Rather asked Krulwich after the debate.

The Republicans, said Krulwich, "chose their ten years, Dan, very carefully, because they stopped counting in 1989, just as jobs in Arkansas took off. In fairness, though, Clinton did not create in Arkansas the high-scale, high-tech, high-wage jobs he's been talking about in his campaign. He brought to Arkansas jobs in the timber industry and poultry jobs, not high-wage jobs."

For all the chaotic circumstances surrounding the 1992 debates, they were by almost any measure a success. It had been Bill Clinton's friend and television counselor, Harry Thomason, who suggested scheduling the four debates like a broadcast miniseries. Over an eight-day period in early October, the debates and their aftermath would absolutely dominate prime-time television. Dumping the tired old press-panel format, much of the time, for fresh alternatives surely helped. So did the prickly presence of a maverick not tied to the record in government of either major party. Better than any of the moderators, reporter panelists or even the "real people" assembled by Gallup for the second debate, Ross Perot posed the questions for which Bush and Clinton had no practiced answers, could not respond to with 90-second soundbursts from their speeches on the stump.

In spite of competing sports events and shifting on-air times, the 1992 debates drew an average viewership of 64 million—on a par with the most heavily watched debates of the past and surpassed only by the 80 million viewers of the solo debate of 1980. On Election Day, over a third of the voters cited the debates as a major influence on how they'd voted—more than checked off any other option in the exit polls. Three out of four voters told a *Los Angeles Times-Mirror* survey that debates had helped them make up their minds how to vote—compared to an even split on the same question after the widely scorned debates of 1988.

THE DEBATES OF 1996

Debates had now taken place in five successive presidential cycles. No future incumbent was likely to risk the beating Bush took in 1992 for appearing to flee his rival. That presidential nominees debate had thus become a settled matter. So too, it appeared, was the role of the Commission on Presidential Debates. The League of Women Voters had abandoned the field; the networks were not likely to forge another alliance to contest it, nor did anyone else appear interested.

As candidates, over the years, had narrowed the role of the sponsor, it was no longer much of a prize. When the commission, in the spring of 1996, announced dates, places, formats and so on for another round, Harold Ickes, the White House campaign chief, said yes, of course, he'd be happy to have the commission raise the money and prepare the sites for the debates. But all the other details, down to the position of the lecterns and the camera shots from the television pool, would be decided by Clinton and Dole—when they (which, given their respective bargaining power, meant primarily Clinton) got around to it.[43]

The commission had called for four debates, three presidential, and one vice presidential, just like last time. Dole, trailing badly in the polls, wanted more. No way, countered the White House, even three was more than the famously workaholic President could crowd into his busy schedule. The first of the commission's four proposed debates would simply have to go.

So, too, would Ross Perot—in spite of what was arguably a better case for his inclusion this time than last time. Perot's 19 percent of the popular vote in 1992 had been the best showing by a minor-party candidate in eighty years. Theodore Roosevelt aside, it was the best since the current two-major-party system was forged in 1856. It not only won Perot a place in the record books, it also entitled him to federal funding for the current campaign.

When the U.S. Treasury wrote Perot a check for $30 million (about half what Clinton and Dole got), Perot assumed that, along with his twenty million votes in the last election, it assured him a place in the debates. Federal funding was one of the "objective criteria" in the commission's published guidelines for judging "viability." Perot had been ruled viable without it in 1992. How could he be rejected now? Simple. Perot never met the commission's criteria for full participation in 1992. He was included then because the major-party candidates, for their own tactical purposes, both wanted him in. This time they both wanted him out.

For Dole, it was a no-brainer. Every poll, and common sense, argued that votes for an independent candidate would be drawn more from the challenger than from the incumbent. On the Clinton side, too, nobody really wanted Perot—a loose cannon with a knack for making trouble—around. With Clinton already well ahead, White House strategists felt no need to boost Perot in order to siphon votes from Dole.

Turning now to the debates themselves, Clinton and Dole finally got rid of the reporter panels altogether. Each debate would have a single moderator and, in the final Clinton–Dole meeting (a "town-hall" session), a hundred or so "uncommitted" voters rounded up in the San Diego area by Gallup. George Stephanopoulos, the resident media specialist in Clinton's White House, and the Dole campaign's John Buckley were assigned to work out the details.

The original idea was to have different moderators for each debate. Stephanopoulos opened the bidding by proposing Oprah Winfrey for the town-hall session. Buckley thumbed that one down with a shudder and countered with Ted Koppel, not exactly a Clinton favorite. Stephanopoulos floated Peter Jennings across the table, and that went nowhere. (Buckley and Dole campaign manager Scott Reed had just lectured the ABC anchorman on what they deemed his broadcast's hostile tilt.) Back came CBS's Bob Schieffer and Lesley Stahl. Schieffer was set aside as a maybe, and then Stephanopoulos tossed in the name of Jim Lehrer of PBS's *Newshour*. The famously unthreatening public television anchorman had a rare appeal for two politicians as wary of reporter self-promotion as Clinton and Dole. Buckley, who'd had Lehrer in mind all along, suggested booking him for the whole series. After checking with the candidates, they called Lehrer and made the deal.[44]

Over the thirty-six years since Kennedy/Nixon and especially since the mid-1970s when debates grew to be expected, there were few examples of their having much affected the outcome of a presidential election. This prior history was a regular feature of pre-debate reporting. So too was the magnitude of the odds Dole had to overcome. In the final CBS News/*New York Times* poll before the first debate, seven out of eight voters had already picked their man. No poll (including Dole's own private poll) showed the Republican trailing by less than fifteen percentage points. "Huge" was Dan Rather's description of Clinton's lead going into the debates. To Peter Jennings it was "vast, insurmountable."

Among the obstacles Dole would have to surmount were the deals Clinton had cut (on health care, the minimum wage and welfare) with Trent Lott, Dole's successor as Senate Majority Leader. All of this bipartisanship on Capitol Hill cut deeply into Dole's talking points for the debates. Having declared in his State of the Union address that "The era of big government is over," Clinton could draw further from the other party's prayer book for his opening statement. "We wanted a government that was smaller and less bureaucratic. . . .

We cut the deficit by 60 percent. Now let's balance the budget. . . . We passed welfare reform. Now let's move a million people from welfare to work."

Dole, meanwhile, having spent all summer crafting a 15-percent tax cut as the central issue of his campaign, had by now dropped it entirely. "The tax-cut stuff never caught on," said his campaign manager, Scott Reed—in part because Dole never could make a convincing case for it. In the opening debate, it was left to Clinton to bring it up in what had become a regular feature of *his* stump speech: "It's a 550-billion-dollar tax scheme that will cause a big hole in the deficit, raise interest rates and slow down the economy." Over and over in their debate preparations, Dole's counselors had drilled him on a spirited rejoinder. When Dole's turn came to reply, however, he simply brushed the matter off.[45]

For the Dole strategists there was only one place to go. "We decided on the ethics stuff," says Reed, "because we didn't have anything else." The only trouble with the ethics stuff, you heard over and over on the air, was that, as ABC's John Cochran put it, "Dole must not revive old images of himself as mean or angry." Given these constraints, Dole needed some cue from the moderator before pouncing on Clinton's character. In the first debate, Jim Lehrer took a maddeningly long time to get there. Finally, fifteen minutes before the end, the moderator asked if there were "significant differences in the more personal area." After briefly citing the tax cut that Clinton once promised and never delivered, Dole backed off with, "Well, my blood pressure is lower, and my weight, my cholesterol, but I will not make health an issue in this campaign." There was little laughter. A few minutes later, Lehrer gave Dole another shot at raising a "personal matter." This time Dole faulted Clinton, in his 1992 debates, for having addressed his adversary as "Mr. Bush" instead of "Mr. President."

Having trivialized the ethics issue in the first debate, Dole and his strategists had nowhere else to go in the second. By now, details of illegal foreign gifts to the Clinton campaign, $50,000 cups of coffee at White House breakfasts, $100,000 nights in the Lincoln Bedroom, were pouring out daily. On the network news broadcasts between the first and second Clinton–Dole debates the burning question was whether Dole would or would not, as the reporters put it, "take off the gloves." Just before the second debate, NBC News put its money on a brawl. "Tom," said Tim Russert on Nightly News, "I can report to you, Dole is going to raise the character issue in his opening statement." *Wrong!* Dole's opening statement was an update on the ball game that had just started on the Fox Network. In a Dole list of seven problems which "this election is all about" the President's character did not come up.

The designated citizens asking questions in this "town-hall" event had clearly paid little attention to network news. They kept bullheadedly asking about other things than presidential character: e.g., taxes, military pay (this was San Diego, and several were in the services), foreign trade, family leave and Medicare. Calling Clinton a liar flat out (there were one or two opportunities for that) would surely have been ruled mean-spirited by the post-debate tribunals, so Dole tried to make this point by swearing up and down that his own character was beyond reproach. "When *I'm* President of the United States, I will keep my word." *Fifteen times* Dole declared that his word was always good, always kept, was above all his bond, you could bank on it, and he never, absolutely never broke a promise.

Finally, with the next-to-last question, fans of the character issue got their day. "Do you feel," said a man who identified himself as a minister, "the office of the President has the responsibility to inspire our young people?" "When you have thirty-some in your administration," Dole replied, "being investigated or in jail or whatever, then you've got an ethical problem. When you have nine hundred files gathered up by some guy who was a bouncer in a bar. . . . I know a person that went to jail for looking at one. . . . So the President has a great responsibility, and that's one I understand and would certainly carry out." And so, at last, the character issue was finally on the table, but Dole was at the end of his 90 seconds. Clinton, completely ignoring the attack (and the question), responded to the minister: "This is the most religious, great country in history. . . . One of my proudest moments was signing the Religious Freedom Restoration Act."

Thus concluded the great debate of 1996 about character and ethics in the White House. The talking heads on the post-debate broadcasts ruled just about unanimously that Dole had escaped the taint of nastiness by his gingerly approach. "Dole," said NBC's Lisa

Myers, "exceeded all expectations . . . he used a scalpel, not a chain-saw." At the same time, could anything less than a chainsaw have brought down the President this late in the day? None of the seers assembled by the networks seemed to think so.

————

Looking back, for the advocates of presidential debates, 1996 had once given signs of being a relatively trouble-free year. For the first time there was never any doubt that the debates would happen. Bill Clinton had given his blessing soon after taking office, and, unlike John Kennedy, lived to deliver on it. The challenger, Bob Dole, was never in a position to dicker over details, and what dickering there was was quickly settled. The most frowned-upon element of past debates with respect to viewer turnoff, the reporter panels, were banished entirely. For the final, climactic debate, moreover, the most highly praised innovation of 1992, "ordinary people" asking questions, was brought back for another anticipated triumph in the ratings.

Yet no such triumph ever happened. Only 46 million people, on average, watched the opening debate—the lowest number since 1960 and 25 percent below 1992. For the final presidential debate of 1996, with its supposedly viewer-friendly "town-hall" format, viewership plunged to 36 million, very likely the fewest ever. For the vice-presidential debate, barely half as many watched as four years before.[46] Some of this 1996 decline presumably reflected the year's more general flight of viewers from political broadcasts. Baseball playoffs on the Fox network during the vice-presidential and second presidential debates (helped along, possibly, by Dole's debate-opening reminder) account for at least some of the especially steep fall in viewership for those later broadcasts.

It's possible, too, that Ross Perot's presence in 1992 enhanced interest, and hence ratings, to a level unlikely to be maintained without a comparable enticement the next time. To whatever degree viewers are drawn to debates by the hope of getting help in making up their minds, in 1996 there were fewer viewers than most years in need of such help at this stage of the campaign.[47] To whatever degree they are drawn to watch by curiosity about the outcome (whether of the debates or the election), in 1996 there were fewer Americans in doubt about either of those things. One could also speculate that the relentless hype about whether one candidate would throw mud at the other just might have encouraged some viewers to watch baseball.

All of that said, the 41 million people, on average, who watched the presidential debates even in a slack year composed nearly half the number that showed up on Election Day. About two thirds of all voters watched at least part of a debate. One survey in 1996 asked voters if they had learned "a lot" about the candidates from (a) watching the debates, (b) reading the newspapers or (c) watching television news broadcasts. Half again as many picked the debates as picked television news or the daily papers.[48]

In their nearly 90 minutes each on ABC, CBS and NBC during the debates, more of Clinton and Dole was seen and heard by more voters than in all the evening news broadcasts of all three networks for the entire year. It amounted to more than twice as much free, roadblocked, prime-time exposure as was sought in 1996 by a "Free Time Coalition" seeking such time—as though none already existed—for the candidates to communicate with voters. (Another 90-minute bloc of guaranteed free time disappeared, wihout even a ripple of concern from free-time advocates, when Clinton rejected a third encounter.)

THE NEXT TIME AROUND

By the spring of 2000, the Commission on Presidential Debates will have formally announced a plan for the 2000 debates, covering all relevant details, including re-examined rules for admission. Much later, some time after the conventions, agents of the major party nominees will then ignore all of this wise counsel as they meet to decide the number, time, place and format of the next round of debates—as well as who, if anyone besides themselves and their running mates, will appear in them. In this negotiation, each side will be motivated exclusively by what it thinks will help it win the election.

Even so, from time to time, there may be ways to nudge them towards the right things to do. One candidate for example, generally the one trailing when negotiations start, will want more debates. The other will want fewer. Since the one who wants fewer is by definition the one with the upper hand, this results most years in only two debates between the presidential nominees.

Assuming the public would be better served by at least three (along with a vice-presidential debate), the networks could do something to encourage that. They could get together, as they did in 1992, and block out four prime-time slots, from 9:00 to 11:00, the first 90 minutes of which would be available for live coverage of debates in which the major party candidates agree to appear. The dates would run from the final days of September through the first twenty days of October—the period generally settled on after a great deal of wrangling for most debates in the past. The Fox network in 1996 bragged a lot about its free broadcast of twenty one-minute soundbites from the candidates (and won an astonishing amount of praise for this nibble). For 2000, Fox could be encouraged to join the other networks in committing six hours of free, unsponsored time for the candidates to make their case to the voters—instead of broadcasting sports events that compete with them for viewers.

This early and specific commitment of broadcast time, and its incorporation into the fall schedules of all the networks, would be much tougher for the campaign that wants the fewest possible debates to reject than would a press release by the Commission on Presidential Debates. The debates would be produced by whomever the candidates chose—most likely the commission. The only network initiative would be to guarantee the airtime.

One decision of the candidates in 1996 with which absolutely no one quarreled was their rejection of the press-conference format and its panel of reporters. It's unlikely anyone will want them back in 2000. The suggestion that Jim Lehrer moderate all three debates came from the Dole side—which worried most about the final debate and felt their man would do better with the same moderator the second time around.

Lehrer, to nobody's surprise, did his job well, but viewers next time would probably welcome some variety. CBS's Bob Schieffer, apparently a runner-up in 1996, would with any luck be offered one of the debates. With a little more luck, both candidates would have the self-confidence to engage ABC's Ted Koppel, the best moderator television news has to offer, and NBC's tenacious Tim Russert. None of these, sadly, would have been the first choice of their own networks under the 1992 proposal.

Were Schieffer and/or Russert chosen, CBS and NBC would have to revisit policies opposed to their reporters appearing in debates where the candidates decide who asks the questions. Though I myself at CBS was always an advocate of that policy, given how much is at stake for the candidates and the power invested in a single moderator, it may be only fair to let them have someone they both trust. It may also be a bit far-fetched to argue that a reporter is seriously diminished by being chosen.

Whoever moderates, something should be done about the pernicious rule that "no follow-up questions by the moderator will be permitted." Another rule of recent years prohibited "cross-questions or cross-conversation between the candidates." These rules give both candidates a license to throw up clouds of misleading or dead-wrong facts and figures on the economy, taxes and crime, among other things, without any direct challenge by the moderator.

Since Lehrer, who was highly qualified to keep the candidates honest, faithfully stuck to the rules, Clinton and Dole were both free to exercise with abandon their license to deceive. For several days afterwards, newspapers would sort out the truth of what thirty to fifty million viewers had been told. On the CBS Evening News the day after the first debate, Eric Engberg did the Lord's work with one of his better "Reality Checks."

On all three networks the night before, however, post-debate analysis dealt mostly with the debate's likely effect on the election— CBS having dropped its truth squad to make room for some more consultants. It is only natural for the horse race to come first, but if the candidates persist in gagging the moderator so he cannot challenge their flights of fancy, the networks could also spare a little time to present some well-chosen facts while their debate viewers are still (hopefully) around. As for the gag rule itself, the candidates obviously like it or it would not be there. On the other hand, a little public agitation on the matter, conceivably by, among others, Lehrer, would not hurt.

Finally, there remains the problem for which no one has ever found a good solution: what to do about candidates other than the major party nominees. The equal-time suspension of 1960, the spot-news exemption adopted in the 1970s and its expansion in the 1980s to include debates sponsored by the media, all had one fairly clear aim: to exclude candidates with no significant national support. Most years that excludes everyone but the major-party nominees. The problem arises when there is a third candidate who does have real support. Where do you draw the line?

Under the past rules, strictly applied, of the Commission on Presidential Debates, only one-third party candidate since 1856 (when the upstart party was the Republican) could have made the grade. Had the guidelines been applied as rigorously in 1992 as they were in 1996, Ross Perot would not have qualified even for the one appearance originally proposed that year by the commission. The commission's guidelines, however, are really beside the point. Neither in 1992 nor 1996 did they have anything to do with whether Perot was in or out. In both cases the major party nominees made it clear that, for any debate *they* appeared in, *their* judgment would prevail.

That, for better or worse, is how the issue will go on being settled. In 1992 Clinton and Bush insisted on Perot's inclusion throughout because they knew that a large number of voters were sympathetic to Perot, and they did not want to irritate those who were still making up their minds. In 1996 Dole and Clinton decided there was nothing to fear. In the end, that may have been the most reasonable guideline of all.

6

AT THE END OF THE DAY

The Evening News and Its Critics

O NE MONTH AFTER THE 1996 ELECTION, MARVIN KALB, Director and Edward R. Murrow Professor at the Joan Shorenstein Center on the Press, Politics and Public Policy of Harvard's John F. Kennedy School of Government, convened a day-long meeting of thirty-four notables in all those fields at the Harvard Club in New York. The central participants and the main topic of the meeting came from television news.

For most of a quarter-century career in broadcasting, Kalb had covered not politics but the State Department for CBS and later for NBC. Since the Center's opening in 1986, however, Kalb had achieved a unique standing for both the Center and himself in the recognition of merit in political reporting on television. Past honorees and keynote speakers in awards ceremonies at the Center included Peter Jennings, Ted Koppel, Barbara Walters, Tom Brokaw, Walter Cronkite, Dan Rather, Mike Wallace and senior executives and producers of all the networks.

It was a Shorenstein scholar, after the Center's first election cycle, who turned the "ten-second soundbite" into the reigning epithet for shallowness in television news. After each election, the Center had convened conferences like this one to scold the networks on their arrogance ("reporters get six times as much airtime as the candidates"), their "poll-driven" obsession with the horse race ("who's up, who's down, who's ahead"), the cynical, negative tone of their reporting (prime suspect in academic research on the roots of low voter turnout) and the invasive scrutiny of private foibles which (it is argued) leads citizens of quality to shun public office. This did not, to be sure, in any way diminish the regularity of the Center's honoring the network celebrities responsible for the coverage.

This time, however, the atmosphere was different. "Let us stipulate," said Kalb early on, that the coverage was better than it had been in previous campaigns. Twice again in the course of the conference Kalb gave his blessing to the 1996 performance of the networks. From Thomas Patterson, the Center's normally sniffy Benjamin C. Bradlee Distinguished Professor of Journalism, came a rare pat on the back. In the last two elections, he noted, clockers at academic centers like the Shorenstein had registered a notable decline in horse-race reporting. A colleague from Wellesley assured him that "the people with the stopwatches" would soon have more good news: once again "Horse race and strategy coverage (were) down and issue coverage up."[1]

Another Shorenstein chairholder, Robert Blendon, reported, from a poll funded partly by the Center, that the great majority of voters (1) were pleased with the campaign coverage they had seen on television and (2) felt they'd learned enough about the candidates to make a reasonable choice. In a quiz about the Clinton and Dole positions on thirty-three issues, the survey found, voters gave the right answers 77 percent of the time (in one instance, suggested Blendon, a professor of government, economics professors would have done no better). As usual, the public's most important source of information was television news.[2]

Each network then showed a sample of the campaign coverage of which it felt most proud. For Mary Flynn, a senior producer at NBC *Nightly News*, that meant "Fixing America." It ran five days a week, through October to Election Day. "We asked a cross-section of real Americans, celebrities, people from all walks of life . . . how they would fix America."[3]

There were *thirty* of these pieces. They ran four or five minutes. Each offered up to five or six fixes for America. Esmeralda Santiago, a published author who "knew only a few words of English" when she arrived from Puerto Rico, called for smaller class sizes in public schools. Olympic swimming champion Janet Evans said it would help America a lot if people would respect other people—"the people you respect can help you along the way." The first thing an Oklahoma City fireman would do if he had "big influence" was "re-establish trust in government." As for Paula Poundstone, the stand-up comedian: "I know exactly what to do to fix America. I've tried several times, nobody listens to me, but I'll try again: campaign finance reform!"

Refreshing and path-breaking as some of these proposals from "all kinds of Americans" (as Tom Brokaw put it) might arguably be, they were odd specimens of a network's *campaign* coverage. None of the people proposing these fixes was running for President or anything else. If any candidate had any of these fixes in mind should he get elected, NBC either didn't know or didn't say.

ABC political director Hal Bruno offered a pair of reports from *World News Tonight* on (*pace* Paula Poundstone) campaign finance reform. The reports ran eight minutes each, "a tremendous amount of time on an evening news broadcast," observed Bruno (it truly was), and, broadcast early in the primary season, was airtime worthily spent.[4]

More interesting, perhaps, was what ABC did *not* do in the critical fall weeks before the actual election. Four years before, in the final six weeks of the 1992 campaign, *World News Tonight* had aired three installments a week of what it called "American Agenda." They ran five or six minutes each, on a total of eighteen issues, and compared the positions of George Bush, Bill Clinton and later Ross Perot on each of them. It was heavy stuff. One week, *World News Tonight* aired three agenda pieces in a row on the environment, another week three on education. Though "American Agenda" got rave reviews at the post-election conferences, there was no repeat performance in '96. *World News Tonight* by then was in a tense ratings struggle with *NBC Nightly News*, and three-parters about Dole's and Clinton's positions on smokestacks or inner-city schools was nobody's idea of a way to win that fight. "You do politics at your own peril," ABC's Roone Arledge once told his producers. He meant their jobs.[5]

ABC's competition this year for "Fixing America" was a daily series called "Solutions." Like "Fixing America," it had no connection with anything being talked about by the candidates for President or for anything else. The solutions being studied "in depth" (as Peter Jennings solemnly presented them) were not Bill Clinton's or Bob Dole's proposed solutions for anything but just plain solutions that somebody ABC had come across might have: for chronic back pain, hard-to-adopt children, helping working families find more time to be together, interracial togetherness on Sunday mornings, things like that.

Barbara Cochran, this cycle's CBS News producer for politics, presented "In Touch with America," her network's showpiece for its 1996 coverage. The prime CBS evening-news broadcast that year was stuck in third place for the first time in the history of broadcasting. Nonetheless CBS, unlike the front runners, did not flinch at relating its "political" pieces to the political campaign going on at the time in the United States.

Cochran showed a sample of what Dan Rather had introduced on air as "part of our effort to bring you in-depth coverage of you, the voters, and the issues that matter to you." In it CBS News correspondent Russ Mitchell "got in touch with . . . Mildred Timinelli, age ninety-four, and her kid sister, Lillian Hunter. She's eighty-eight." Mitchell gets in touch with them at a retirement home in Palm Beach. "What," he asks, "would it do to both of you if your social security was cut?" "We would have to go to the poorhouse," replies Lillian.[6]

Both sisters are Republicans, we're told, but, says Mildred, "Dole has his eagle eye on Medicare and Social Security and that has me really worried." Mitchell then presents, in about a minute, a medley of double-talk on these topics from both camps and summarizes crisply the real differences between them. At the close, Lillian still plans to vote Republican. Mildred isn't sure.

NBC News vice president Bill Wheatley, a sometime fellow of the Shorenstein Center, noted that listening to "the voters," as the CBS "in-depth" report had sort of done with Mildred and Lillian, was a good thing, and NBC had done its own share. "We built on the trend from '92 in spending more time with the voters."[7]

Amid all these euphoric assessments of a job well done, it was Wheatley who finally noted perhaps the most remarkable thing about the campaign coverage on network news broadcasts of 1996: how little there was! Four years earlier, between Labor Day and Election Day, the three evening broadcasts combined had aired nearly a thousand minutes of campaign stories—over seven minutes per night, about a third of each broadcast. During the same period in 1996 the networks aired less than half of that—a little over three minutes per show.[8]

In those last four weeks of the 1996 campaign, *CBS Evening News*, a half-hour broadcast since 1963, actually spent less time on campaign news than did the network's *fifteen*-minute broadcast during the corresponding period of 1960. In 1968, the first year for which there exist copies of the half-hour broadcasts, CBS and ABC devoted about twelve minutes a night to the campaign in its final weeks, more than half of that year's twenty-three-minute news hole. NBC devoted only a little less. As recently as 1992, at least one-third of the broadcast was the norm for campaign reporting in the fall. In 1996, that fraction plunged to one sixth. Why were all involved so pleased with themselves? How was this progress?[9]

"HERE THEY COME, THERE THEY GO"

In the fall of 1960, Norman Gorin was a young field producer for the CBS News flagship broadcast, *Douglas Edwards with the News*, and he had a plum assignment: covering Richard Nixon during that year's campaign for President. Here's how Gorin told me he and the correspondent traveling with him spent their day:

> We got up, got a plane, went to a morning event, filmed it. Late morning we covered a speech. If it was near New York or a bureau (which meant Washington, Chicago or Los Angeles) you might get in a one or two o'clock event. San Francisco and Denver and Atlanta were also possible cities. Des Moines or Louisville were not possible unless you ordered a "loop" (a broadcast-quality telephone line) in advance.
>
> In some cases, if the event was early enough, you could get on a plane and get to a more distant processing center (i.e., a bureau or one of the relatively few affiliates with high-speed film-processing equipment). Then you had to rejoin the campaign, God knows where, that night or in time for the first event the next day. If the event was too late and the candidate had left, that usually meant chartering a plane.

You had to get the film in the "soup" (developing fluid) no later than four o'clock. It took thirty or forty minutes to get four hundred feet of film through the soup before you could edit it. When you cut it, you had to pick out cutaways—shots of reporters, cameramen, spectators—so you could link one piece of sound to another without getting a jump cut. You'd see the candidate arriving, shaking hands, maybe a ground-breaking ceremony.

We'd find a forty-second to a minute soundbite—we called it "track" then, because it was the optical soundtrack from "single-system" sixteen-millimeter film. Somewhere along the line you'd tell New York what you had, maybe argue about the lead, because they had the wire story, and find out how much time you had. The reporter would set the whole thing up with something like "Vice President Nixon indicated today," and then you'd get the soundbite. Then you'd feed the whole thing to New York.

The correspondents and field producers assigned to such manic workdays were usually relatively young and chosen for their stamina and doggedness as much as for their command of national issues and electoral politics.

The correspondent often had to record most of his report while the camera was scanning the event, sometimes from a moving car. Only in the "standup" or "close" at the end, where he faced the camera, could he say something substantive without fear of "fighting the picture." Much of the correspondents' "voice-over," accordingly amounted to a description—or, if skillfully done—an embellishment of the accompanying pictures.

For the broadcast producers and more assertive anchormen like Walter Cronkite (who succeeded Edwards in 1962), this was not the highest form of journalism. Av Westin, a network producer whose career spanned CBS News in the 1950s and 1960s and PBS and ABC News after that, wrote:

> The pictures and the excitement of the campaign dominated the coverage. Crowd counting became a measure of a candidate's success. A typical evening news report during the campaign consisted of pictures of crowds, a snippet of natural sound like a band, more crowds, per-

haps a cut from a news conference or speech, and then the stand-up close, wrapping up the piece. There had been so much going on that caught the camera's eye that hardly any attempt was made to analyze the speeches or to put the campaign strategy into perspective.[10]

The customary putdown of these pieces from on high was "Here they come, there they go." The best a campaign report from the field could normally hope for was a passing grade (e.g., "They got the lead right"). That grading came with the next day's *New York Times*, the gold standard in that era which television news managers aspired daily to measure up to. (In 1964, the *Times* headlined its review of the election night broadcasts, "CBS by a Landslide." CBS News President Bill Leonard later recalled the effect on his entire organization: "We were the best. We knew it. The *New York Times* had confirmed it.")[11]

FACE TIME FOR THE CANDIDATES

Whatever their limitations, between Labor Day and Election Day in the 1960s, reports from the campaign "trail" on the nominees for President and Vice President, their supporters, their wives and their children took up roughly half the news hole on the evening news broadcasts. No one at the networks, however, saw this coverage as meeting the obligation, which all acknowledged, to inform their viewers about the candidates and issues.

It was a time when genuine zeal to do something more engaged not merely the news divisions but the top executives at all three networks. The most memorable product of all that zeal was the debates of 1960 and the strenuous efforts every four years to get Congress to reauthorize them. More than that, throughout the 1960s all of the networks scheduled weekly prime-time reports "in depth" with series titles like "Presidential Countdown" (CBS), "The Candidates and the Issues" (NBC) and "Campaign Roundup" (ABC). Needless to say, the time preempted for this voter education tended to be up against the more popular entertainment shows on the rival networks. Still, the viewership of these broadcasts did not trail an average evening news broadcast by very much. In 1965, the *Journal of Broadcasting* summed it all up:

There was a total of about 61 hours in 1960 and 51 hours in 1964. In both years these programs had an average rating of eight with a share of audience of about 20. Though it is a gross over-simplification, this means that some form of political program was broadcast on the national television networks for about one hour each day of the campaign in September and October.[12]

The threshold problem for these prime-time campaign broadcasts was the same as for debates. Under the equal-time rule, showing the Republican and Democratic candidates for President for any significant amount of time required, in most cases, giving equal amounts to the Prohibition, Vegetarian, Greenback, and Socialist Worker (Trotskyite) Parties, and many, many others. Equal time for everyone, whatever appeal it might have in the abstract, in the real world meant that there would be little or no face time for anybody.

The exemption to this rule enacted by Congress for 1960 covered not only four hours of debate but four additional hours, which the networks applied to their prime-time specials. In CBS's case, that meant half-hour interviews on alternate Monday nights with Kennedy, Nixon, Johnson and Lodge. A few days after the 1960 election, Frank Stanton had breakfast with the president-elect. The CBS president politely declined a series of government posts (Secretary of Commerce; Secretary of Health, Education and Welfare; Under Secretary of State). He then asked for and got what he'd come for: Kennedy's support for another equal-time waiver in 1964.[13]

Three years later, on November 21, 1963, confident of the backing of the President, Stanton formally proposed that, starting on Labor Day, 1964, CBS "have a stand-off between the two major candidates. The host would explain that we were giving an hour every Sunday night at nine for the candidates to take a single issue and hammer it out. On the final Sunday before the vote, they would summarize the campaign as they saw it."[14] The next day, of course, Stanton lost his White House backer for all that equal-time-free Sunday airtime in 1964. A few days after Lyndon Johnson (a CBS affiliate owner and personal friend of Stanton) moved in, he had Stanton over for dinner. Right off, Stanton recalled, Johnson "poked me in the side and said, 'Forget it. I'm not going to do it.' "[15]

Down the chute with the 1964 debates went any other kind of free time for the Republican and Democratic nominees. There would be no equal-time exemption for "Presidential Countdown" or "The Campaign and the Candidates." Those broadcasts would become in effect weekly prime-time digests of the campaign essentially *without* the candidates. The FCC relented to the extent of allowing two minutes for each presidential nominee. That left 24 minutes to fill with surrogates, supporters, pollsters, party officials and local reporters from "battleground" states. The final product amounted for the most part to *Hamlet* not only without the Prince but without the King, and broadcasts peopled largely by retainers were inevitably boring.

There was just one exception to the equal-time rule: "regularly scheduled" newscasts. Broadcasts that appeared year in and year out could do what they do any other time even if it involved putting a candidate on the air. There were just a few such broadcasts. One was the weekly sitdowns with Washington "newsmakers" in the Sunday morning "ghetto" of public-affairs broadcasts—a time slot in competition with hunting, fishing, golf, church and sleeping late. Politicians did not go on *Meet the Press, Face the Nation* or ABC's *Issues and Answers* to make an impression on likely voters (few of them watched) so much as to provide copy for the headline writers of the Monday-morning papers.

The most important of the "exempt" broadcasts were the morning talk shows and the evening news. Face time on the evening news, in particular, brought the full reach of network television to an obscure candidate trying to get known or a known candidate with something to say. Viewership on these broadcasts, especially at NBC and CBS, approached that of prime-time entertainment. In the late summer of 1963, the airtime available on those broadcasts abruptly doubled.

THE THIRTY-MINUTE EXEMPTION

A year earlier, in the long struggle to overtake Huntley and Brinkley in the ratings race ("This program," NBC bragged every night, "has the largest daily news circulation in the world") CBS had installed

Walter Cronkite at the helm of its *Evening News* broadcast. It booked more time than either of its rivals on the newly launched communications satellite to bring in same-day foreign reports, and it expanded its overseas bureaus to keep the satellite occupied.[16]

CBS could afford all this, because its cash cow, the prime-time entertainment schedule, was overwhelming its competition as decisively as Huntley and Brinkley dominated the evening news period. Given CBS Chairman Paley's irritation at being Number Two in anything, Stanton freely paid for whatever his News division wanted.[17] Expanding *CBS Evening News* to a half hour, which would cost a lot, might enable CBS to exploit its overall advantage in reporting assets to overcome Chet and David's edge in loyal fans.

"Good evening from our CBS newsroom in New York," said Walter Cronkite at 6:30 P.M. on September 2, 1963, "on this the first broadcast of network television's first daily half-hour news program." The highlight of the broadcast, using up more than half the extra time, was an interview with President Kennedy. Cronkite devoted the entire first segment of that interview to re-election politics—though the election was nearly a year away. Would the civil rights issue hurt Kennedy in the South? Kennedy said it had cost him votes in 1960 and might very well again. Which Republican would he like to run against? "I'll let them decide . . . I recall, three years ago, some of *them* were hoping they'd get *me*."

A week later, Huntley and Brinkley also went to a half hour at NBC. At ABC, which would wait till four years later, an unidentified newsman told *Newsweek:* "What are they going to keep filling thirty minutes with? Sometimes you can't even fill fifteen minutes."[18] As it turned out, between the civil-rights struggle and a Vietnam war reported live by satellite, filling thirty minutes would never be a problem in the 1960s—or later. The 23–24-minute nightly news holes on television's two leading networks would become a decisive theater in the world's first "living-room war" and transform forever the making of U.S. strategic policy. The broadcasts also became, by virtue of their exemption from the equal-time rule, the only way aside from paid advertising for presidential candidates to reach a mass television audience.

THE SOUNDBITES OF '68

1968 was the first presidential-election year in which all the major networks had half-hour broadcasts daily in which to report the campaign, and there was no shortage of campaign news to report. For the first time in the television era, both parties had serious primary struggles for the nomination. In one of them an incumbent President was driven from the field, probably against his will, and the main rival to his hand-picked successor was murdered moments after winning the final primary. Richard Nixon, though nominated by a large margin on the first ballot, actually came within a few votes at one point of facing a precarious multiballot struggle with Ronald Reagan and Nelson Rockefeller. Hubert Humphrey, though never seriously threatened for the nomination itself, got it only after four days of riot in downtown Chicago.

In the fall contest there were three campaigns that warranted, and got, virtually equal coverage night after night. A mid-September Gallup poll had George Wallace in third place but trailing Hubert Humphrey by only seven points. In some electoral-vote estimates, moreover, Wallace (who was reckoned to have clear leads in half the Southern states, while Humphrey in September led almost nowhere) actually ran ahead of the Democrat until well into October.

Wallace's running mate, retired Air Force General Curtis LeMay, repeatedly said things that got him on the broadcasts. One day at a news conference, Jack Nelson of the *Los Angeles Times* asked the general what he thought of using nuclear bombs in Vietnam, and LeMay explained that nukes were "just another weapon in our arsenal"—no big deal. Another day LeMay volunteered that racial integration had worked well in the Air Force, and it ought to work just as well in the public schools of the country, and, said LeMay, Wallace agreed with his position. Opposition to school integration was, of course, the reason why Wallace was running in the first place.

Night after night, accordingly, there were Nixon, Humphrey and Wallace stories, along with LeMay, Spiro Agnew (who also had a way of saying things that got him on the broadcasts) and Ed Muskie stories—as well as exhaustive coverage of the networks' own effort to get Nixon's supporters in Congress to allow a revival of debates. Since those efforts ultimately failed, what voters saw at 6:30 or 7:00 on ABC, CBS and NBC was their main source of information on what the candidates stood for in the fall of 1968.

In the meantime, only a little had been done to improve the logistics of television reporting from the field. Picture and sound were still recorded on film. That meant long delays to develop the film and reliance for editing it on the unpredictable skills of the editor assigned at the affiliate from which you fed to New York. A "double chain" system was now used to align sound film carrying the soundbite and narration with a separate "b-roll" carrying the picture. Tight editing of the soundbites, or running a bunch of them, was generally out of the question.

Here, for example, is Bill Plante's report on the CBS *Evening News* of October 1, 1968. Humphrey, in a speech the night before, has proposed a halt in U.S. bombing of North Vietnam—a proposal carefully drafted to make peace with the antiwar faction of his own party without opening a breach with his patron, President Johnson. Plante is traveling with Richard Nixon:

> *Plante:* Nixon called his opponent's statement possibly his fifth or sixth position on the bombing, recalling that he had earlier agreed with him—no bombing halt without a reciprocal announcement by Hanoi. He said that, unless clarified, the Humphrey offer could destroy the only trump card the United States had in the (Paris peace) talks.
>
> *Nixon:* The representatives of the government of Hanoi read everything that is said by prominent political figures in the United States, including editorials and in particular statements by presidential candidates. I think it is possible that the men in Hanoi could interpret this particular statement as offering them a concession in January that they could not get now. It is possible; I do not charge it. And I think that he should clear up that possibility with a very forthright statement that all he was trying to do in making that statement is that he was simply saying that in January he would negotiate exactly as President Johnson is doing now. He either has to be for the bombing halt, as some of his prospective supporters or present supporters would like, or he has

to support the negotiators in Paris as he indicated in his speech that he would and at the present time I'm not sure which side he is on, and I think he leaves it very much in doubt.

Plante: Richard Nixon is now very much aware that whatever the Vice President means exactly, this could develop into a brand new ball game. This is not unexpected. The Nixon staff has been waiting for the Humphrey camp to make some sort of dramatic move to reunite the party, and it has come. Bill Plante with the Nixon camp in Detroit.

The soundbite is classic Nixon. Three times he has hinted broadly ("It is possible; I do not charge it") that Humphrey would give away the store if it were left to him to negotiate with Hanoi. Nixon's analysis of Humphrey's double-talk deftly exposes the Democrat's dilemma. To bring home the doves in his own party, Humphrey needs them to believe he would do precisely what Nixon suggests ("I do not charge it"): give Hanoi something Lyndon Johnson would not. Saying that flat out, however, which Humphrey had not done the night before, would have provoked à very risky break with the President who put him where he was. It would also, since Johnson *was* still the President, have undermined the negotiations going on in Paris.

It took Nixon barely a minute to make all these points, rather long for a soundbite even in the era of the jiffy film developer, a-roll and b-roll, and pick-up editors patching the pieces together with splicing tape. Not every viewer, to be sure, would have grasped all of Nixon's strategic thrusts, including his sham profession of objectivity, on a single viewing. A decade later, Plante might have given them some help. He could have isolated Nixon's central points in two relatively crisp segments: "I think it is possible that the men in Hanoi could interpret this particular statement as offering them a concession that they could not get now" (9 seconds) and "He should clear up that possibility with a very forthright statement that in January he would negotiate exactly as President Johnson is doing now" (10 seconds).

A decade later, the candidate himself, knowing how evening-news pieces were put together, would have made his point about undermining the negotiators in Paris in such a way that it could have formed another brief soundbite on its own. In between the two or three Nixon quotes, Plante would have underlined, for anyone who needed help, what the candidate was hoping to accomplish.

That, of course, is what political reporters in every other medium have always done. Hardly ever in a newspaper or a magazine account of a speech do you get a single quotation as long as the Nixon quote in the 1968 Plante report. If the evening news soundbites are seen as a daily entitlement of free airtime in a medium with few other places to be heard, Nixon's full minute in one gulp on the October 1 broadcast was something he had coming to him. (Over time, Humphrey and Wallace were getting just as much.) To the television correspondents' peers in the writing press, however, and among themselves, it was not campaign reporting as it should be.

In the mid-1970s, technology came to the aid of network reporters in the field. Videotape cameras finally became portable (by a strong back), and replaced 16-millimeter film. No time was wasted any more in putting film through the "soup." The correspondent could review the taped sound during the day and decide well ahead of time which statements he wanted to use. It did not have to be a single statement, or at most two. He could weave a narration in and out of the soundbites, and the editor could bind sound and pictures together electronically, without razor blades and tape. Here, in consequence, is how Bill Plante could report on Ronald Reagan's day for the *CBS Evening News* of October 10, 1980:

> *Plante:* Reagan toured the Youngstown Sheet and Tube mill, which for the past two years has been 90 percent shut down. His motorcade rolled past the great hulking dilapidated sheds over the now-inactive blast furnaces. Thirteen thousand basic steel jobs have been lost in Youngstown in the last three years, and Reagan blamed the Administration.
> *Reagan:* I said it was closed down for two reasons: dumping, and the EPA forcing costs on them for environmental protection to meet their mandates that could not be afforded.
> *Plante:* Reagan told a questioner he was angered by what he had seen, and again blamed government regulation.

Reagan: The federal government over the years has created—there's 5,600 regulations imposed on the making of steel, administered by twenty-seven different government agencies. Now, you tell me how these guys can sit in a bureau in Washington and make rules and regulations that run the steel industry, and they've never even been out here to take a look at it.

Plante: Reagan's anger over regulation led him into a thicket of extemporaneous remarks last night in Steubenville, Ohio, where he criticized the philosophy of no growth, and ventured the opinion that the eruption of Mount St. Helens had caused more pollution than automobiles.

Reagan: I have a suspicion that one little mountain out there in the last several months has probably released more sulfur dioxide into the atmosphere of the world than has been released in the last ten years of automobile driving or things of that kind that people are so concerned about.

Plante: The Environmental Protection Agency points out that automobiles do not emit sulfur dioxide pollution. EPA Administrator Douglas Costle responded to Reagan's charge:

Costle: Sulfur oxides emitted by Mount St. Helens add up to about what one major power plant does in the course of a year.

Plante: The EPA says Mount St. Helens has pumped an average of 1,500 tons of sulfur dioxide into the atmosphere every day in recent months, but that 81,000 tons a day enter the atmosphere from man-made sources, principally coal-fired generating plants. . . . Pressed for sources on Reagan's statistic, aides said they must have come from the candidate's own reading. Facts and figures recalled off the cuff like that caused Reagan trouble during the primaries, because they were often inaccurate, but he has largely steered clear of the problem since. Bill Plante, CBS News, Chicago.

The three takes of Reagan in this 1980 report run an average of 13 seconds, compared to a minute for Nixon's one soundbite in Plante's 1968 report. Other values besides those of journalism apply here. For television producers in the videotape era, the crisp use of sound to achieve "pace" in news reports, aside from any issues of content, is a cardinal principle. Plante's 1980 piece meets that test, as the 1968 report, given the equipment of the time, could not.

For the presidential candidate, however, the new state of the art could make his nightly appearance on the news an uncertain blessing. In this instance, the reporter's ability to isolate three different statements by the candidate (instead of just taking one and letting it run on) allows him to raise questions about each as it is presented and even to bring on a highly credentialed employee of the man's opponent to rebut two of them.

CRITIQUING THE PICTURE

While Plante and his colleagues at CBS and the other networks were dissecting the message of the candidate in their daily reports, one of his colleagues at CBS found a new specialty: critiquing the pictures. "What did President Carter do today in Philadelphia?" asked White House correspondent Lesley Stahl at the top of her report on September 3. Her answer:

> *Stahl:* He posed—with as many different types of symbols as he could possibly find. There was a picture at the day-care center, and one during the game of bocce ball with the senior citizens. Click—another picture with a group of teenagers. And then he performed the ultimate media event: a walk through the Italian market.
>
> The point of all this, obviously: to get on the local news broadcasts and in the morning newspapers. It appeared that the President's intention was not to say anything controversial lest he draw attention away from what his strategists call Ronald Reagan's gaffes. Simply, the intention was to be *seen,* as he was, and he was photographed, even right before his corned beef and cabbage at an Irish restaurant with the popular Mayor Bill Green—the one in the center—who supported Senator Kennedy in the primary.

The piece got its edge, of course, from what cannot be shown here: the succession of pictures of an outgoing "Jimmy" Carter mixing lightheartedly with the people while the correspondent pinpoints the underlying calculation. This report, one of many like it by Stahl, was seized on after the campaign by two political scientists writing a book still highly cherished at media studies centers like the Shorenstein. Michael Robinson and Margaret Sheehan chose "What Carter did today in Philadelphia" as a symbol of their own: of how network news reporting seeds cynicism in the land. This was Robinson and Sheehan's take on Lesley Stahl's day in Philadelphia:

> The premise that the Italian market was the "ultimate media event" seemed to us somewhat less than objective, if not inaccurate, given that several thousand reporters had covered the Democratic Convention three weeks before. . . . Stahl's piece was all campaign strategy, which in the media is one of the higher orders of horse-racism.
>
> [Helen Thomas's UPI wire] story of the same event pretty much covered what Carter had said and not why he said it. CBS in a longer piece used Carter's words or ideas only once. . . . The UPI piece neither said nor implied anything critical about Carter. . . . Stahl painted Carter as a cynical poseur—a practitioner of media-based, symbolic politics.[19]

Robinson and Sheehan's disparaging (in this instance) comparison of UPI and CBS was not a rap that would trouble anyone then engaged in television news. Walter Cronkite, who got his start in news at the wire service and was always proud of it, had retired the year before. To the brash generation of television reporters who succeeded him, the straight ahead, "upbeat," stick-to-the-facts doctrine of the wire services was no model to emulate. For Stahl, every knock in the Robinson/Sheehan review was a boost.

There were two ways, essentially, to fight the efforts of campaign manipulators to shape the look of the network report. One was simply to shun the designated photo ops and look hard for other things to shoot. Alternative shots as interesting or attractive as those arranged by the campaign, however, were not always that easy to find. Back in New York, moreover, at 6:30 P.M. the show producers of each network are watching all three reports. If a particularly neat picture arranged by the campaign appears on the other two reports, the correspondent and field producer can expect to hear about it from New York if that picture is not in theirs.

The other way was to do what Stahl made a regular practice of doing: show the pictures slickly laid out by the campaign, but expose the artifice, make it clear that you are not being taken in and you are not going to let your viewers be taken in. In 1984 Stahl met her match.

"HOW DOES RONALD REAGAN USE TELEVISION? BRILLIANTLY!"

It would become one of the most discussed, analyzed and invoked reports in a half century of television news. Far into the *CBS Evening News* of October 4, 1984 several hundred Republicans running in the election just a month away were shown standing on the South Lawn of the White House to have their picture taken with the President. It was, said Dan Rather, "but one example of a presidency that projects a personality and an image that, even in the view of harsh critics, is almost picture-perfect in its use of television. But in using the medium, what is the Reagan message? Does it distort the big picture of reality? Lesley Stahl has been looking into this." This was Stahl's report:

> *Crowd cheering; band playing "Hail to the Chief"*
> *Stahl:* How does Ronald Reagan use television? Brilliantly! He's been criticized as the rich man's President. At seventy-three, Mr. Reagan could have an age problem. But the TV pictures say it isn't so. Americans want to feel proud of their country again and of their President, and the two pictures say you can.
> This orchestration of television coverage absorbs the White House. Their goal? To emphasize the President's greatest asset, which his aides say is his personality. They provide pictures of him looking like a leader. Confident, with his Marlboro Man walk. A good family man. They also aim to erase the negatives. Mr. Reagan tries to counter the memory of an upopular issue with a carefully chosen backdrop that actually *contradicts* the President's policy. Look at the Handicapped Olympics, or the opening ceremony of an old-age home. No hint that he tried to cut the budgets for the disabled and for federally subsidized housing for the elderly . . .

Another technique for distancing the President from bad news: have him disappear, as he did the day he pulled the Marines out of Lebanon. He flew off to his California ranch, leaving others to hand out the announcement. There are few visual reminders linking the President to the tragic bombing of the Marine headquarters in Beirut. But two days later, the invasion of Grenada succeeded, and the White House offered television a variety of scenes associating the President with the joy and the triumph . . .

In running the Presidency, the White House often prevents reporters from questioning Mr. Reagan. . . . This tight control has baffled those who think Mr. Reagan is at his very best when he's spontaneous, say in dealing with hecklers.

Reagan: I'll raise his taxes. (*laughter, cheers*)
Stahl: Or in tossing off one-liners. He can be masterful at deflecting a hostile question.
Woman: Do you mean to give a signal to other Republicans that if they don't conform that off will go their heads?
Reagan: How can you say that about a sweet fellow like me?

Stahl: President Reagan is accused of running a campaign in which he highlights the images and hides from the issues. But there's no evidence that the charge will hurt him, because when the people see the President on television, he makes them feel good, about America, about themselves and about him. (*Women singing about America over the loudspeaker; crowd cheering*) Lesley Stahl, CBS News, the White House.

From four years worth of Reagan b-roll, Stahl's producer, Janet Leissner, had assembled a greatest-hits reel of Reagan receiving the Olympic torch, getting a hug from Mary Lou Retton, pumping iron, honoring veterans of the Normandy landing under a glorious sun at Omaha Beach on the fortieth anniversary of D-Day, listening attentively to farmers in the field, retirees in a nursing home. It was superb evidence of Stahl's premise that Reagan (and his staff) used television brilliantly.

Once again, and far more elegantly than in the Carter years,

Stahl had exposed herself to the charge of painting a President of the United States as a cynical poseur. That, it could be said fairly, was her intent. In her mind the piece was "tough"—in television news there is no higher praise. It was the kind of piece that draws applause in the newsroom the night it appears and compliments the next day from colleagues in the White House press room.

Tough pieces, however, are supposed to draw blood, to provoke intemperate outbursts from their subjects, a freeze on private briefings, on returning phone calls. As Stahl steeled herself for the expected scolding, she got a far more deflating reaction.

"Way to go, Kiddo," said Richard Darman, the White House staff secretary—on the phone to Stahl, moments after the broadcast was over. "We loved it—five minutes of free media. We owe you big time." "Why are you so happy," replied the stunned correspondent, "didn't you hear what I said?" Nope. What about Reagan's cutting back on funds for the disabled, going AWOL after the bombing in Beirut, hiding from the issues? Surely there was something the President's man found offensive? Sorry. "You guys in televisionland haven't figured it out, have you? When the pictures are powerful and emotional, they override if not completely drown out the sound. I mean it, Lesley, nobody heard you." Stahl told the story widely. Martin Schram, a political reporter in transition to the media beat, used the White House put-down of the network reporter to set the theme for a popular book on television news.[20] Next time Stahl would have lots of company on the picture watch, and this time the politicians in their sights wouldn't love it at all.

1988: THE YEAR OF THE FLAWED VISUAL

Throughout the 1980s and 1990s the struggle for control of campaign visuals grew more intense with every cycle. For the candidates, in their contests with the networks, there were some winners—and a lot of losers.

"Don't call Michael Dukakis soft on defense," said Chris Wallace, on the *NBC Nightly News* of September 13, 1980. "Today he rolled across the the Michigan plains like General Patton on his way to Berlin." It was probably the most self-destructive act ever performed in public by a candidate without saying a word. Reporters in every medium salivated over it, but only television could show it. This was Bruce Morton's attempt, on CBS, to match the pictures, at which the entire newsroom broke out laughing as they appeared on the monitors.

> Biff! Bang! Powie! It's not a bird. It's not a plane. It's presidential candidate Michael Dukakis in an M-1 tank as staff and reporters whoop it up. In the trade of politics, it's called a visual. If your candidate is seen as weak on defense, put him in a tank.

There had been a lot of that since the campaign began. In one of the Shorenstein Center's first research efforts, Kiku Adatto, a Center fellow, tabulated *twenty-nine* instances of network news stories based on such disasters of attempted image management. Many still find a place on anybody's all-time joke reel of politics on television.[21]

There was Gary Hart's formal announcement of his candidacy—atop a boulder in a downtown park in Denver. To shoot Hart from the position to which the cameras were assigned, you had to frame his head and shoulders against a mountain peak. Hart did not quite invoke Edwin Markham's "a man to match the mountains;" but that was the idea. Sadly, however, Hart's image makers had not reckoned on the wide-angle lens. Though they got the majestic shots they wanted at some point in the network stories, what stuck in everybody's mind was a truly weird long shot, in which Hart is posed all by himself on a huge rock proclaiming his vision for America while far below, where they can hardly see him, are the hometown supporters gathered for his great moment. "That's the loner image we don't need," said one of those supporters when she watched the evening news.

Much of the merriment in covering the more elaborately staged campaign appearances came from the doomed attempts to make regular fellows out of the starchy 1988 nominees: two gaunt, austere men, both given to three-button Brooks Brothers suits, with button-down collars, regimental stripes, Phi Beta Kappa keys and diplomas, between them, from Andover, Swarthmore, Harvard and Yale.

Three days after George Bush finished behind Bob Dole and Pat Robertson in the Iowa caucuses, the mythic Republican image shapers calling the shots for Bush ran across a promising remedy for their man's stubbornly upper-class persona. (At a diner, earlier that day, Bush made his famous request for a "splash" of cream in his coffee.) The opportunity came in the parking lot of a truck stop in New Hampshire, where an enormous eighteen-wheel Mack truck and its driver were about to take off. Instead the Vice President of the United States, a hard hat perched unsteadily on his head, climbed up to the cab and led his motorcade in a race around the parking lot. For some reason, it was hard to shake the notion in some quarters that, unlike the visual howlers committed by the Democrats, Republicans are so masterful at this sort of thing that even their blunders come out all right. Without describing the size or nature of the viewers in their sample, Jack Germond and Jules Witcover wrote, "The rank phoniness of this 'media event' staged for television seemed obvious to us, and we expected the whole scene to be greeted with hoots of derision by viewers who saw it that night. Instead, it apparently was taken as genuine evidence of his interest in the common man."[22]

The mother of all phony visuals aired on all three networks on September 20, 1988. "Today," reported CBS's Bob Schieffer, "George Bush took homage to the flag to new heights. Like a pilgrim going to Mecca, Bush traveled to a New Jersey flag factory." On ABC, Brit Hume: "Politicians who campaign on their patriotism are sometimes described as wrapping themselves in the flag. . . . Today George Bush came close to actually doing it." Even Lee Atwater acknowledged that it was "one flag factory too far." The bantering tone of the network reports was not offset by any visual charm. Bush surrounded by red, white and blue fabric, telling factory workers that "flag sales are going well and America is doing well" was not the same as Ronald Reagan on Omaha Beach, with the blue sky and blue water at his back, saluting "the boys of Pointe de Hoc, the men who took the cliffs."

———

Much tougher to deal with than the often inept visual stunts of the candidates was the challenge to network news posed by a very ugly trend in campaign advertising. In the off-year election of 1986, the nastiest commercials ever seen on television had turned stomachs from coast to coast. Some of the very worst appeared late in the campaign, often too late for their victims to prepare ads and secure television time in response—assuming they had money left to do so. It was the start of a phenomenon in campaigning at all levels of American politics that television news has ever since struggled, seldom well, to deal with.

The responsibility for dealing with it in an off-year election fell mainly on the local stations, which conveyed this advertising to the voters and collectively made a lot of money at it. At the networks, which aired none of these ads as such, the news broadcasts all ran reports about the most ruthless cases. With graphic excerpts from the ads themselves, they made compelling stories.

In 1988 we all expected a lot of mean advertising in the fall campaign. Roger Ailes, who was doing media for Bush, had produced some of the sleaziest ads of 1986 and was in fact a pioneer, going back several decades, of this advertising genre. Mike Dukakis's original campaign manager, John Sasso, also had a history, in Massachusetts politics, of playing thirty-second hardball.

We did not have to wait for the fall. On the final weekend of the New Hampshire campaign, when television station managements had locked up their commercial schedule and left, Governor John Sununu, a Bush supporter, called the station operators at home and got them back to air what became known as the "straddle" ad. It showed two faces of Bob Dole, one on each side of the screen, with the legend "Straddled." An announcer then rattled off the issues on which Dole was said to have played both sides of the fence: among others, the oil-import tax (affecting fuel-oil prices in icy New Hampshire), the pledge signed by the other candidates not to raise taxes, sure turnoffs for New Hampshire Republican (and for that matter Democratic) voters. Bush bought enough airtime that weekend to hit the average New Hampshire voter eighteen times with the straddle ad. Dole had nothing.

On the Democratic side, Dick Gephardt and Mike Dukakis launched attack ads at one another in the early primaries and caucuses, until Dukakis launched one that wiped his rival out. Over a dozen years in the House of Representatives, Gephardt had migrated to the left on a host of issues from what had once been fairly conservative positions for a Democrat. The resulting voting record provided rich material for a standard attack-ad formula: the flip-flop. What the Dukakis ad contrived this time, however, was no routine flip-flop ad. Chris Black and Tom Oliphant, in their intimate chronicle of the often clumsy Dukakis campaign, describe with zest this rare example of its doing something spectacularly well:

> The idea was to find an acrobat, spray his hair Gephardt strawberry blond, and show him flip-flopping on the screen to represent Gephardt's shift on issues. They auditioned gymnasts and chose a young man who looked a bit like Gephardt. They sprayed his hair, put him in a Robert Hall suit, white shirt and red power tie. They pulled up his pants legs and then made him jump, flip and flop for six hours. They used video tricks to make him go faster, slow, backward, forward.[23]

In the resulting 30-second spot the acrobat flipped and flopped, while an announcer said: "Congressman Dick Gephardt's been for and against Reaganomics, for and against raising the minimum wage, for and against freezing Social Security benefits. He acts tough towards big corporations but takes their PAC money." A stern-looking Dukakis was then seen talking to supporters while the announcer continued: "Mike Dukakis refuses PAC money, opposes Reaganomics and supports a strong minimum-wage act. You know where Mike Dukakis stands." Back to the red-headed acrobat doing a final flip and freezing in place: "But Congressman Gephardt, he's still up in the air." [freeze frame]

Nothing ever done to Dukakis by the Bush campaign in the fall would surpass what this ad did to Gephardt. We all did stories on it. It was genuinely funny—mean but altogether legitimate. Gephardt had indeed been all over the lot, as the ad said, on a lot of things. His own people had known he would be hit with a television spot like this one sooner or later, even predicted it in conversations with reporters. They simply had not reckoned on its being so lethal.

In what became a maxim of political practice in America, these negative commercials *worked*. For Bush the straddle ad turned around a campaign that was on the edge of defeat and delivered a blow to

Dole from which he never recovered. Before "The Acrobat" began appearing in the Super Tuesday states, Gephardt had been alternating caucus and primary wins with Dukakis and was well ahead in unelected superdelegates. After those ads, on which Dukakis made an enormous buy, Gephardt was through.

It was not, however, as a perpetrator but as the victim of killer ads that Dukakis became famous. The first and cleanest of the Bush campaign's many hits came in the governor's home waters. Dukakis had once turned down nearly a billion dollars from Washington to clean up Boston Harbor because he could not come up with his state's share of the cost. Roger Ailes' "Boston Harbor" spot took viewers on a truly disgusting thirty-second tour of floating sewage, debris and oil slicks—ending, "Think what [Dukakis] could do for the country." Suddenly, in a very rare moment, the Republican had become the environmental candidate.

When the Bush attack ads kept hitting home, the Dukakis campaign cried foul—especially as Roger Ailes got careless with his facts—and prodded the networks to expose them. On ABC's *World News Tonight*, Richard Threlkeld did network news's first ad watch. A Bush ad had asserted, "Michael Dukakis has opposed virtually every defense system we developed." That, like some other things in the ad, was a stretch. Countered Threlkeld: "[Dukakis] supports a range of new weapons systems including the Trident II missile." Bush ad: "He opposed anti-satellite weapons." Threlkeld: "Only if the Soviets did the same."

And so on. One of the most controversial television spots of all time came next, and Lesley Stahl at CBS took it on this way:

Stahl: The Bush ad which has had the biggest impact . . . is the revolving-door commercial criticizing Dukakis's furlough policy. Why is that a good ad?
Tony Schwartz (Democratic media consultant): Because it's what people know is true.
Stahl: But the irony is that part of the ad is false.
Voice of Man (in Bush commercial): His revolving-door prison policy gave weekend furloughs to first-degree murderers not eligible for parole.

[*"268 Escaped" appears on screen*]
Stahl: Two hundred and sixty-eight murderers did not escape. . . .
The truth is that only four first-degree murderers escaped while
on parole. The number that appears on the screen as the announcer says "first-degree murderers" refers not to murderers but
to all furloughed prisoners.

These two attempts to straighten out the facts in just two of
1988's more fallacious ads represent the year's entire effort on the network news broadcasts. One reason there were so little, as would become apparent in the "ad watch" efforts of future years, is that many
of the most odious ads actually had their facts straight.

The most odious of all, the obviously racist "Willie Horton" ad
produced by an "independent" group of Bush supporters, displayed a
sinister-looking Afro-headed African-American as it told how he'd
been sentenced to life without parole in Massachusetts for a hideous
murder, had nevertheless been granted ten weekend furloughs, and
on the tenth had taken off on a criminal spree that ended with the
rape of a woman and the knifing of her boyfriend. Unlike the misleading Roger Ailes ad, however, which Stahl had skewered over its
"268 [murderers] escaped," there were no inaccuracies in the Willie
Horton spot for an ad watch to correct.

CLOCKING THE SOUNDBITES

No one knows who started it, but the term *soundbite* was used as far
back as the 1960s for the short takes of audiotape in radio news
broadcasts, when its newsfilm counterpart in television was still referred to as "[sound] track." At some point after videotape replaced
film in television news, *soundbite* gravitated to the editing rooms of
television. By the early 1980s the word had already broken out of the
editing rooms and become part of the cant of political consultants
and media critics. The consultants bragged of how they taught their
clients to speak in soundbites that would shout "take me" in those
editing rooms. For media critics, the prepackaged soundbites and the
market for them became fresh evidence of the gullibility of television
news.

It was a young scholar in the formative years of the Shorenstein (then Barone) Center who turned the soundbite issue on its head. Far from being suckered into putting the candidate's carefully crafted, easily recalled message on the air, she argued, the network broadcasts had pitilessly shrunk the time allotted to candidates to less than a quarter of what had once been their due.[24] Using Vanderbilt University's unique archive of television news, the Shorenstein's Kiku Adatto clocked the soundbites from the network news broadcasts of 1968 between Labor Day and Election Day. She found an average duration of 42.3 seconds. The same exercise conducted on the 1988 broadcasts yielded an average of 9.8 seconds.

The first of Adatto's numerous reports on her findings appeared on the Op-Ed page of the *New York Times* on December 12, 1989. Reformers of television news promptly found a new, bite-sized issue to rally round: the "ten-second soundbite." What Adatto did not mention in her widely read and cited *Times* article was that by her own count there had been three times as many soundbites in 1988 as in 1968. George Bush, as a result, had been heard on network news air a total of 58 minutes, as compared to 74 minutes for Richard Nixon— less than in 1968, to be sure, but but not 80 percent less.

It was not a matter of choice, as I showed earlier, that the single 40- to 60-second soundbite became the nugget around which network news stories were usually shaped in the 1960s. In the 1970s reporters and producers in the field got other choices. Long before Adatto and others put their stopwatches to work on the Vanderbilt files, videotape had replaced film in the editing rooms and multiple short soundbites in a story were the rule. By 1980, the average soundbite had already shrunk to twelve seconds, and in 1988 both Adatto and Daniel Hallin, a scholar at the University of California, San Diego, clocked it at ten.[25]

Network correspondents and executives were stung by the assaults on their coverage of the 1988 campaign and on the taut little soundbites that became a mantra for the medium's detractors. It was something they found themselves having to defend at dinner parties. Well into the 1992 campaign season, CBS's Dan Rather collared his executive producer, Erik Sorenson, and said that he, Rather, had taken enough guff from people whose opinions he respected. Henceforth, on *his* broadcast, soundbites of presidential candidates would run at least thirty seconds. However, this entitlement did not extend to persons not running for President, and it was not coupled with any lengthening of the political pieces encompassing the soundbite.

Correspondents and producers struggling to produce reports under this edict found themselves reduced in effect to packaging the elongated soundbites at the expense of reporting stories of the campaign. Instead, moreover, of reaping the warm praise of a greatful nation, Rather found little notice taken of his gesture—aside from newspaper stories describing (accurately) the confusion into which it had thrown his own staff. Within a few weeks, thirty seconds had shrunk to twenty, and before the month was out the anchorman's quixotic tilt against the windmill of standard television practice was quietly abandoned.

The idea, nevertheless, of giving candidates a chance to be heard, at least a little, in their own voice on the evening news kept cropping up at the networks. While nobody besides Rather wanted to provide this nightly in routine campaign reports, there was a strong inclination to do *something*. The most ambitious proposal came from the political high priest at NBC News, Washington bureau chief Tim Russert. "Can the networks do better?" Russert asked on the Op-Ed page of the *New York Times*. Heading Russert's list of answers to his question: "Early in the campaign the networks should broadcast the stump speech (of each candidate) in its entirety . . . on their news programs."[26]

Anything approaching a basic stump speech "in its entirety" would suggest the commitment of perhaps half an evening news broadcast to each of the numerous candidates found in the early stages of a campaign. In the fierce ratings war then going on, no network broadcast (least of all the doggedly competitive NBC) figured to embark on such a public-spirited program all by itself. The primary season of 1992 came and went without any entire stump speeches on Russert's NBC, or any other commercial network. In June, *Nightly News* finally came through with three minutes each for Bush, Clinton and Perot. (CBS nearly a year earlier had given two minutes each to the principal contenders for the Democratic nomination. In the summer, it too presented Bush and Clinton in three minutes of "stump speech.")

———

Some of the critiques of network coverage in the 1990s clashed with one another. The heavily edited soundbites, often sharply introduced and followed with skeptical asides, brought calls to let the candidates get their message out "unfiltered," by reporters with agendas of their own. At the same time there were arguments, just as urgent, that the networks should take a more active role in pressing issues that the candidates were ignoring, and in exposing lies and deceit—whether in paid advertising or on the stump. At CBS, that mission was assigned to Eric Engberg, a 25-year veteran with hashmarks from Watergate, Iran-*contra* and innumerable campaigns.

REALITY CHECK

"Reality Check" was Engberg's vehicle, and with it came a mandate to be bold. The pieces generally ran a little under three minutes, not quite epic-length; part of their style was to be crisp. Engberg would typically open with some wholly unqualified claim by Bush, Clinton or Ross Perot, on the stump or in a campaign ad. After a beat, the correspondent would generally pronounce (some might say snarl), "Time out!"—while on screen a bright red "Reality Check!" would be stamped with a heavy metallic "thunk." Here is how one "Reality Check" in late October began:

> *Engberg:* Out for his morning jog, President Bush dished out his own spin on how reporters should write about new figures showing surprising growth in the overall economy in the last three months.
> *Bush:* And here we are with a sixth quarter of growth. This one is 2.7 percent, leading every country in the world practically, and it's good news for the American taxpaper and the American people. There's no way to write this one, no other way.
> *Engberg:* Time out! The President is seizing on a quarterly bump of 2.7 percent in the gross national product. . . . Economists say

that's a notoriously volatile number that does not necessarily mean a trend.

Oops! History has since told us that Bush had it right after all. Engberg, to be sure, never said flatly that Bush got it wrong, but to see that takes careful reading. As a rule, if not in this case, the Reality Checks stand up well to close inspection years later.

One of the best took a shot at Bill Clinton's reading of the same economy.

Engberg: As he dwells on the recession, his exuberance for gloom-and-doom numbers sometimes gets the best of him.

Clinton: This president promised us fifteen million new jobs. He is over fourteen million short.

Engberg: True.

Clinton: And now, for the first time in American history, there are more people going to work in government offices every day than in factories throughout the United States.

Engberg: True, but only if you lump in every cop, meter maid and bus driver who works for local and state governments, most of which are run by Democrats.

Clinton: . . . A fifty percent increase in people who get up every day, play by the rules and do their best to raise their children and they're still living below the poverty line, eighteen percent of the work force, nearly one in five Americans.

Engberg: Census figures show eleven percent of American families live in poverty. Clinton makes it sound twice as bad through statistical chicanery. . . . On the explosive question of passing a treaty to lower trade barriers with Mexico and Canada . . . with unions against and consumers for, the candidate is in the middle and stalling . . .

Clinton: When I have a definitive opinion, I will say so. It's a very long and complex document . . .

Engberg: Time out. Clinton has a reputation as a committed policy wonk who soaks up details like a sponge, but, on an issue which will likely cost him votes no matter what side he takes, the one-time Rhodes Scholar is a conveniently slow learner. Eric Engberg, CBS News, New York

Engberg, his producer and several researchers had checked out the claims and counterclaims with economists in both camps as well as academic sources without any recognized connection. It might well be a textbook case of how candidates use numbers and slogans to envelope an issue in fog, and how television news can help its viewers penetrate at least some of that fog.

As it turned out, this particular Reality Check did find its way into a textbook. Thomas Patterson, the Shorenstein Center's Benjamin Bradlee Professor, used it to demonstrate "the unrelenting negativity of the press" as a superficial, self-indulgent game played by reporters at great cost to the public:

> The rise of the press-centered campaign has coincided with a decline in voter turnout and an increase in voter cynicism. There are many reasons aside from the reporting of the campaign for this tendency. However, negative news surely adds to it.[27]

In combating the cynicism sown by obsessively negative reporters, Patterson had a staunch ally in the Shorenstein's then long-time director and Murrow Professor of Politics, Press, etc., Marvin Kalb. Kalb describes himself as "one who spends a lot of time teaching young people and trying to drive out the cynicism and drive out the skepticism" which he too often finds.[28] (Some might think it odd for a teacher bearing Murrow's imprimatur to counsel the young against skepticism in reporting the news.)

As 1996 began, the war on cynicism found recruits beyond the halls of learning. In the course of a twenty-year writing career, James Fallows had taken two of the country's most basic institutions, the car industry and the military, to the woodshed. "These institutions," he later wrote, "reversed their decline only when they recognized and corrected the defects in their internal values." In search of a fresh institution to correct, Fallows did not have to look far. "The most fundamental parts of the media," he wrote in a widely read book, "have lost sight of or been pushed away from their central values." How so?

> The working assumption for most reporters is that most politicians will deceive them most of the time. The coverage we see is a natural result—which aggravates today's prevailing despair and cynicism in

public life. . . . Four-fifths of the public believe that politicians' morals were worse than those of the average citizen. Four-fifths thought that political authorities could "never" be trusted.[29]

In this passage from his book *Breaking the News*, Fallows, not atypically, had his facts wrong on the survey he cited. Only 3 percent said "never."[30] Nor do most reporters believe politicians will deceive them most of the time. The trouble is, there is no flashing light to tell you which are the times when you can safely rely on what they tell you. It is a relatively new thing for a journalist to imply, as Fallows does, that reporters owe it to their country to err on the side of trust. Monica Lewinsky aside, the U2 flight over the Soviet Union, Tonkin Gulf, the Cambodian "incursion" and Watergate, let alone Iran-*contra* and Bill Clinton's air strike on a pill factory in Khartoum, all occurred during the lifetimes of most readers of this book.

A more temperate recruit to the war on cynicism was Andrew Heyward, the latest president of CBS News. Speaking to the Radio and Television News Directors' Association on the "Seven Daily Sins of Television News," Heyward ticked off the first half dozen (e.g., laziness, hype). Following which, without any roll of the drums (that would be hype), Heyward concluded: "Which brings me to the seventh daily sin: cynicism. I think we are cynical about our ability to make a difference in people's lives. . . . Now more than ever ours is a business for idealists, true believers, not cynics."[31] After getting an earful from Fallows (a Harvard classmate) at a panel somewhere, Heyward invited him to a sitdown with correspondents and producers at the CBS Washington bureau—not famous as a hangout for idealists and true believers. Some highlights of the meeting:

> *Heyward:* The crux of [Fallows'] argument is that journalists are undermining democracy by some of the things we do—turning everything in politics into a sporting match, who's up, who's down. Spreading cynicism in the population.
> *Linda Douglas (correspondent, covering health care, now at ABC):* I'm new to Washington. I was amazed how quickly we moved away from the substance of health-care proposals to the politics. During the last six months, I could not get one story on the air about the substance of the issue.

Heyward: Is this because somebody like me said it wasn't interesting? [Laughter]

Douglas: If you don't deal with the politics behind Senator X or Senator Y's proposal, you're told you're not covering the story.

Eric Engberg: Why do we cover these things in terms of strategy—what will Clinton's next move be, what will Dole's be, how does this hurt him, how does it help him—instead of whether it's a good idea or not? Because, if you're with a Congressman or Senator or White House aide, that's the way *they* approach every issue.

Fallows: It's a matter of habit. This is the way the whole culture we live in operates. You get it in 90 percent of the reporting. Fifty/fifty would be a step along the way.

Heyward: To be fair, if you [told an evening news producer] I want to give you in-depth coverage on the budget, it would be a harder sell than here's what is going on behind the scenes in terms of political maneuvering.

In a way Heyward, who until recently had been executive producer of the evening news, had finally got to the heart of his problem. Every morning at each network, from up to a dozen bureaus around the world as well as special units in New York, "pieces" are offered. Some are related to the news of the day, some are developed over a period of days or weeks to help viewers understand a complicated issue, and some are there because viewers seem to want them: medical, entertainment, sports, unusually gruesome crimes, scandals affecting the famous. At a time when a network's evening news is trailing the other two (the case then at CBS) or clinging nervously, like NBC and ABC, to higher rungs, a correspondent soon learns not to pitch too many "hard sells" to the broadcast.

From the numerous graders of television coverage in the academic world has come a steady stream of data on 1996. Most of it confirms the buoyant mood of the Shorenstein conference that opened this chapter. On the most ancient of measures in this field of research, "horse-race" reporting as a fraction of the whole, all the clockings were on the downside. From the University of Pennsylvania's Annenberg Public Policy Center, Shorenstein's main rival in the horse race among the media centers, came a heavily funded revisionist study of negative campaigning professing to "debunk" the notion that campaigns over the last few cycles, or the reporting of them, have grown more negative.[32] The Annenberg study also reported that ad watches were fewer, something which in other years might have occasioned some chilly comment, but academic opinion on these was now mixed. Some media scholars now worry that, by suggesting politicians lie or mislead, critical stories about campaign ads augment the cynicism of Americans about their elected leaders. (I'm not making this up.)[33]

Whatever the final academic verdict on the evening news broadcasts, negativity was certainly (as we have seen) in short supply at the conventions and debates. For two election cycles, the centers had been as uniformly on-message to the networks as the most disciplined campaign for office: issues, not horse race; stop pounding viewers with unwanted strategy and progress reports; enough with the polls; allow the faces and voices of ordinary people to be seen and heard; stop picky-picky fault-finding about the public-spirited Americans who at great personal sacrifice serve in elective office; and, by doing all this, purge the land of cynicism and reverse the deplorably low turnout on Election Day. In 1996, it appeared, network news may have taken at least some of this counsel to heart.

So why in 1996, after all that, did thirteen million fewer voters than in 1992 go to the polls—even as the voting age population had grown? The answer is probably that none of the proscribed past practices of television news ever had much to do, one way or another, with voter turnout. Whatever benefits might have resulted from more correct conduct by the networks, higher voter turnout never figured to be one of them. The real roots of low turnout, still something of a mystery, clearly lie elsewhere.

CONCLUSION

The Control Room, the Internet and the Politics of 2000

SIDE FROM HAVING BOTH SPENT SOME TIME UNDERWATER IN the Navy, John Kennedy and Jesse Ventura do not seem at first glance like a pair of politicians with a huge amount in common. It wasn't long, however, after the Body was elected governor of Minnesota in November 1998, that the evangelists of on-line politics were declaring them two of a kind.

As often happens, it was Philip Noble, the South Carolina–based consultant whose clients rule Britain, Italy, Sweden and Australia, who got the buzz among the Web heads out to the off-line community. On the Friday after the election, Noble told the *New York Times* that the question of the moment was, "Do you mean to tell me Jesse is the JFK of the Net?" By that Noble's fellows in the wired world of politics meant that Kennedy—by blowing away a supposedly more formidable rival in the first televised debate with Richard Nixon—had launched the era of television's sway over campaigns for office. Ventura, whose not exactly state-of-the-art Web site might just conceivably have generated the 55,000 votes by which *he* won, had arguably performed the same feat for the Internet.

Within a month that argument had been carried to campus conference halls full of academics, politicians, journalists and on-line professionals at Harvard, George Washington and American universities. At American, Noble stated his case: Minnesota in 1998, he declared, had witnessed "the birth of digital politics. . . . The day of television politics is over. . . . 2000 will be the year of the Internet in politics."

One conference attendee who could not have agreed more was Philip Masden, Web master of Ventura for Governor. Not only, reported Masden, had more than a third of Ventura's contributions come by way of the Internet, but most of the volunteers whose efforts in the final days may have produced the winning margin were recruited there.

In a fairly close election, to be sure, many campaign elements may reasonably claim credit for having made the difference. One of the more obvious in Ventura's case was, well, televised debates. There were ten of these old-media events in the Minnesota race. Like Kennedy, Ventura had to most people's surprise excelled in them. Before the first debate, his support in the polls was barely 10 percent. On Election Day, in the three-man race, he won 37 percent. If Masden gave his Web site credit for the 55,000 votes in Ventura's winning margin, I asked him, how many of the remaining 700,000 votes did he attribute to the debates on television? "Half," he acknowledged—"or more."

At Harvard's Kennedy School of Government, Elaine Kamarck, a scholar with unusual experience in presidential politics, wondered if all the year's campaign Web sites (89 percent of candidates for senator or governor in one survey had Web sites) were not mostly "preaching to the converted."[1] Do all those electronically tabulated "hits," "impressions," "page views" and "unique visits" (among the many varied measurements of digital achievement) come from voters windows shopping to make a choice, or have those visitors mostly already made a choice when they click on one site as opposed to another? The unique power of television, news as well as advertising, has been its ability to reach, as well as the converted, the entire universe of the unconverted—and even the not very interested.

That unique franchise would have to be in jeopardy before the control rooms of network television news, like the smoke-filled hotel suites of a prior era, were ruled a spent force, or even a secondary force, in presidential politics. It is hardly news, in the final years of the twentieth century, that the political reach and influence of the major broadcast networks are not what they have been in the past.

The year 1996, as noted in earlier chapters, brought steep declines in viewership of broadcast conventions and debates and in campaign coverage on the daily network news broadcasts.

Between 1980 and 1994, estimates by Nielsen Media Research of the combined number of households in which these news broadcasts are watched dropped by about a third. The drop presumably was due in large measure to their networks' overall loss of viewership to cable-originated, pay-per-view and previously taped television and, perhaps, to some other forms of recreation. In the past four years, however, while the overall Nielsen ratings of the major networks have continued to erode, the combined network news measurements have remained remarkably stable—in any event, by almost any standard, tremendous. For thirty minutes on an average weeknight in 1998, 30 million Americans watched one of these broadcasts. [2]

In the same year, sources of political news on the Web, aside from the candidates' own Web sites, were still fairly limited. Among the most popular were on-line spinoffs of network news itself. In no case, however, did the number of "eyeballs" (in the on-line idiom) reached by any of these Web sites compare to those watching the television parent. The most far-reaching Internet-originated source of campaign news, America Online's *Election 98*, reported 15 million "page views" over an eight-week cycle—about half the number of network news viewers on a single night. [3]

In the Voter News Service exit poll of 1998, 40 percent said they make regular use of the Internet. VNS did not ask if they had learned much about the campaign from it. A national telephone survey in late October did ask. Six percent in that survey cited the Internet as a major source of campaign information; 72 percent cited television (mostly local, to be sure—this was an off-year election); 72 percent cited newspapers. [4]

Few speakers at the postelection conclaves of the on-line brought as broad a perspective to their assessment of the new medium's challenge to the old as Douglas Bailey. In the 1960s and 1970s, Bailey and his partner, John Deardourff, who are Republicans, ran the most successful television consulting firm in either party. Today Bailey's daily on-line political news report, *Hotline* (all 40 to 50 page views of it), is the universal noontime nourishment of political reporters in America. "I have yet to see," said Bailey at George Washington University, "the first campaign in which it is said at the outset, 'our Internet site is the major deal by which we are going to win this campaign.'" That campaign, Bailey ventured, "has yet to happen. It will probably happen in 2000."

Bailey did not suggest that this would be the typical campaign of 2000, nor does anyone else see it, that year, as the way to get to the White House. The common mantra of most political sophisticates at the conferences (not, to be sure, the view here) was that the most important requirement for a presidential contender in 2000 would be to raise at the very least $20 million in 1999—mostly for, yes, television. As imaginations run wild, however, on the future "dog years" by which the wired measure the evolution of their medium, hardly anything is off limits for campaigns to come in the twenty-first century.

Bailey envisioned campaigns as early as 2002 posting on-line "positions on demand": delivered by the candidate him/herself in audio-video form at a time of the eyeball's choosing. America Online's Kathleen DeLaski worried that there might be so much on-line traffic in the days leading up to the next election that even the most richly fortified server (presumably hers) was apt to crash. Most Web visionaries take it for granted that, sooner or later, elections themselves will be conducted on line. (Several can tell you right now how ballot security can be taken care of, though they acknowledge it will not be an easy sell to Congress or state legislatures.)

Party-run primaries and chat rooms (in lieu of caucuses) on line are anything but far-fetched notions for the presidential, not to mention lower-level, politics of the next century. By the campaign of 2000, or soon after, the number of Web-wired households could easily overtake those with cable television. In such an environment, with the vastly lower costs of Internet communication and so much of the public's future life itself likely to occur on the Net, with campaign funds and volunteers destined to be increasingly raised and recruited and then deployed on line, there may eventually be little off-line politics for the soon-to-be-dinosaurs of network television to cover.

That, however, is a topic for another century—and another book. This one concludes with some thoughts about the control

room and its still central role as the first president is about to be chosen for an era likely to be defined by the Web.

ANOTHER "REFORM" BACKFIRES

In the past five elections of the twentieth century, every Republican
nomination has been decided by the middle of March. Only once did
the Democratic race go past early April. The great majority of both
parties' voters, in states with primaries further down the line, had as little to say about their parties' tickets as they did when the party bosses
ruled. When Bob Dole wiped out his rivals for good on the first Tuesday
of March 1996, barely one out of four Republicans (even among those
rarities just dying to get out and vote) had had a chance to do so.

When that year's Republican contest sputtered to a record early
close, party chairman Haley Barbour named a task force to find
some remedies. As a result, in 2000, states that held their primaries
or caucuses later would get some extra delegates to the Republican
convention.

Almost no one took the bait. Far from pressing their legislatures
to help them secure those bonus delegates, Republicans in voter-rich
states like California, New York, Ohio and Michigan chose relevance
instead and joined Democrats in moving their primaries still earlier
in March—and even into February.

The "front-loading" of the system thus became, if anything, more
severe than ever. Not the least fazed by the threatening approach of
the states where most of the country's voters live, Iowa and New
Hampshire kept their place at the head of the line by moving to January and the start of February, respectively.

There used to be a case of sorts for giving Iowa and New Hampshire their edge. They were still small enough, went the argument,
for candidates to run old-fashioned campaigns, meeting with small
groups of voters and answering their questions. It was supposed to be
a good way of testing the candidates' people skills with voters who got
a chance to know them. Every four years, reporters recycled the tale
told by 1976 Democratic candidate Morris Udall about the New
Hampshire gas-station attendant who, when asked what he thought
of So-and-So, said, "Don't know yet. Only met him three times."

Iowa and New Hampshire also, the argument continued, gave candidates who might not be famous or have huge campaign chests a chance to become better known by "doing well" and then to raise money down the line. State spending limits on candidates getting federal funds proved useful equalizers for a time. The spending limits, Iowa's hard-to-target caucus-goers, and the peculiar nature of New Hampshire's media markets also kept a lid on the role of television ads—another arguable gain.

After 1996, it was hard to make that argument. Since 1976, when federal funding and state spending limits went into effect, so many loopholes to the limits have been found that they no longer have much effect. Bob Dole, who took the money, was still able, legally, to spend many times the official limits on both states. By far the largest chunk of this money went not for grassroots organizing but for television ads. Phil Gramm, the candidate with the most highly regarded "ground game" in Iowa, finished fifth.

In a rational world, all the state primaries and caucuses would be replaced by one national primary, giving all of the country's Republicans and Democrats an equal opportunity to cast an effective ballot. A national primary in May with a June runoff between the top two would give all supporters, wherever they live, the same chance to influence their party's choice of nominee.

By then the issues that would be on voters' minds in November would more likely be in focus than in February. Network television could help by creating forums for the candidates—at a time when most voters could put what they learned to use at the polls. Quite apart from doing good works, the networks would have more everyday incentives as well. There is no reason why these broadcasts could not (with some obvious restrictions) carry advertising. Making the primary and runoff national events would generate viewer interest as well as voter turnout. Pre-runoff debates between the final contenders in particular would very likely get excellent ratings.

That, of course, is what would happen in a rational system. No such system, however, is in sight. Practicing politicians in both parties for the most part hate the idea. Nor is the irrationality of the current system very high on the public's list of things needing to be fixed. In contrast to the 1970s, when the Democrats were constantly tinkering with their nominating process, the Republicans are now the tinkerers. Having failed in their prior efforts to arrest the front-loading of the primaries, both parties in 2000 have new commissions charged with devising a remedy.

At the networks, skeptical veterans will wish them well. Since the early sixties, television has been the chicken or the egg (take your pick) in a relationship that led to both the special status of Iowa and New Hampshire and the front-loading of the rest of the primary calendar. By no means alone among the news media, television covers the actual casting and tabulation of votes in Iowa and New Hampshire with the kind of resources reserved for major national events.

Candidates who don't make respectable showings (however that is defined) in at least one of these states will most likely never get to make their case in the remaining forty-eight. Given how critical it is for a campaign's viability to make such a showing, by far the most actual campaigning in the whole year before the primaries and caucuses begin takes place in those states, and so inevitably does a great proportion of the campaign coverage.

Moreover, given the huge costs of television campaigns in the big states whose primaries follow, campaign strategies inevitably focus on the Tuesdays that come first. Candidates who survive Iowa and New Hampshire are compelled to spend most of their time and money trying to get past the Super Tuesday that comes next. States that want attention, accordingly, keep elbowing their way towards the front.

An idea advanced for some years in academic quarters, and by journalism's influential David Broder, is a system of regional primaries. States in each of the country's generally recognized quadrants (Northeast, South, Midwest, Far West) would hold their primaries or caucuses on or about the same Tuesday at monthly intervals starting in March. The sequence in the first cycle would be decided by lot. In succeeding cycles, the region that was originally first would go last, and each of the other regions would move up a notch. In 1999, the state officials generally charged with administering primary elections took a formal stand (with some dissents) in favor of such a system.

The National Association of Secretaries of State is not, to be sure, composed for the most part of heavyweights in the politics of their respective states. Getting their plan off the ground would require the concurrence of both national parties. In the case of the Republican party, this concurrence would have to occur no later than the national convention of 2000, since Republican rules require that the terms for each nominating cycle be determined by the previous convention.

Once adopted by the national party bodies, the scheme would pose formidable obstacles in enforcement—especially in the region that learned its place at the head of the line would come in the year 2016. The secretary of states' plan, moreover, unaccountably removes Iowa and New Hampshire from their respective regions and leaves them once again, indeed even more so than in the past, as gateways to the process, thus reinforcing the worst of all the distortions in the current system.

One solution widely supported by academic conclaves would be a collective act of restraint on the part of television in covering these early events whose importance they did so much over the years to enhance. Such forebearance would encounter resistance from the powerful executives who control network news budgets and worry about evening news (and the increasingly competitive morning news) ratings. It would also require an unlikely level of cooperation from the other news media.

The problem is that almost any level of reporting on the early contests will take a heavy toll among the candidates who fare poorly, especially since all the candidates will spend themselves silly to keep this from happening to them. Therein lies the dilemma that the networks created for themselves a third of a century ago—when they made a media circus of the "first in the nation" New Hampshire primary and set it on the road to becoming the troublesome anomaly it is today. A decade later (the author being more than just a bystander) the nuisance was compounded when they did the same thing for Iowa's caucuses. Now network news, and the country's presidential politics, appear to be stuck with them. Having created these monsters, how can the networks—or anybody else—kill them, or even ignore them? In the control room, knowing how to do the right thing is not always easy.

"WHAT ARE WE DOING HERE?"

As the network news divisions were packing up in Chicago in 1996, after eight nights there and in San Diego of "What are we doing here?" there were oaths all around that weeklong convention coverage was history. Public as well as shareholder interest is on their side: combined major network viewership hit an all-time low during the 1996 conventions.

It's always possible, of course, to write scenarios in which a party and the press arrive at the convention site, no one has a sure majority, the networks throw away the minute-by-minute lineups from the convention programmers and go out and cover a story. That hasn't happened, though, since 1976. If it ever does again, it does not take a lot of notice to preempt some August reruns when the front-runner has made a deal that puts him or her over, or when it's learned that the vote on a platform amendment will be a test vote on the deal. At such a convention, no one could write a minute-by-minute program, or if anybody did, television producers would use it for scratch paper. They would be playing by ear in reporting an unpredictable, open-ended news event.

In the more likely event of another pair of coronations for nominees decided in the spring, and platforms adopted without debate, the networks should simply set aside one evening, all of it, for each party's nominees to make their case without interruption and without competition from other network programming. The press could then go home and leave the politicians to raise money, plan strategy, conduct workshops and revel to their hearts' content for as many days as they choose—or as their contract with the host city requires.

Without making explicit deals, the networks might undertake additional programming, not necessarily the same for every network, to make up for the airtime recovered by limiting convention coverage to a single night. It could take the form of weekly half hours in the fall devoted to what the candidates said on the stump that week. Or an hour in each of the weeks with no presidential debate. There is enough talent at all the network news divisions to put that time to better use in the fall than eight nights of sham reporting at made-for-TV conventions in August.

The formal proposal made by CBS in November 1963 (see pp. 171–172) would be an excellent model for what CBS (or any other network with the kind of leadership CBS had then) could do for its country—at a relatively modest cost to the shareholders. Were it, or they, to propose such a plan for 2000, under current law no politician could stop them—as Lyndon Johnson stopped Frank Stanton.

1996 was a year in which free time for candidates became a rallying cry for network critics who think (rightly) that these very profitable companies should pay more dues for their use of a valuable national asset. Little attention was paid, however, when four and a half hours (90 minutes per network) of absolutely free network time, most of it for direct communication by the candidates with voters, was left on the table—at the insistence of just one of the candidates.

Since 1960 the networks have always been prepared, generally indeed eager, to air four debates, and there has never been any doubt that they would air as many as the major party nominees agreed to. When the time comes, however, for the candidates to negotiate the terms of the debate, there is usually one who wants fewer. In the fall of 1996, Bill Clinton, like any incumbent with a large lead in the polls, saw little to gain from debates—even against a challenger who wasn't much good at them. Clinton stood his ground and, including the vice presidential debate, there were just three.

There was not, to be sure, any great cry of outrage from the public (or even from the Free Time for Candidates Coalition) over being denied another Clinton–Dole debate. Even so, it's a bad precedent. And for those who feel there was not enough airtime provided for the candidates to convey their views on public policy to the voters (I am one of them), it was a serious loss.

Disappointing as the networks' 1992 effort may have been, they ought to try once more to incorporate four general-election debates into their fall schedules well ahead of time (say a year), so that they are spaced at reasonable intervals throughout the fall—without conflicts from contracted sports events tied in with complex arrangements among leagues, clubs, municipalities and a variety of independent business entities. Furthermore, the debates should be held in network studios so that local arrangements do not become a complicating factor in scheduling or financing.

Negotiations between the networks and the Commission on Presidential Debates in 1992 for joint production of the debates broke down over, among other things, network insistence that each network get to pick a moderator, presumably its evening news anchorman. A more limited proposal by the networks could confine their role to clearing the airtime and providing the facilities.

A joint network announcement on the evening news broadcasts with dates and places would be much harder for either candidate to thumb a nose at a year later than the usual news conference by the commission on its own. Attendance at the designated times would not, obviously could not, be compulsory. If only one candidate showed up, however, the networks and the commission could assemble reporters and hold a news conference with the candidate who did—or a debate with a significant third candidate if there was one.

POLLING AT THE POLLS—AND ELSEWHERE

After a narrow escape in New Hampshire, disaster in Arizona and nothing much for anyone to boast about on election night, you might suppose the networks learned a lesson from 1996. You might think they would stop trying to whip one another in a contest the rest of the world will notice only if they blunder.

But you would be wrong. Consultants are under contract, computer programs have been refined, the systems for making unilateral calls from the very same data by five networks (actually four, since CNN and CBS share the same consultants) are in place. An educated guess at the combined cost of this foolishness to all concerned: about $3 million.

What is especially foolish is that, while racing to beat each other on risky and often unimportant calls (like the Senate race ABC blew in 1996) they go on withholding often more important results that they know for certain. Whatever strides for freedom may be taken in the next century, there is little relief from the Pledge in sight for the networks. Still, while they may again have to wait all evening to even hint at a result in California that they've known since late afternoon in the east, they don't have to hide the fact that they know it. They don't have to be shy about letting viewers know they could report the news sooner and let them get to bed earlier if the government would stop hounding them not to. More candor about these restraints might generate impatience in the more easterly time zones to counter the paranoia of the west.

In reporting polls, the search for news in the horse-race numbers too often implies a precision in the data that simply isn't there. Pollsters should not, in making a case for stories, fail to make pests of themselves about the real size of their error margins. There is more to be learned from the polls than the current, approximate level of support for the candidates. Too little of that issue-related information makes the broadcasts.

Executive producers will continue to be skeptical (not without reason) about whether real, outside-the-beltway Americans are more eager to learn what the rest of them (or, say, single white non–college-educated working women with preschool children) think of a flat income tax than whether the candidate they want to win has more chance than a month ago of doing so. They ought, however, to apply their skepticism with equal energy to much of the seeming ups and downs in the horse-race margins.

As for the voices out there urging the news media, especially television, to temper their reporting with an eye to its effect on confidence in government, any impulse to be good guys should be sternly resisted. There is no more slippery slope in journalism than the one that begins with doubts about the people's sense of proportion—in this case as to their ability to form their own judgment about what matters and what does not in the behavior of their officials.

There *have always been* people to whom the personal character of their presidents matters. Even after the country's recent binge on this topic, it will surely still be of interest to a few fussy voters in 2000. If something arguably shameful turns up regarding a candidate, there is nothing wrong with letting them know about it. They can decide for themselves whether it disqualifies that person from running the country. That decision may of course be influenced by the consequences of the judgments made in 1992, 1996 and 1999.

Different news organizations may have different standards about how zealously they want to pursue this kind of news. There is no need for a uniform code. Journalists, no matter how eminent, should stop trying to police the behavior of other journalists.[5] If viewers really don't want to know about the private lives of candidates, some network should swear that it will never tell them, and reap a rich reward in ratings from all the people who tell pollsters that is their wish. This is not, to be sure, on the evidence of 1998, a bet many high rollers at the networks are apt to place.

When a story is "out there" because some other organization has done the legwork, there is nothing sneaky about letting your own viewers know about it. This is not a case of letting someone else do the dirty work and then piling on. It simply goes with the job of keeping Americans informed. Obviously news organizations should exercise some judgment about the credibility of the story and the level of public awareness already attained, and give people affected by it a chance to be heard. This is not necessarily easy or pleasant work, but those who do it don't need to kvetch endlessly in public over how much it troubles them.

———

In a book noted earlier, James Fallows ascribes to some British newspaper editor a defining maxim for a good journalist: "to see life steady and see it whole." It is a splendid maxim—though its author happens to be Matthew Arnold, who had Sophocles in mind. Minds as spacious at that of Sophocles, or even Matthew Arnold, however, do not apply for jobs in newsrooms every day. For the generally honorable, well-intentioned and for the most part astute men and women who do, I have a maxim of my own. It comes from St. Paul by way of John Milton, the unmatched mentor for a free press:

Prove all things, hold fast to that which is good. For books are as meats and viands are: some of good, some of evil substance, and yet God in that apocryphal vision, said without exception, Rise Peter, kill and eat, leaving the choice to each man's discretion.[6]

As for books, so for the news. Prove all things, hold fast to what is good. And leave the choice to each reader's, or viewer's, discretion.

NOTES

Unless otherwise sourced, quotations in this book are from statements made to or in the presence of the author. Quotations from broadcasts are made in most cases from transcripts, occasionally from videotapes or kinescopes, and in most cases are not separately noted here. Some other sources beyond the author's own observation, recollection and analysis are noted below.

Among the books cited, a few call for special recognition. Four on which I drew gratefully are the work of men who helped shape the history of television news: Sig Mickelson (*The Electronic Mirror*, New York: Dodd Mead, 1972) and Bill Leonard (*The Storm of the Eye*, New York: Putnam, 1987) of CBS, Reuven Frank of NBC (*Out of Thin Air*, New York: Simon & Schuster, 1991) and Av Westin of CBS, PBS and ABC (*Newswatch*, New York: Simon & Schuster, 1982). The successive editions of Sidney Kraus's authoritative *The Great Debates* and *Televised Presidential Debates* (most recent, Hillsdale, N.J.: Erlbaum, 1998) were a valuable resource for Chapter 5. So too, for the early years covered in this book, was Michael Russo's doctoral dissertation at New York University (*CBS and the American Political Experience*, 1983), a fine work of research into both archives and institutional memories.

Introduction

1. John Elvin, "Inside the Beltway." *Washington Times*, June 7, 1992, A6.

2. NBC's star reporters, headed by Tom Brokaw, were appearing with Public Broadcasting's Robert MacNeil and Jim Lehrer on a live PBS broadcast until NBC News took the air at 10:00 P.M. with its own broadcast. In the calculations of the political managers, however, it was what appeared on the big three commercial networks that mattered.

3. Author's interview with Bill Wheatley.

4. Roper Center for Public Opinion Research, Storrs, Conn.

5. Vice President Spiro Agnew (from a text prepared by Patrick J. Buchanan in collaboration, by Buchanan's account, with Richard Nixon, Des Moines, Iowa, November 13, 1969). "A small group of men, numbering perhaps no more than a dozen anchormen, commentators and executive producers, settle upon the twenty minutes or so of film and commentary that's to reach the public [every night]. . . . We'd never trust such power as I've described over public opinion in the hands of an elected government. It's time we questioned it in the hands of a small and unelected elite." For considerably though not entirely different views from the left, see Mark Hertsgaard, *On Bended Knee* (New York: Farrar, Straus, & Giroux, 1988), Danny Schechter, *The More You Watch the Less You Know* (New York: Seven Stories, 1997) and Norman Solomon and Jeff Cohen, *Wizards of Media Oz* (Monroe, Me.: Common Courage, 1997), Chapter 3, "The Myth of the Liberal Media."

Chapter 1. In the Beginning Was New Hampshire—and the Networks

1. "The direct effect of video on those who voted in the New England state," wrote Jack Gould in the *New York Times* (March 16, 1952), "was practically nil. There are no television receivers to speak of in New Hampshire. But there was undoubtedly a very great effect on citizens hundreds of miles from New Hampshire. That is the new and unknown wrinkle in politics in 1952." In 1956 and 1960, however, neither party had a contest in New Hampshire, so it was left till 1964 for television news to confirm for this state's primary voters the significant franchise they have enjoyed ever since.

2. Theodore Sorenson, *Kennedy* (New York: Harper, 1965), 128.

3. Paul David, Malcolm Moos and Ralph Goldman, *Presidential Nominating Politics in 1952* (Baltimore: Johns Hopkins University Press, 1954), 37. Estes Kefauver, a Tennessee senator challenging the prevailing powers in the Democratic Party, used the sitting President's remark against him tellingly and won a stunning upset in New Hampshire. Truman, who promptly took himself out of the race, later said what he meant by "eyewash" was that winning primaries in that era did not bind the delegates to vote for you. Not only, said Truman, did he respect and favor primaries that bound the delegates, he would actually support a binding *national* primary.

4. Iowa's emergence as a rival to New Hampshire was a consequence of the Democratic Party's effort to reform the caucus system. Under new rules, the Iowa party produced a statewide tally the night of the caucuses. This created a contest, prior to New Hampshire, on which the networks could project winners and highlight losers to keep an eye on. Rather than compete among themselves, however, Republicans and Democrats in both states have shrewdly worked as a team in their respective national bodies to preserve a joint hegemony, eight days apart, at the head of the nominating table.

5. Harold Stanley and Richard Niemi, *Vital Statistics on American Politics* (Washington, D.C.: Congressional Quarterly Press, 1994), 60–61.

6. David Broder, *Washington Post*, January 9, 1972; Martin Nolan, *Boston Globe*, February 3, 1972; R. W. Apple, Jr., *New York Times*, February 14, 1972.

James Perry, *Us and Them* (New York: Crown, 1973), 85–86. Author's interview with Maria Carrier. The author, too, was a player in this game. Early in January, while Broder, Nolan and Apple were laying down markers for Muskie in New Hampshire, CBS News went for the big picture. Not just in New Hampshire but across the country, Muskie was backed by the kinds of people (governors, senators, party chairmen) who historically had something to say about where votes go at a convention. Under the new rules, caucus and primary voters would have more to say than in the past, but in state after state Muskie led the field in polls as well. On a *Sixty Minutes* segment entitled "Can Anyone Here Beat Muskie?" Mike Wallace summarized a survey I conducted among five hundred or so state and county Democratic officials on how they thought the delegates would go *if their primaries or caucuses were held at that time.* This was the resulting graphic for estimated delegates:

Muskie   1,199
(310 less than needed to nominate)
Hubert Humphrey   311
Henry Jackson   198
George McGovern   194

"Does that lock it up for Muskie?" No, said Wallace, offering the obvious disclaimers. Years later, Max Kampelman, Humphrey's career-long political ally, recalled to me that, as the graphic appeared on *60 Minutes*, a contributor about to sign a large check for Humphrey put his pen away.

7. One place you found a lot of these people, along with the reporters who cover them, was at "One year to . . ." parties my wife, Susan Morrison, and I have held since the early seventies. They are generally scheduled a year before the presidential election as well as a year before some other landmark event (Iowa, New Hampshire, Super Sunday) in the presidential calendar. In the foyer is a ballot box that used to serve a precinct in Northwest Chicago. Guests get a ballot and are asked to predict the national tickets in both parties as well as the winning ticket. The poll is fallible, to say the least. In November, 1991, for example, the Morrison/Plissner guests picked Mario Cuomo not only to run but to go all the way. Washington insiders, however, were impressed when Bill Clinton, who was still barely visible in the national polls, ran close behind Cuomo. It was one of a number of things, at that point in the race, that raised Clinton's head above the crowd.

8. Jack Germond and Jules Witcover, *Whose Broad Stripes and Bright Stars* (New York: Warner, 1989), 148.

9. According to Richard Cohen, Rather's political producer at the time, Donilon's presence at the warm-up for Bush (a popular topic at the time among conspiracy theorists of the right) was a coincidence—he was in New York and just happened to drop by. Soon afterward, when Jack Kemp's presidential campaign folded, CBS hired Kemp's press secretary, John Buckley, to provide insights on the *Republican* campaigns. Both are very smart fellows and were good company to have around. See Note 15 below.

10. *Campaign for President: The Managers Look at '88* (Auburn: Dover, 1989),

67. In this transcript from a conference at Harvard, Ailes says the CBS whistle-blower talked to Ailes himself. In Roger Simon's *Road Show* (New York: Farrar, Straus, & Giroux, 1989), 39, Ailes tells essentially the same story but says *Bob Teeter*, the campaign pollster, was the man who got the call. Queried on the matter in 1998, Teeter drew a blank.

    11. Bob Schieffer and Gary Paul Gates. *The Acting President* (New York: Dutton, 1989), 348. Author's interview with Mary Martin.

    12. Germond and Witcover, *Whose Broad Stripes*, 118.

    13. *Television News Index and Abstracts*. Nashville, Tenn.: Vanderbilt University Television Archives.

    14. According to Ken Bode, the NBC correspondent on the story, by the time his network's appetite for it had been whetted by the *Times*, the staffer to whom the Dukakis camp had leaked the "attack video" had tucked it away and left for the weekend. NBC recovered smoothly and mobilized its Des Moines affiliate and its London bureau, on a Saturday afternoon, to produce the Kinnock and Biden soundbites for the early evening broadcast. At NBC and some other places, hesitation about making much of this story reflected an awareness that Biden had injected the lines from Kinnock into his stump speech a number of times and rarely, as on this one occasion, failed to acknowledge where it came from.

    15. So, too, for a while, was the status of John Sasso as mastermind of the Dukakis campaign. In penance for his video mugging of Joe Biden, and the clumsy effort at a cover-up, Sasso was forced out of his campaign job. It was this incident that led indirectly to Dan Rather's retinue of political consultants. A rumor that, with time on his hands, Sasso was providing NBC's Tom Brokaw with hot tips and shrewd insights led Rather to feel that he needed a Sasso of his own. As it happened, the sinking of the Biden campaign had left Biden's main strategist, Tom Donilon, also free to smarten up anchormen. For a tidy sum, CBS snapped him up.

    16. When Clinton, more than a half hour into the speech, paused and then said, "In conclusion . . . ," the hall broke into loud cheers and sustained applause.

    17. Compiled from *Television News Index and Abstracts*, Vanderbilt University.

    18. White House transcript, March 18, 1992. In the *60 Minutes* interview, McCurry noted, Clinton had made only one flat denial—of a twelve-year affair. When Steve Kroft asked the obvious follow-up, ". . . and so you're denying a sexual affair," the classically Clinton response was, "She has denied that in the past, and so have I." "And are you denying it now?" Mike Wallace would have shot back without a beat, but Kroft apparently settled for ". . . and so have I." When Clinton and his supporters subsequently insisted that he had told the truth on *60 Minutes*, well, perhaps he did. In any event, for twelve years or one night, what Clinton finally acknowledged having done with Flowers met even *his* definition of sexual relations—and that, it might be noted, of Webster's unabridged *Third New International Dictionary* (Springfield, Mass.: Merriam-Webster, 1986)—as his meetings with Monica Lewinsky famously did not.

    19. *Television News Index and Abstracts*.

20. Jeffrey Birnbaum, "Clinton Received a Draft Deferment for an ROTC Program He Never Joined," *Wall Street Journal*, February 6, 1992, A22.

21. Ted Koppel and Kyle Gibson, *Nightline* (New York: Times Books, 1996), 391–98.

22. CBS, fortunately perhaps, had no way to play a card in this particular primary-night rubber—the network's entire prime-time schedule had been preempted for the Winter Olympics.

23. Andrew Tyndall, *The Tyndall Report* (New York: ADT Research, 1995 Archive Edition).

24. Ibid.

25. As an example of judge-made law, the freedom of self-financing candidates from most campaign-finance regulations is hard to beat. When originally passed by a Democratic Congress and signed by a Republican President (Ford), the law severely restricted contributions to federal candidates as well as spending by presidential candidates who receive federal matching funds. It also prohibited presidential candidates from spending more than $65,000 of their own money.

In *Buckley v. Valeo*, the Supreme Court declared the cap on personal spending unconstitutional but left in place the contribution limits. This holding turned a statute designed to level the playing field for federal office into one that created a huge advantage for the very rich. It empowered a man like Forbes, with a half-billion-dollar private fortune, not only to outraise his rivals by writing one check but to legally spend, as they could not, whatever he liked wherever he chose.

26. Derived from *Tyndall Report* data, January 1996.

27. Author interview with Scott Reed, campaign manager, Dole for President.

28. Interview with Scott Reed; *Campaign for President—The Managers Look at 1996*, edited by Harvard University Institute of Politics (Hollis, N.H.: Hollis, 1997), 80–81.

29. Dole spending figures and most others in this report are based on Federal Election Commission records. Figures on Forbes spending in specific states were given by the campaign to the CBS News Election Unit. Since Forbes was not subject to the state spending limits, he was not required to file this data in his FEC reports.

Chapter 2. From Gavel to Gavel to Ten to Eleven

1. Sig Mickelson, *The Electronic Mirror* (New York: Dodd Mead, 1972), 221–28; Sig Mickelson, *From Whistlestop to Soundbite* (New York: Praeger, 1989), 32–38.

2. Author's interview with Don Hewitt.

3. Mickelson, *Electronic Mirror*, 222.

4. Paul David, Malcolm Moos and Ralph Goldman, *Presidential Nominating Politics in 1952* (Baltimore: Johns Hopkins University Press, 1954), 53. "In this case, the rustlers stole the Texas birthright instead of the steers."

5. David, Moos and Goldman, 69–70.

6. Reuven Frank, *Out of Thin Air* (New York: Simon & Schuster, 1991), 55–56.

7. Mickelson, *From Whistlestop to Soundbite* (New York: Praeger, 1989), 37; Mickelson, *Electronic Mirror*, 226; Walter Cronkite, *A Reporter's Life* (New York: Knopf, 1996), 91. "Only sixteen years later," Mickelson notes, "NBC producer Enid Roth was hailed into court on a charge of invasion of privacy [at the Democratic convention in Chicago] for a similar bugging episode."

8. David, Moos and Goldman, 91.

9. Mickelson, *Whistlestop*, 37.

10. Michael Russo, *CBS and the American Political Experience: A History of the CBS News Special Events and Election Units, 1952–1968* (Dissertation at New York University, 1983), 86–88. Charles H. Thompson, "Television and Presidential Nominating Procedure," internal report to the Brookings Institution, November 14, 1955, 42.

11. Russo, 87.

12. Mickelson, *Whistlestop*, 26.

13. Ibid., 27.

14. Frank, *Out of Thin Air*, 106.

15. Author's interviews with Frank Jordan, director of NBC News Election Unit, and Robert "Shad" Northshield, executive producer of special events in the 1960s.

16. Author's interview with Frank Stanton, CBS president 1946–1973.

17. Author's interviews with Richard Salant, CBS News president 1960–63 and 1966–78, and Bill Eames, CBS News Election Unit producer in the early 1960s.

18. Interview with Bill Eames.

19. Author's interview with CBS's Bill Leonard. For other networks, see "TV Networks Throw $23 Million, Big Armies into Fight for Viewers," *Wall Street Journal*, November 15, 1964.

20. Frank, *Out of Thin Air*, 215–16; Russo, 352–53.

21. This was the first use of exit polling to call an election and was a closely held secret even within CBS at the time. See Chapter 3, pages 81–82, and Chapter 3, note 19.

22. Marvin Barrett, ed., *The Politics of Broadcasting* (New York: Crowell, 1973), 49. It was in May of 1972 that political pollster (and NBC consultant!) Oliver Quayle thrust on Walter Cronkite the designation "most trusted man in America"—for any reporter, an epithet to die for. In surveys done for candidates in eighteen states, Quayle included a "thermometer" question regarding the level of public trust for candidates for the Senate and governor in those states as well as most of the men running for President. For reasons not entirely clear, Quayle added Cronkite's name to the list. The top seven scores reported by Quayle from nearly 9,000 responses were

Cronkite	73%
Average senator	67%
Edmund Muskie	61%

Average governor	59%
Richard Nixon	57%
Hubert Humphrey	57%
George McGovern	56%

The most trusted man in America's political potential did not go unnoticed by the practicing politicians of his time. In New York both Republicans and Democrats at one time or another urged him to run for the Senate. (The Democratic overture came from Robert Kennedy at a lunch in which Cronkite instructed Kennedy that, given his views on Vietnam, the Senator had a "duty" to run for President.) In an interview, Cronkite told me that Governor Hugh Carey joined former New York Mayor Robert Wagner and other "high-level Democrats" in a plea to run for mayor. They even offered to build him a boathouse next to Gracie Mansion, recalled Cronkite—a dumb idea, in the anchorman's authoritative view, should he ever seek re-election. At a private strategy meeting during John Anderson's 1980 run for the Republican presidential nomination, the candidate floated the idea of announcing a running mate during the primaries. He gave Cronkite, whose regard for Anderson had not escaped attention on the air, as an example of someone who might give his campaign a lift. When Morton Kondracke, then at the *New Republic*, called Cronkite and floated the trial balloon past *him*, Cronkite told Kondracke he would be "honored if asked." He failed, he said later, to make it clear that if really asked he would have turned the honor down. For days after Kondracke's story appeared, Cronkite was off on his boat—out of radio contact—while CBS executives in New York went crazy dealing with press calls for comment.

23. Theodore H. White, *The Making of the President 1968* (New York: Atheneum, 1969), 244.

24. Not widely known, largely because CBS News never got a chance to report it when it happened and no one else had staked the meeting out, was the 19-to-15 vote by which Nixon defeated Ronald Reagan in an after-midnight caucus of the Florida delegation. As a result, under a winner-take-all rule, Nixon got all but one of Florida's 34 votes on the presidential roll call the following night. South Carolina, Mississippi and Georgia, all closely divided between Nixon and Reagan supporters, were poised to follow Florida—whichever way it went. The 80 votes of those four delegations put Nixon over the top. Had Reagan won them, as he very nearly did, Nixon might never have been President. By the time we had the story, however, CBS News had signed off for the night. The next day, when we returned to the air, the presidential nomination was a lock, and the story under pursuit became not how Nixon almost blew it but who he'd pick for Vice President.

25. While the Kennedy banners were floating about the floor, I got a call from Patrick Lucey, then lieutenant governor (and later governor) of Wisconsin. Lucey had been the delegate tracker in Robert Kennedy's campaign. He was now the convention manager for Eugene McCarthy. There was a real chance, said Lucey, that Ted Kennedy would accept a draft. He gave me a list of people, headed by McCarthy and Chicago's Mayor Daley, who would help to make it happen. Did *I* see any way Kennedy could get the votes? I'd gone through the same exercise earlier in the day with Larry O'Brien, Humphrey's

convention manager, so I saw no reason not to do it with Lucey. Most of the people on his list, I pointed out, were not part of the Humphrey hard core to begin with, and putting Kennedy's name in play would set the Vice President's Southern support in concrete. Lucey thanked me and went off to see Steve Smith, the Kennedy brother-in-law who was handling the senator's affairs from a hotel suite on the other side of town. When a formal disavowal of the draft effort was announced a few hours later, I figured this was linked in part to the gloomy assessment I had given Lucey. Apparently not. Years later, Lucey told me it had taken four hours to get through Chicago's riot zone to the hotel, and by then the die was cast.

26. Howard K. Smith, *Events Leading up to my Death* (New York: St. Martin's, 1989), 341–43. Russo, 468–69. After its late start every night, ABC's capacity to cover news at the convention was further limited by the soon-to-be-legendary spats of its marquee attraction, "our odd couple" (as resident ABC commentator Howard K. Smith described them) of "special commentators, William F. Buckley, Jr., and Gore Vidal." Perhaps the most weird of the odd couple's on-air eye-gougings came after demonstrators ran up a Viet Cong flag on a flagpole in Grant Park and Smith suggested this could be considered provocative—like running up the Nazi flag during World War II. Said Vidal, dissenting: "There are no Nazis here, except Bill Buckley, a crypto-Nazi." Responded Buckley: "Listen, you queer, stop calling me a crypto-Nazi or I'll sock you in the goddamn face." Among the more sobering findings in the post-mortems on the 1968 conventions: ABC won the prime-time ratings every night.

27. Theodore H. White, *The Making of the President 1968* (New York, Atheneum, 1969), 277–80. John Connally, *In History's Shadow* (New York: Hyperion, 1963), 201–203.

28. Frank, *Out of Thin Air*, 270–71.

29. Ibid.

30. Russo, 478.

31. Frank, *Out of Thin Air*, 275. Mike Wallace and Gary Paul Gates, *Close Encounters* (New York: Morrow, 1984), 119.

32. George Gallup, *The Gallup Poll: Public Opinion 1935–1971*, Volume III, 1959–1971 (New York: Random House, 1972), 2160.

33. There is not, of course, any constitutional bar to the President and Vice President being "inhabitants" of the same state. The only problem is that electors cannot vote for more than one person from their own state. In a very close election, therefore, California's electors might have been unable to vote for Ford, and a President Reagan might have found that his Vice President was Walter Mondale. Ford made it clear to Cronkite (and the whole world) that he, *and the Reagan camp*, had consulted widely on how to deal with even this eventuality:

> [Some people] say, "Well, Jerry, you can move back to Michigan . . . or you can go to Colorado, where you own property . . . and now some lawyers have filed a memorandum [Cronkite: These are Reagan staff lawyers, I've heard] Yes, they went back and researched the Federalist Papers and . . .

34. Ronald Reagan, *An American Journey* (New York: Simon & Schuster, 1990), 215–16. Before watching the Cronkite interview, according to Reagan,

"for several days I had expected Ford to be on the ticket and hadn't given any thought to other candidates."

35. Phyllis Schlafly, the matriarch of the party's anti-abortion plank, at one point complained that CBS, in polling on public support for the pro-life position, had not allowed for a unique exception when the mother's life is in danger. In this respect, however, the survey was simply reflecting the actual position formally adopted by the Republican platform—a position more absolute than his Holiness's or even Ms. Schlafly's.

36. The opening night address by Powell, by far the most popular Republican of the day, was seen by the Dole campaign as the most valuable of all the cards it had to play on the convention broadcasts. Part of the price for Dole of having this model of the straight-shooting soldier appear in his behalf was that Powell could not, like Bill Weld four years before, be asked to note his dissenting position on the party's most inflammatory issues in an aside. "You all know," Powell declared right up front, "that I believe in a woman's right to choose and I strongly support affirmative action." As Powell approached this line in his prepared speech, CBS floor cameras were tight on Buchanan himself—a study in smiling, serene attention—and nobody stormed the podium or the exits.

37. Howard Kurtz, "A Convention Scripted to Mirror TV Broadcasts," *Washington Post*, August 10, 1996, A12.

38. Howard Kurtz, "GOP Offers Images, Media Seek News," *Washington Post*, August 14, 1996, A25.

39. Author's interview with Mike Berman, Democratic convention programmer; Dick Morris, *Beyond the Oval Office* (New York: Random House, 1997), 325.

Chapter 3. For Whom the Networks Call

1. Thomas Bohn, "Broadcasting National Election Returns: 1916–48," *Journal of Broadcasting*, Summer 1968, 267–86.

2. Thomas Bohn, "Broadcasting National Election Returns: 1952–1976," *Journal of Communication*, Autumn 1980, 140–53.

3. Ibid.

4. Michael Russo, *CBS and the American Political Experience: A History of the CBS News Special Events and Election Units, 1952–1968* (Doctoral dissertation at New York University, 1983), 250.

5. Ibid., 254.

6. Author's interview with Lou Harris.

7. Author's interview with Bill Eames, CBS News Election Unit producer in the 1960s.

8. Theodore H. White, *America in Search of Itself: The Making of the President, 1956–1980* (New York: Harper, 1982), 170–72.

9. Not, to be sure, entirely without precedent. This was what NBC's Kaltenborn had famously done, without benefit of computers or sample precincts, in the matter of President Dewey.

10. Author's interview with Richard Scammon.

11. Author's interview with Frank Jordan.

12. Author's interview with Robert "Shad" Northshield, NBC News executive producer for special events in the 1960s (later at CBS).

13. Ibid.

14. "TV Sticks to Computer Despite Election Goofs," *New York World Journal Tribune*, November 11, 1966.

15. Author's interview with Bill Eames.

16. Author's interview with I. A. "Bud" Lewis, director of NBC Election Unit in the late 1960s and early 1970s.

17. *Newsweek*, April 19, 1976, 88.

18. Ibid.

19. Author's interview with Lou Harris; Bill Leonard, *The Storm of the Eye* (New York: Putnam, 1987), 103–107. Strictly speaking, Harris conducted no *interviews*, the customary way in which most exit polls have been done ever since. He told me that at 120 precincts throughout the state he had posted persons who offered voters a choice of beans (white for one candidate, black for the other) and asked them to pick one. The estimate on which he made his call, says Harris, was based on that bean count. According to the late I. A. "Bud" Lewis, NBC conducted interviews at ten polling places out of a 21-point sample during the same primary, which reinforced indications from the hard-vote sample to be very patient about calling a winner; see Chapter 3 in Paul Lavraka and Jack Holley, eds. *Polling and Presidential Election Coverage* (Newberry Park, Calif.: Sage, 1991), 64. For Leonard, who was in charge of the CBS broadcast, this particular instance of getting it first and getting it right was no feather in anybody's cap. "All through the evening, I continued to whistle in what I hoped was not the dark. . . . As the last VPA precincts reported in, our final estimate of the race—while still showing Goldwater ahead—was actually below the guideline figure, which meant that, had we had that figure early in the evening, I would never have made the call, nor would Lou Harris have recommended it."

20. *Congressional Quarterly*, August 8, 1981.

21. Ibid.

22. Author's interview with Roy Wetzel, director of NBC Election Unit, 1976–1989.

23. An even more dramatic outcome occurred on November 5, 1996, when CBS and CNN conducted their own general election for President. On the Voter News Service exit poll, the two networks exercised their option to order special questions by having voters in the survey asked how they would have voted had the candidates been Colin Powell as the Republican, Bill Clinton as the Democrat and Ross Perot as the Reform Party Candidate. The result:

Powell: 48%
Clinton: 36%
Perot: 8%

24. "Talk of the Town," *New Yorker*, November 18, 1996.

Chapter 4. *Masters of All They Survey*

1. Robert Chandler, *Public Opinion: Changing Attitudes on Contemporary Political and Social Issues* (New York: Bowker, 1972), 137.

2. Author's interview with I. A. "Bud" Lewis.

3. Author's interview with David Jones, national editor, *New York Times*.

4. U.S. Census Bureau, *Current Population Survey, 1998* (Washington, D.C.: U.S. Government Printing Office, 1998).

5. Michael Wheeler, *Lies, Damn Lies and Statistics* (New York: Liveright, 1976), 66–71. Bernard Roshco and Irving Crespi, "From Alchemy to Home-Brewed Chemistry—Polling Transformed," *Public Perspective*, April/May 1996, 8–12.

6. Roshco and Crespi, 12.

7. Wheeler, 75.

8. Wheeler, 73.

9. Bruce Altschuler, *LBJ and the Polls* (Gainesville: University of Florida Press, 1990), 69.

10. Author's interview with David Jones.

11. Warren Mitofsky, "The 1980 Pre-Election Polls: A Review of Disparate Methods and Results," *Proceedings of the American Statistical Association*, 1981; John Stacks, "Where the Polls Went Wrong," *Time*, December 1, 1980; Alvin Sanoff, "The Perils of Polling 1980," *Washington Journalism Review*, January/February 1981.

12. "Face Off—A Conversation with the Presidents' Pollsters," *Public Opinion*, December/January 1981.

13. Paul Taylor et al., *Washington Post*, October 13, 1992, 1. David Moore, *The Superpollsters: How They Measure and Manipulate Public Opinion in America* (New York: Four Walls Eight Windows, 1992), 250.

14. Author's interview with Hal Bruno.

15. Kathleen Frankovic, "Reading Between the Polls," *New York Times*, June 27, 1992, A23.

16. James Bennet, "Polling Provoking Debate in News Media on Its Use," *New York Times*, October 4, 1996, A24.

17. Michael Kagay, "Experts Say Refinements Are Needed in the Polls," *New York Times*, December 15, 1996, 34.

18. Everett Ladd, "The Pollsters' Waterloo," *Wall Street Journal*, November 19, 1996, A22; David Butler and Dennis Kavanagh, "The Waterloo of the Polls," in *The British General Election of 1992*.

19. This is not to deny that the Democratic tilt of most final polls in the last two presidential elections is curious and worth study. Warren Mitofsky (*Public Opinion Quarterly*, Summer 1998, 245) reviewed the final reports of the country's major pre-election polls since 1956. Through 1988, he found pretty much a draw: thirteen cases of a tilt favoring the Democrat and eleven cases favoring the Republican. In contrast, for 1992 and 1996, twelve were high on Clinton, none on the Republican. Michael Barone ("Why Opinion Polls Are Worth Less," *U.S. News and World Report*, December 9, 1996, p. 52), noting that pre-election

polls during the same period in Britain, Italy and Israel showed a similar tilt against conservative parties, speculates that "mainline media coverage" in most places "often makes it seem disreputable to vote for the right. So voters may hide their intentions." It would take more instances of such a global phenomenon and more specific research as to motivation to sustain this hunch.

The most persistent partisan tilt in pre-election polling, it should be noted, took place during the period just prior to that covered in Mitofsky's research. From 1936 to 1948, George Gallup, by far the most influential pollster of his time, overstated the vote for the Republican every time. Could there have been a media-induced stigma in voting for FDR or Truman? Perhaps. A stigma theory of conservative nonresponse today, however, is hard to square with the regular overstatement of the vote for Patrick J. Buchanan in primary exit polls.

20. "Polling Council Analysis Concludes Criticisms of 1996 Presidential Poll Accuracy Are Unfounded," press release, February 13, 1997, National Council on Public Polls, Fairfield, Conn.

21. Or take this example, from ABC *World News Tonight*, September 16, 1992. "The race," says Jennings, "is somewhat closer." In a survey of 623 likely voters, 49% favored Clinton, 41% Dole. A week earlier a similar sample had come up 54/35. From a 19-point to an 8-point gap sure seemed like good news for the candidate at the south end. The problem was that the potential sampling error on the margin both times was 8 points, and no other poll that week showed the sizable shift heralded later in the evening of September 16 on *Nightline* as "Good News Tonight for Senator Dole."

22. Moore, *The Superpollsters*, 288.

23. Moore, 289. Alvin Sanoff, "ABC's Phone-In Polling: Does It Put Credibility on the Line?" *Washington Journalism Review*, March 1984, 49–50. Sheldon Gawiser and Evans Witt, *A Journalist's Guide to Public Opinion Polls* (Westport, Conn.: Praeger, 1994), 101.

24. Kathleen Frankovic, "News Media Polling in a Changing Technological Environment," Van Zelst Lecture in Communication, Northwestern University, May 25, 1994.

25. *This Week*, ABC, August 27, 1995.

26. Dick Morris, *Beyond the Oval Office* (New York: Random House, 1997), 235. Kenneth Starr, et al.: *The Starr Report* (New York: Public Affairs, 1998), 149. Far transcending, for its prospective impact on the history of the country, any of the surveys recounted in Morris's book is the one told to a grand jury and made public in Starr's report:

Morris suggested that he take a poll on the voters' willingness to forgive confessed adultery. The President agreed. Mr. Morris telephoned the President later that evening with the poll results, which showed that the voters were "willing to forgive [the President] for adultery but not for perjury or obstruction of justice. When Mr. Morris explained that the poll results suggested that the President should not go public with a confession or explanation, he replied, "Well, we just have to win then."

27. E. J. Dionne, "The Illusion of Technique: The Impact of Polls on Re-

porters and Democracy," in *Media Polls in American Politics*, Tomas Mann and Gary Orren, eds. (Washington: Brookings Institution, 1992), 151.

Chapter 5. The Less Than Great Debates

1. Abraham Lincoln, *Speeches and Writings, 1832–1858* (New York: Library of America, 1989), 479.

2. Joel Swerdlow, ed., *Presidential Debates 1988 and Beyond* (Washington, D.C.: Congressional Quarterly Press), 11.

3. Samuel Becker and Elmer Lower, "Broadcasting in Presidential Campaigns," in Sidney Kraus, ed., *The Great Debates: Background, Perspectives, Effects* (Bloomington: Indiana University Press, 1962), 39–40.

4. Michael Russo, *CBS and the American Political Experience: A History of the CBS Special Events and Election Units, 1952–1968* (Dissertation at New York University, 1983), 155.

5. Sig Mickelson, *The Electronic Mirror* (New York: Dodd, Mead, 1972), 196.

6. Russo, *CBS*, 171.

7. Ibid., 176. NBC saw no reason why the broadcasts should not carry advertising. Stanton, however, remembered how close the networks had come to having sixteen hours of "free time for candidates" shoved down their throats. CBS announced that it would forgo advertising on the four hours of debates, and the other networks promptly fell into line.

8. Richard Nixon, *RN: The Memoirs of Richard Nixon* (New York: Grosset, 1978), 41.

9. Khrushchev, referring to the U.S.-sponsored "Captive Nations Resolution" at the United Nations: "This resolution stinks. It stinks like fresh horse shit, and nothing smells worse than that." Nixon: "I am afraid that the Chairman is mistaken. There is something that smells worse than horse shit—and that is pig shit." Steven Ambrose, *Nixon, Volume I: The Education of a Politician 1913–1962* (New York: Simon & Schuster, 1987), 522–23.

10. Nixon, *RN*, 214–17.

11. Mickelson, *Electronic Mirror*, 195–97.

12. Ibid., 200–203.

13. Herbert Seltz and Richard Yoakum, "Production Diary of the Debates," in Kraus, ed., *The Great Debates: 1962*, 77.

14. Ibid, 78–79.

15. Nixon, *RN*, 219.

16. Seltz and Yoakum in Kraus, ed., *The Great Debates: 1962*, 85.

17. Michael Schudson, *The Power of News* (Cambridge, Mass.: Harvard University Press, 1995), 116–18. From its nightly marketing surveys, Sindlinger Research reported that radio listeners picked Nixon as the winner of the first debate while television viewers picked Kennedy. The data, says Schudson (with some others) was "never reported in a manner that made serious analysis possible." At the same time, the notion that Kennedy scored better when he and Nixon were seen as well as heard, though perhaps unproven, hardly seems unlikely.

18. Samuel Lubell, "Personalities vs. Issues" in Kraus, ed., (1962), 158.

19. Sidney Kraus, *Televised Presidential Debates and Public Policy* (Hillsdale, N.J.: Erlbaum, 1988), 29. Kraus suggests a total audience for the entire 1858 series of under 100,000.

20. Herbert Terry and Sidney Kraus, "Legal and Political Aspects: Was Section 315 Circumvented?" in Kraus, ed., *The Great Debates: Carter vs. Ford 1976* (Bloomington: Indiana University Press, 1979), 41–53.

21. Ibid.; Peggy Lampl, "The Sponsor," in Kraus, ed. (1979), 83–105.

22. Herbert Seltz and Richard Yoakum, "Production Diary of the Debates," in Kraus, ed. (1979) 110–15.

23. Ibid., 118–21, 132–36.

24. Ibid., 125–27. Richard Salant, "The Good But Not Great Nondebates," in Kraus, ed. (1979), 175–86. "We did not even know [the candidates] played any role [in selecting the panels] until it was disclosed to us by a League representative at a cocktail party." The League president, when pressed, acknowledged that candidates got a peek "as a courtesy" before the panels were announced. Should there be amy objection, she said, "We'll cross that bridge when we come to it." For Salant, the official "CBS News Standards" had already crossed that bridge: "The subject of an interview shall not have any voice in the selection of the interviewer." Since the CBS legal position was that debates were spot news over which it had no control, Salant's indignation did not really have a leg to stand on. But he could hold his own correspondents to the network's standards.

25. Henry Kissinger, *Diplomacy* (New York: Simon & Schuster, 1994), 760.

26. David Lanoue and Peter Schrott, *The Joint Press Conference*, (New York: Greenwood Press, 1991), 20.

27. Kraus, ed. (1979), v.

28. Hamilton Jordan, *Crisis* (New York: Putnam, 1982), 353.

29. It was the then relatively new Federal Election Commission that led the way. The FEC had raised a question whether news organizations that hold debates but don't invite everyone on the ballot are in effect making in-kind contributions to those they do invite. The National Association of Broadcasters made a convincing argument that such a ruling would lead to fewer debates and less voter opportunity to appraise the major candidates for office. Emboldened by this sucess, the NAB made the same argument to its main master, the FCC, and this time carried the day.

30. Author's interview with Frank Donatelli.

31. "New Question in Race: Is Oldest U.S. President Now Showing His Age?" *Wall Street Journal*, October 9, 1988, 1.

32. Robert Hunter, ed., *Electing the President: A Program for Reform, the Final Report of the Commission on National Elections* (Washington: Center for Strategic and International Studies, 1986), 14.

33. Ibid.

34. Sandy Johnson, "Parties Win Agreement from Candidates for Four Debate Dates," Associated Press, July 7, 1987.

35. Jack Germond and Jules Witcover, *Whose Broad Stripes and Bright Stars* (New York: Warner, 1989), 3.

36. Author's interviews with Tad Devine of the Dukakis campaign and Charles Black of the Bush campaign. Both sides give the Dukakis side credit for having initiated this particular advance in the state of the art.

37. Letter from Roone Arledge, Tom Johnson, Eric Ober and Michael Gartner to Ron Brown et al., September 24, 1991.

38. Ibid.

39. Shirley Anne Warshaw, "The Presidential Debates," presented at annual conference of Center for the Study of the Presidency, Washington, D.C., March 20, 1992.

40. Frank Fahrenkopf and Paul Kirk, "Debates and the Networks' Role," *Washington Post*, October 27, 1991.

41. The last time in which there had been an arguable third contender, in 1980, the League of Women Voters adopted two main criteria—presence on enough state ballots to win a majority in the Electoral College and 15 percent support in public opinion polls. For the Neustadt panel, however, ballot access and poll numbers were only the beginning. Under its guidelines, the candidate would need to have a "realistic [i.e., more than theoretical] chance of being elected President." To meet that standard, there were five tests for "national organization," five more for "newsworthiness and competitiveness" and three more for "public enthusiasm and concern."

When the commission asked for a ruling on Perot, he was already on the ballot in nearly every state, and he met most of Neustadt's other "objective criteria." But did he have a "realistic chance of being elected President"? To decide that, the committee was supposed to weigh "significant public opinion polls and the opinions of major Washington bureau chiefs, campaign consultants and political scientists."

As it happened, the latest CBS News/New York Times poll pegged Perot at barely 7 percent. He did little better in other polls. Neustadt and his colleagues gave no report on their soundings of bureau chiefs, handlers and other scholars. They simply recommended that Perot be invited to the first debate and leave the others up in the air. The commission suggested to Bush and Clinton that, if this was a deal-breaker, they consider other sponsors for the last two debates. The candidates responded that the deal was for all the debates or none. During this time, I had a call from one of the campaigns about whether the networks were prepared to warm up their studios if the commission bolted. After consulting some colleagues at CBS, though not at the other networks, I allowed that it could certainly be done and offered my personal guess that the other networks, if asked, would go along. Faced, however, with the prospect of going out of business then and there, the commission swallowed hard (lawsuits by other minor-party candidates were hanging on this decision) and overruled its panel of scholars.

42. Anthony Corrado, "Background Paper" in *Let America Decide: The Report of the Twentieth Century Task Force on Presidential Debates* (New York: Twentieth Century Fund Press, 1995), 131–32.

43. Author's interview with Harold Ickes.

44. Author's interviews with John Buckley and Doug Sosnick, White House Political Director.

45. Author's interview with Scott Reed.

46. Nielsen Media Research, New York, N.Y.

47. Ibid.

48. Media Studies Center/Roper Center Survey, September 1996.

Chapter 6. At the End of the Day: The Evening News and Its Critics

1. Transcript, *Campaign '96: TV News Issue Coverage* (sponsored by the Joan Shorenstein Center and the Kaiser Family Foundation, Harvard Club of New York City, December 4, 1996), 29, 35, 45.

2. Ibid., 56–62. Robert Blendon et al., "Did the Media Leave the Voters Uninformed in the 1996 Election?" *Harvard International Journal of Press/Politics*, Spring 1998.

3. Shorenstein transcript, 20–21.

4. Ibid., 10.

5. Tom Rosenstiel, *Strange Bedfellows* (New York: Hyperion, 1993), 245.

6. Shorenstein transcript, 12–13.

7. Ibid., 29–30.

8. Andrew Tyndall, *The Tyndall Report* (New York: ADT Research, 1995 archive edition).

9. Data for 1996 and 1992 from *Tyndall Reports*, various dates; for 1968 from Vanderbilt University Television Logs; for 1960 from the author's clocking of kinescopes at the Library of Congress.

10. Av Westin, *Newswatch* (New York: Simon & Schuster, 1982), 171.

11. Bill Leonard, *The Storm of the Eye* (New York: Putnam, 1987), 114–15.

12. Lawrence Lichty, Joseph Ripley and Harrison Summers, "Political Programs on National Television Networks: 1960 and 1964," *Journal of Broadcasting*, Summer 1965, 217.

13. Author's interview with Frank Stanton.

14. Speech by Frank Stanton at the National Institute of Social Sciences, Washington, D.C., November 21, 1963.

15. Corydon Dunham, *Fighting for the First Amendment: Stanton of CBS vs. Congress and the Nixon White House* (Westport, Conn.: Praeger, 1997), 63.

16. Gary Paul Gates, *Airtime* (New York: Harper & Row, 1978), 93–96; Reuven Frank, *Out of Thin Air* (New York: Simon & Schuster, 1991), 180–83.

17. Author's interview with Frank Stanton.

18. "CBS and NBC: Walter vs. Chet and Dave," *Newsweek*, September 23, 1963, 62.

19. Michael Robinson and Margaret Sheehan, *Over the Wire and on TV—CBS and UPI in Campaign '80* (New York: Russell Sage, 1983), 6–8.

20. Martin Schram, *The Great American Video Game* (New York: Morrow, 1987). Michael Schudson, in his delightfully contrarian *The Power of News* (Cambridge, Mass.: Harvard University Press, 1995, 115–18), parts company not only with Schram but also with a whole choir of media wisepersons (e.g., Hedrick Smith, David Broder, Kathleen Jamieson) on the moral of Stahl's story. "The story's punch," Schudson argues, "depends on our belief that the White

House official knew what he was talking about. But did he?" Not to Schudson, who argues that none of the magical powers of the Reagan White House to dictate visuals on television did anything for the President's approval ratings so long as the economy was in the tank. Even on television, argues Schudson, it was not the *visuals* which made the sale for Reagan:

I suspect that we will one day recall Reagan as one of the least visual but most auditory of our presidents. What is memorable is the Reagan with the slight choke in his voice when he told a melodramatic story about a G.I. or read a letter from a little girl, his quick intelligence with a joke or a quip . . . Reagan knew, if his critics did not, that it was his voice, his long-lived radio asset, that made his television appearance so effective.

21. Kiku Adatto, *Picture Perfect* (New York: Basic, 1993), 48.
22. Jack Germond and Jules Witcover, *Whose Broad Stripes and Bright Stars* (New York: Warner, 1989), 137.
23. Christine Black and Thomas Oliphant, *All by Myself* (Chester, Conn.: Globe Pequot, 1989), 109.
24. Kiku Adatto: "TV Tidbits Starve Democracy," *New York Times*, December 10, 1989, A23; "Soundbite Democracy: Network Evening News Presidential Campaign Coverage, 1968 and 1988," Shorenstein Center, June 1990.
25. Daniel Hallin, "Soundbite News: Television Coverage of Elections, 1968–1988," *Journal of Communication*, Spring 1992.
26. Timothy J. Russert, "The Networks Have to Do Better," *New York Times*, March 4, 1990, A23.
27. Thomas Patterson, *Out of Order* (New York: Knopf, 1993), 204.
28. "Ethics in Journalism," panel discussion at National Press Club, Washington, D.C., February 27, 1972.
29. James Fallows, *Breaking the News* (New York: Pantheon, 1996), 65.
30. Ibid., 203, 290; *Ordinary Americans More Cynical than Journalists: News Media Differs with Public and Leaders on Watchdog Issues* (Los Angeles: Times-Mirror Center on the People and the Press, May 22, 1995); *Deconstructing Discontent: How Americans View Government* (Washington, D.C.: Pew Research Center for the People and the Press, 1998), 87.
31. Keynote address, Edward R. Murrow Awards Ceremony, Radio and Television News Directors Association, Los Angeles, October 9, 1996.
32. Shorenstein transcript, 45; Kathleen Jamieson and Paul Waldman, "Mapping Campaign Discourse," *American Behavioral Scientist*, August 1997, 1133.
33. Courtney Bennett, "Assessing the Impact of Ad Watches on the Strategic Decision-Making Process," *American Behavioral Scientist*, August 1997, 1165.

Conclusion

1. Web site data from Michael Cornfield of George Washington University's Graduate School of Political Management.
2. Nielsen Media Research, *1998 Report on Television* (New York, 1998), 25–28. Additional data from Vincent Nasso, Nielsen Media Research, New

York (the broadcast industry standard for nearly half a century) and public opinion surveys by the Pew Research Center for the People and the Press diverge significantly on trends in network-news viewing. Pew reports a large decline between 1993 and 1995 in Americans who "regularly watch . . . the nightly network news," as does Nielsen to a lesser degree for television households in the same period. For the last four years, however, Nielsen has reported little change, whereas Pew Center surveys report the decline continuing.

3. Kathleen DeLaski, director of news and political programming, America Online, at "Politics on the Net" conference at Kennedy School of Government, Harvard, December 3, 1998.

4. Voter News Service exit poll, 1998, sample size 10,000, sampling error 1 percent. Figures from Pew Center telephone survey presented by Andrew Kohut, director, at Harvard conference, December 3, 1998.

5. In late 1998, Howard Kurtz, the peerless media reporter of the *Washington Post* and CNN and author of *Spin Cycle* (New York: Free Press, 1998), took aim at the big feet of his trade, after noting with obvious relish that the Gennifer Flowers story of 1992 had turned out to be "an important story after all" (*Washington Post*, December 14, 1998, D1). Coverage at the time, he reminded his readers, "was described as 'sickening' by James Gannon of the *Detroit News*, 'grab your crotch journalism' (David Nyhan of the *Boston Globe*) and the 'degradation of democracy' (the *Post*'s David Broder). Max Frankel, then the editor of the *New York Times*, said he was 'ashamed for my profession.' "

6. John Milton, "Areopagitica: A Speech for the Liberty of Unlicensed Printing," in *Milton's Prose*, Malcolm Wallace, ed. (Oxford University Press, 1925), 288.

ACKNOWLEDGMENTS

Several election cycles back, my wife, Susan Morrison, who was teaching graduate courses in journalism, asked for a list of books on presidential politics from the point of view of the television broadcasters who cover it. Aside from a handful of chapters in not very recent works, I could not point her toward very much.

It took a while, and some prompting from others, before I began a serious effort to fill this apparent void. Bob Barnett, the superlawyer of Washington politics and journalism, circulated a proposal. The late Martin Kessler, then president of Basic Books, offered some structural advice as well as a quite reasonable advance. David Burke, then president of CBS News, approved and strongly encouraged my moonlighting on the project.

Beyond the debts incurred during years of often intense teamwork, I need to thank my closest colleagues at CBS—Warren Mitofsky, Kathy Frankovic and Dotty Lynch—both for refreshing my memory about many of our common efforts and for reading this manuscript. It has, as a result, significantly fewer flaws than it might have. Joan Richman's wonderful critical eye also caught its share. To E. J. Dionne, the most thoughtful political writer practicing today, I owe some valuable advice on the presentation of this book following his reading of the manuscript.

For all my own thirty-odd years of experience, the television networks had covered a lot of presidential politics before I joined the

CBS News Election Unit in 1963. Among the CBS veterans who helped fill gaps in my knowledge of the pioneer days were Walter Cronkite, Frank Stanton, Don Hewitt, Blair Clark, Bill Small, Bill Eames, Norman Gorin and the late Eric Sevareid, Richard Salant and Bill Leonard—as well as Lou Harris, the indispensable consultant at the Election Unit's birth. Among the NBC veterans who filled me in on their side of what was then largely a two-network rivalry are Sander Vanocur, Frank Jordan, Robert "Shad" Northshield (whose later years were spent at CBS) and Richard Scammon.

For my own years at CBS, a very partial list of colleagues who in sometimes repeated interviews shared ideas and experiences reflected in this book includes Bruce Morton, Lesley Stahl, Eric Engberg, Susan Zirinsky, Brian Healy, Mary Martin and Murray Edelman— now the brains of Voter News Service. Many more, to whom I am deeply grateful, are cited in the course of this book.

Sources of important insights and anecdotes at NBC include Bill Wheatley, Roy Wetzel, Mary Klette, the late Bud Lewis and Ken Bode—who, during several decades as a treasured source on politics and television, happened to be at NBC when I interviewed him. Hal Bruno, for many years my counterpart as political director of ABC News, provided not only good companionship at uncountable campaign sites but also valuable insights and recollections for this book. Also at ABC, Jeff Gralnik, Tom Bettag and Jeff Alderman were helpful in many ways, as was Tom Hannon of CNN.

The political figures who over the years have confided, often quite heatedly, their strong views on the subject of this book are too numerous to provide a complete list, or even a selective one, but many of those views are noted directly in the course of the book.

Dog years ago, Phil Noble, whose *url* (www.PoliticsOnLine.com) is only one indication of his ability to get there fastest, gave me (along with numerous paying clients who run countries) an early heads-up on the political promise of the internet and has helped to keep me current. So too has Jonah Seigar@campaignwebreview.com.

In developing this book I had the immense benefit of the CBS News Reference Library—with its superb archive of books and documents on both presidential politics and broadcasting. My gratitude to Laura Kapnick and Cryder Bankes, as well as to Bob Tomlin for supplying network logs and transcripts and Neil Waldman for making videotapes available, cannot be overstated. Bob Lichter, president of Washington's Center for Media and Public Affairs, and its research director, Rich Noyes, made their valuable (and, so far as I know, unique) collection of network news transcripts available—with a rare tolerance for both the time of day and the urgency with which many of my requests were placed. John Lynch of Vanderbilt University's indispensable Television News Library could not have been more helpful.

Tom Mann of the Brookings Institution enabled me to use its fine reference library. The wonders of the Library of Congress for almost any type of research made relatively light work of several tasks that might otherwise have been burdensome indeed. Madeline Matz of the Motion Picture and Broadcasting Collection steered me to numerous records of network broadcasts which are not available from the networks themselves. If today's network managers were to resume the former practice of supplying archival material to the country's premier repository of knowledge, it would be a great service to scholarship and to public understanding of what they do.

Research assistance was ably provided by Diane Beasley and Jinghua Zou. Cheryl Arnett at the CBS News Survey Unit was a constant source of both data and helpful ideas.

Martin Kessler, my original editor, did not live to read the final manuscript. He took an earlier draft with him when he moved to The Free Press and established his own imprint there. After Martin's death—a great loss to public affairs publishing—Bruce Nichols helped me over the final hurdles of getting my first book into shape, judiciously weeding out, along the way, some particularly inside lore and some fine writing that I loved perhaps too much. My copyediting supervisor, Edith Lewis, brought to the manuscript a vigilance, with respect to clarity in particular, from which readers will benefit as I have.

INDEX